THE GOD SHIFT

ABOUT THE AUTHOR

Adrian B. Smith MA is the author of fourteen previous books, the most recent of which include: *The Christ* (CANA Publications, 2002); *A New Framework for Christian Belief* (John Hunt Publishing, 2002); *A Reason for Living and Hoping: A Christian Appreciation of the Emerging New Era of Consciousness* (St Paul's Publishing, 2002); and *God and the Aquarian Age* (McCrimmon Publishing, 1990). He is a Catholic missionary priest who is much in demand to give lectures and retreats on aspects of the emerging New Era of Consciousness.

THE GOD SHIFT

Our Changing Perception
of the Ultimate Mystery

Adrian B. Smith

The Liffey Press

Published by
The Liffey Press Ltd
Ashbrook House, 10 Main Street
Raheny, Dublin 5, Ireland
www.theliffeypress.com

A catalogue record of this book is
available from the British Library.

ISBN 1-904148-47-6

Printed in Spain by GraphyCems

CONTENTS

ACKNOWLEDGEMENTS

I wish to thank my many friends who have encouraged me to present in written form the thoughts we have shared together.

I am particularly grateful to those friends with expertise in Theology, Biblical Studies and Physics who read my draft text and enriched it with their recommendations.

I wish also to express my gratitude to innumerable authors over the last decade whose insights have inspired me, particularly those whose works I mention.

Seed Thought

In all aspects of life — scientific, sociological, political, cultural, ethical, psychological — we no longer express ourselves nor understand our world as our parents did.

Yet we are expected to believe in and worship a God with concepts that have remained unchanged since the Middle Ages. Hence the sense of unreality about God, about religion, about the Church experienced by so many Christians today.

INTRODUCTION

What do a Catholic-turned-Quaker marriage counsellor, an ex-Lutheran spiritual healer and a Catholic missionary priest (myself) have in common? In 1990 we formed *The More-to-Life Partnership* to offer people weekend non-religious retreats.

During these retreats we make no mention of such "religious" subjects as the Bible or the Church or Christ. Nor do we pronounce the name God. We do, however, refer to The Divine Mystery, since participants come to these retreats precisely because they are on a spiritual search and are aware of the transcendental.

At every retreat we see confirmation of the view expressed by the late Gerald Priestland, the religious broadcaster, that our western world is becoming less and less religious but more and more spiritual. Not all retreatants come from a Christian background, but among those who do one might say that their perception of God puts them into one of three categories.

There are those — few in number — who cling desperately to a belief in a set of truths they were taught as children. This provides them with a basic security even though, and especially now, they are meeting apparent contradictions. Fear of letting go these childhood images, fear perhaps of judgement and of eternal punishment which are features of this faith-package — even a fear of God — restrain their exploration. That which seems to contradict their experience they simply label "a mystery". And yet they are left feeling uncomfortable, schizophrenic. So, tentatively, they join the searchers.

The second group has been on the searchers' road for some time. They have been able to make the step — a big one in some cases — of letting go what they were brought up to believe because it just does not seem to match up with the way they are experiencing their lives or the world. They experience a gap between the expression of these truths and Truth. Having let go, they feel they have nothing to lose. They are real explorers, excitedly following the trail wherever it leads at the time, and experiencing a liberation in doing so.

The third category, while acknowledging the Christian influence on their culture, were never brought up with any Church connections and religious practice played no part in their education. Having arrived at middle age, they feel they are missing out on a vital dimension of life — the spiritual, if not the religious — and are pursuing any path their intuition prompts them to follow. They are urged on in their search because they feel there is "more to life".

The large majority of participants belong to the second category and it is to these especially that I offer this book. I believe they represent a very large and rapidly increasing number of people in our western culture for whom our traditional Churches are no longer sources of spiritual nourishment. While people in the third category feel no attraction towards any Church because in their eyes no Church offers the answers to the questions they are asking, these people of the second category were once deeply religious and loyal members of their Church congregation but now feel that their spiritual growth has taken them beyond where their fellow parishioners are. But it is more than that. They feel that their continued participation in Church activities, in its worship, in discussions with staunch Christians, is actually holding them back from the spiritual journey to which they feel attracted: it is dragging them back to a stage they have left.

What I offer in these pages are not answers to the questions being raised. Nor am I proposing one particular route. I am offering a compass which I hope will assist spiritual explorers in the

Christian tradition to locate where they are on their journey and, I would like to think, to help them on their way.

This is why I have not loaded the pages with footnotes and references as if it were some academic work, nor supplied a bibliography to prove how many authors agree with my views! Indeed, the authority of this book lies in the reader's judgement as to whether or not it articulates their own experience. I have, however, suggested a few easily digestible books at the end of most chapters for those readers who would like to explore further some of the points I have been able to touch upon only lightly.

Full Circle

by Erna Colebrook

The idea of God is born from
        the hearts and minds of earthlings.
The hearts and minds of earthlings are born from
        the bodies of earthlings.
The bodies of earthlings are born from
        the ancestors of earthlings.
The ancestors of earthlings are born from
        the web of life.
The web of life is born from
        the unfolding of the earth.
The unfolding of the earth is born from
        the death of a star.
The death of a star is born from
        an ever-emerging universe.
An ever-emerging universe is born from
        the heart and mind of God
who is the ground of all being and becoming.

God who is the ground of all being and becoming
        gives birth to an ever-emerging universe.
An ever-emerging universe gives birth to
        the death of a star.
The death of a star gives birth to
        an unfolding earth.
An unfolding earth gives birth to
        the web of life.
The web of life gives birth to
        the ancestors of earthlings.
The ancestors of earthlings give birth to
        the bodies of earthlings.
The bodies of earthlings give birth to
        the hearts and minds of earthlings.
The hearts and minds of earthlings give birth to
        the idea of God who is pure love.

(Reproduced from *Resurgence* magazine, with permission.)

"Let us invoke Him as the inexpressible God, incomprehensible, invisible and unknowable. Let us avow that He surpasses all power of human speech, that He eludes the grasp of every mortal intelligence, that the Angels cannot penetrate Him, nor the Seraphim see Him in full clarity, nor the Cherubim fully understand Him. For He is invisible to the Principalities and Powers, to all creatures without exception. Only the Son and the Holy Spirit know Him."

— *St John Chrysostom, c.347–407*
Doctor of the Church

Chapter 1

AN EVOLVING GOD

In a previous book, *God and the Aquarian Age,* I read the "signs of the times" to identify the developing trends in society, chiefly, though not exclusively, in the western world.* I suggested there that all these trends can be classified under four major heads, what I call four Key Trends: that these provide a key to the understanding of all the changes taking place with increasing rapidity today.

Key Trends in Society

I listed these Key Trends as:

1. **An increasing humanisation.** By this is meant, very briefly, that people of our technological age are taking more responsibility for their lives: they desire to be in control of their human situation and to participate in the planning of their own and their children's futures. They are drawing more fully upon all their human abilities.

2. **A global movement towards unity.** This is apparent at three levels:

   a. *The personal*: there are signs of growth towards personal integration, shown by increasing concern for whole food,

---

* The word *world* can have a number of meanings. To avoid ambiguity I use it in this book only in the sociological sense of the place humanity inhabits. To describe the totality of creation I refer to the *Universe* or the *Cosmos*. I use the *Earth* to refer to our planet from the ecological, evolutionary point of view.

yoga, complementary medicine, the popularity of personal growth workshops, and the many means sought to bring about greater body-mind-spirit balance in life.

b.   *The social*: manifested by such groupings as the United Nations, the European Union, the African Union, etc., and at a planetary level the sense that we belong to one global village, demonstrated by the tremendous response to disaster appeals at the other side of the world. On the Christian scene, illustrated by the growth in ecumenical endeavour between Churches and the increasing dialogue with people of other religions.

c.   *The cosmic*: the many signs of humanity's concern for the environment and for ecological issues, ranging from the Green Party in politics to Creation Theology in the Church.

3   **The emergence of a new era of consciousness and the increasing recognition of this.** Among the manifestations of this are a greater awareness and interpretation of the synchronicity of events and encounters in our daily lives, the re-emergence of feminine energy, the Gaia hypothesis, the return to Vedic science, the popularity of meditation techniques, the new cosmology, appreciation of the influence of the Morphic Field, a more widespread belief in reincarnation, a desire to move from religious knowledge to spiritual experience, increasing instances of channelling.

It is when I name what I believe to be the fourth Key Trend that eyebrows are raised, especially when I do so in a lecture to non-Church people. I identify this as:

4   **A new perception of the Divine Mystery.** For I am convinced that the spiritual dimension of life plays a prime role in ordering our manner of living and relating to others and to our environment, even if, for many people, it is at the subconscious level and outside any adherence to a structured religion.

A Challenged Perception of God

If our personal experience verifies all or some aspects of the first three Key Trends as descriptive of our present world, is it any surprise that within this scenario, within these everyday experiences, we find ourselves struggling with an unchanged, static perception of God? In all aspects of life — scientific, sociological, political, cultural, ethical, psychological — we no longer express ourselves nor understand our world as our parents did. Yet we are expected to believe in and worship a God explained in theological concepts that have remained unchanged since the Middle Ages.

We are faced with a number of disjunctions between our day-to-day experience of life and what is proposed for our religious belief. Let us just look at some of these.

We are taught that the human species is "the only creature on Earth which God willed for itself" (Second Vatican Council, 1965, GS 24) as if we were the final product of creation for the sake of which all that went before (including the 99 per cent of species that inhabited the Earth previously but are now extinct) were no more than a means to an end, the end being us! But today we accept that creation was not a once-for-all-time event but is an ongoing process, always evolving. We recognise our true place within the total picture of this emerging creation. We are appreciating that the human being is only one species among many, albeit the most recent arrival, one with a developed self-consciousness, a stage on the evolutionary flow. Do we feel comfortable believing that God created the billions of galaxies millions of light-years away from Earth, simply for our benefit?

While astrophysicists explore the immensity of the Universe and geologists tell us of the composition of the Earth's core, we still do our God-thinking with the cosmology of the Israelites of 2,000 years ago. We raise our eyes to Heaven, a place where God is, from which Jesus "came down on earth" and to which he "ascended" back to his Father. We speak of Heaven and Hell as if

they were geographical places rather than modes of being and relating, life in another dimension of energy.

We continue to have proposed for our belief an account of
humanity's Fall from a perfect Eden state and the consequences
for us of inheriting through conception the Original Sin of an
original pair of parents uniquely created by God; yet our knowledge of prehistory reveals that human beings developed from different pairs of primates in different continents over a period of
two million years.

We live in a technological age in which we are able to control
most natural forces — from genetic engineering to atom-splitting
— yet we still presume in a God who is attendant upon us to answer our prayers, to change the laws of nature in our favour, to
bring about instant climatic changes — according to our whims.

We profess our faith that Jesus saved us by his suffering and
death on a cross, by shedding his blood to pay a debt for our sins,
a belief we express in terms of redemption, ransom, sacrifice —
words which belong to the era when slaves were bought and sold
and rulers had to be appeased and which leave us dissatisfied as
an explanation, meaningful for our times, of just how the Jesus-
event touches our lives 2,000 years later.

We continue to address God in archaic emperor-worship titles
— Lord, Judge, King, Almighty, Creator — rather than by those
words which relate to the deepest dimensions of our lives — Truth,
Wisdom, Love, Life — adjectives which Scripture applies to God.
After Hiroshima, can we continue to think of God and address him
as uniquely all-powerful when we have taken upon ourselves the
task of guarding the balance between sustaining creation and the
obliteration of all life on Earth, the potential for omnicide?

We maintain our dualistic approach to life — a legacy of the
Greek philosophers of 2,000 years ago — distinguishing the natural from the supernatural, thereby dividing into two distinct zones
the secular and the religious. We act as if God can only be found
and communicated with by our withdrawing from the human and

secular and entering the "holy" part of life where God belongs. The implication is that the religious part of life holds a primacy over the secular. Yet for most Christians today, to turn away from the secular seems irresponsible. They feel God must be present at the centre of the totality of their lives where they invest most of their intellectual and emotional energies. Today we are more aware of offending other people than we are of offending God because we relate to other people more immediately than we relate to God.

These are just a few reminders of the schizophrenic life we lead in our God relationship!

An Evolving God?

God does not evolve. Not because God is stagnant but because God *is*: always fully in the eternal *now*. It is we who are evolving in consciousness, in our understanding of our place in the historical and physical totality of creation. Our perception of God evolves as we evolve and as our God–human relationship evolves. This evolution took a great leap forward when humanity emerged from a state of pre-consciousness into a state of self-consciousness and it is now, I firmly believe, making another great step forward, rising to a state of super-consciousness in our own times.

Is God going to be left out? Is God going to become redundant? No. Whatever the future holds for religion, we cannot dispense with the spiritual. Since our emergence into self-consciousness, spirituality has been a constituent part of our human make-up.

Our Religious History

Our distant ancestors, going back some 100,000 years, who had discovered fire and were making tools, must have been aware of a spiritual dimension to life. They believed in an afterlife, as is indicated by their burial customs. It is only comparatively recently in human history — around 2,000 BCE — that humanity started to

structure its spiritual experience, that the major religions began to
appear. Formal religion comprises only about six per cent of human religious history.

Today, despite Church leaders bemoaning the fact that Europe
is no longer Christian, our western culture is still fundamentally a
Christian culture, formed by centuries of Christian influence and
belief. Eastern cultures are influenced by Hinduism, Buddhism
and Taoism, while a fifth of the world's population is guided by
the beliefs, moral values and laws of Islam.

Religious and cultural pluralism is, however, spreading
throughout the world as never before, on account of migration,
borders being more open, the ease of intercontinental travel as
well as through the increasing transmigration of the refugee
population. (For example, Britain is home to more than five hundred different religious groups.) It is also promoted by our easy
access to knowledge of other cultures through the media. The
world's major religions are no longer confined to specific areas of
the globe. So one finds, for instance, people in Britain embracing
Islam or Hinduism or Buddhism in preference to the Christianity
of their upbringing.

There is increasing dialogue between the leaders of the major
religions, not only at the level of belief but even more on subjects
of common human concern such as justice and peace and environmental issues.

Almost all major religions have this in common: they believe
in a Divine Power, a Divine Being greater than the human, in
which we have our origin; and that our ultimate destiny is the fulfilment of our happiness through some form of union with the
Divine. Furthermore, all are agreed that the human condition is
flawed in some way, but they differ in the means they offer to
right it; they propose different paths by which to reach our journey's end (see figure opposite).

Different Religious Understandings of the Flaw in our Human Condition and the Different Ways of Addressing the Root Problem

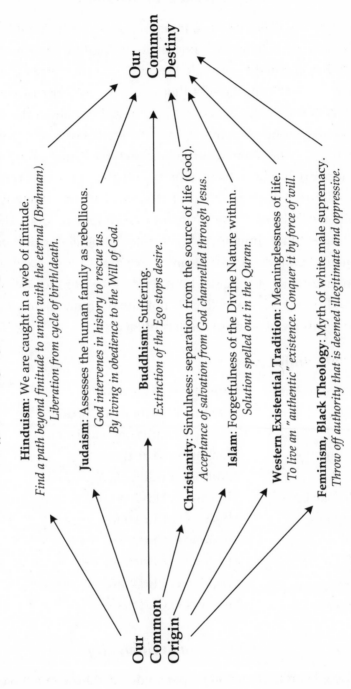

Our Common Origin

Our Common Destiny

Hinduism: We are caught in a web of finitude. *Find a path beyond finitude to union with the eternal (Brahman). Liberation from cycle of birth/death.*

Judaism: Assesses the human family as rebellious. *God intervenes in history to rescue us. By living in obedience to the Will of God.*

Buddhism: Suffering. *Extinction of the Ego stops desire.*

Christianity: Sinfulness: separation from the source of life (God). *Acceptance of salvation from God channelled through Jesus.*

Islam: Forgetfulness of the Divine Nature within. *Solution spelled out in the Quran.*

Western Existential Tradition: Meaninglessness of life. *To live an "authentic" existence. Conquer it by force of will.*

Feminism, Black Theology: Myth of white male supremacy. *Throw off authority that is deemed illegitimate and oppressive.*

Source: Inspired by an article by Ellen Z. Charry in *Toward a Universal Theology of Religion*, Orbis Books, 1987.

Divisiveness of Religion

What is so tragic is that since their emergence within only the last 3,500 years, each religion, while maintaining that love is its foundation, has claimed to provide *the* right, and therefore *the* unique, path. It is a sobering thought that while the majority of wars and conflicts in our world in recent years have been about the right of a particular group of people to govern themselves as a people — tribal wars — the main factor giving each particular group its cultural identity has been its loyalty to a religion, or an interpretation of a religion, which is different from that of its antagonist. Put simply, we fight over our different perceptions of God. The German philosopher, Immanuel Kant, said in the eighteenth century that nature employed two means to separate peoples: differences of language and of religion, both tending to produce mutual hatred and pretexts for war. This is not always immediately evident. Let us be aware of some of these conflict areas.

War and Conflict Areas

Northern Ireland	Catholics v. Protestants
Cyprus	Muslims v. Orthodox Christians
Israel	Jews v. Muslims and Christians
Lebanon	Muslims v. Christians
Sri Lanka	Hindus v. Buddhists
India/Pakistan	Muslims v. Hindus
Philippines	Muslims v. Christians
Sudan	Muslims v. Christians
Chad	Muslims v. Christians
Georgia	Muslims v. Christians
Azerbaijan	Muslims v. Christians

Our Common Humanity

If all people on Earth could be persuaded just how much we share with one another in our common humanity and that so many of our differences arise from the roots of our differing God-concepts, we might be more willing to accept other people as our brothers and sisters. In these pages, I contend that our deepest physical, psychological and spiritual experiences are the same for all of us and arise not from a religious belief nor from a religion-formed culture, but out of our humanity. They are the same because human beings do not differ in terms of their sense perception or in the way their brains work. It is our interpretations of these experiences and the causes to which we attribute them that are coloured by our religious beliefs.

It is my contention also that on the part of Christians one of the causes of world problems is that for too long we have over-emphasised the transcendence of God at the expense of appreciating God as immanent. The former causes us to think of God as aloof from creation and ourselves as miserable sinners seeking to placate a father-God or to win the love of a tolerant God. To restore the balance by emphasising more the immanence of God will enable us to appreciate that spark of divine life within all people and cause us to treat the natural world not as a dead, soulless machine existing purely for our use but as a reflection of its creator. The lack of this sense of the Divine within ourselves causes us to lack self-esteem and seek our self-worth instead in our role in society, our possessions, our personal achievements and our sense of superiority over others. Happily, we can recognise in some current trends — the feminist, ecological and human rights movements — a reawakening to the immanence of God.

While I offer this book in the hope that its reappraisal of the God–humanity relationship will contribute to the growing together of the human family across the frontiers set by different religions, its particular concern is to examine the meaning of that tiny word "God" for those of us who like to call ourselves Christians.

The very word *God* is problematic. This word with which we name the Ultimate Mystery stems from a Germanic root meaning "good" as opposed to "evil". Therein lies the seed of a dualism which has probably had a profound but unconscious effect on western religious thinking. Whereas, if we turn to the Middle East where our Judeo-Christian religion originated, we find names like *Elat* (Old Canaanite), *Elohim* (Hebrew), *Alaha* (Aramaic) and *Allah* (Arabic) which stem from roots more correctly translated as Oneness, the All, Divine Unity or the Being of the Universe.

Surely no reader would deny that a great deal of rethinking about God is going on amongst ordinary Christians in our culture today. Even in theological circles we have been through the "Death of God" phase and are now hearing about Secular Christianity: that belief in God is not intrinsic to Christianity. However, the reason for our disquiet about the traditional, orthodox concept of God cannot be attributed to any one event or to a single emerging philosophy. I propose in these pages that there are a number of factors — each chapter deals with one of these — in our present evolution of consciousness which, not individually but collectively, are pushing us towards new horizons in our perception of the Divine Mystery. Although chapter follows chapter as one might expect, their sequence is of little significance. Each is like paint on an artist's pallet. It is for the reader to "pick and mix" the colours in order to create that picture of the Divine Mystery which speaks to them most appropriately at the present moment.

CB

"Looking at the Earth from afar you realise it is too small
for conflict and just big enough for co-operation."
— *Yuri Gagarin, the first human being in space.*

For further exploration

Adrian B. Smith (2002), *A Reason for Living and Hoping: A Christian Appreciation of the Emerging New Era of Consciousness*, St Paul's Publishing, London.

James Redfield and Michael Murphy (2002), *God and the Evolving Universe*, Transworld Publishers, London.

Ray Grasse (2002), *Signs of the Times*, Hampton Roads Publishing Co. USA.

Chapter 2

THE KNOWLEDGE FACTOR

Even if a man is deeply versed in the understanding and knowledge of all spiritual things ever created, he can never by such understanding come to know an uncreated spiritual thing . . . which is none else than God! But by recognising the reason for the limitation of his understanding, he may. Because the thing that limits his understanding is God, himself alone.

— *The Cloud of Unknowing*, fourteenth century.

How can we know God? One meets a great deal of confused thinking about the way in which God makes Himself* known to human beings — what is called in theological terminology "Divine Revelation". (We will go into this more deeply when considering the Revelation Factor.)

It would seem that the root of the problem lies in the classical theologian's approach to the subject by starting from God. It is presumed that we have been given a package of information about God — albeit a package which has been added to from time to time — and in the light of that all else can be understood and put into perspective. The scholastic theologians of the Middle Ages claimed that this revelation reached its climax in the teaching of Jesus and that thereafter there was nothing new to learn. As it used

---

* I use the capital "H" with He, Him, His, Her for God as distinct from a gender "he" or "she".

to be said, Divine Revelation ended with the death of the last Apostle. In other words, this knowledge of the divinity takes a top-to-bottom, a God-to-humanity, direction. And, what is more, there is a lot that we would not know about God if God had not deigned to make it known to us. These theologians, therefore, make a distinction between Natural Revelation — knowledge of the Divine Mystery that can be known by us without God's intervention — and Divine Revelation, which is channelled to humanity through the Church, the guardian of divine truth, and, in particular, through the Church's interpretation of the Bible. Consequently, the knowledge that other religions have of God is only Natural Revelation and certainly quite deficient. Or so it used to be said. I would suggest that the approach has to be bottom-upwards.

Human Consciousness: The Key to All Knowledge

The recurring theme of this book is that human consciousness is the source, and the only source, of all we know about creation and about whatever is beyond the confines of our time-space creation — about God.

I deliberately say "human consciousness" and not human knowledge because our perception comes from two sources: our rational knowledge which informs us *about* the spiritual, the divine, and our intuitive knowledge which gives us a *direct* experience of the spiritual and the divine.

At a tender age when I was first made to learn the answers of the catechism — answers to questions I never thought of asking at that age — I learnt that human beings were "created in the image and likeness of God". This presumed that we knew a lot about God in the light of which we could understand the fundamental questions about human life on Earth.

I propose that it is more true to say — and I am not the first to say it — that we make God in our own image and likeness; that we can do nothing else than start where we are and from that understanding reach upwards to learn something of that which is higher and greater. Human consciousness is the key to open up all our treasury of knowledge.

In what pertains to our understanding of the Divine Mystery, the top-down approach gives the Church the last word, the ultimate power, over our knowledge. But this is only because we allow the Church to exercise this power over us. We become passive subjects, whereas, in fact, the Church would not be able to exercise this power if we did not let it do so by surrendering our minds to it. This may have been an acceptable practice in medieval times but it is not being accepted by educated, free-thinking people today. Today we feel freer to question everything and to accept only what we feel to be authentic, by which we mean that which makes sense within the parameters of our own experience. And this surely is what it means to be fully human.

There is Only One Consciousness

As human beings we know things humanly! There are not two different ways of knowing: a way that pertains to our life on Earth and a different way of knowing what we call the Divine. All our knowledge is dealt with by the same human mind. There is not a special mind for knowing the Divine, nor a special channel of thought or of language through which God communicates Himself to humanity. There are not two parallel systems of communication, as if, so to speak, one had the choice between receiving via land cables or by satellite, or between receiving on this or that waveband. The human mind is both the transmitter and the receiver of all knowledge which we are capable of handling.

Even what is proposed to us as Divine Revelation has to be received and interpreted by the same human mind that receives information about all that is around us. There are not two different departments of the mind: one for knowledge of material things and another for spiritual truths.

Outer and Inner Sources of Knowledge

While there is only one knowledge that the human mind handles there are, however, two channels by which such knowledge enters our consciousness. Again, the difference is not between human and natural or divine and supernatural. I choose to call them an outer source and an inner source. Both provide us with a single knowledge but in a different form.

By the outer forms of knowledge I mean all the information which reaches our minds from an outside source. Our "receivers" for taking this in are our five senses: touch, smell, hearing, taste and sight. I am not listing them as hands, nose, ears, tongue and eyes: these are the physical instruments through which the information enters, while touch, smell, hearing, taste and sight are the experience we have when the mind has applied itself to what it encounters through our "sensors" and identifies it. So the mind needs to do something with the information it receives. We call this information rational knowledge because it is processed by our reason. The information is only of use to us once the mind has identified it, catalogued it, compared it with previous experiences, reflected upon its source, decided how to respond or react to it. These are just some of the ways the mind handles this incoming information. We edit our experiences to fit pre-conceived ideas. As the French writer Anaïs Nin (1903–1977) observed, "We don't see things as they are, we see them as we are."

Applied to God-knowledge, this is the information that has come to us from outside ourselves, in fact, through other people, and it is always *about* God and *about* divine truths: it is not a direct experience of them. As I shall explain later, it is about truths, not about Truth.

All during our lifetime we have been picking up pieces of information about the Divine and building up a mental picture. The "truths" have come to us through our various senses and in a variety of ways: in our earliest days, perhaps, seeing our parents on their knees praying and realising there must be Someone even greater than they, from our catechism or Sunday School classes, through those prayers we had to learn by heart, from Bible stories, from holy pictures, by feeling a sense of awe in a beautiful cathedral, through our participation in an impressive liturgy, through the words of the hymns we sang together — in innumerable ways. But perhaps the most lasting impressions were made by the teacher or parent who explained the meaning of all these disjointed messages and helped us to assemble them into a whole. This probably awoke our first awareness of there being something greater than our everyday experiences. Indeed, those first childhood ideas made a very deep and lasting impression on us and often lurk in the background even when our adult mind has rethought its way through them. This is particularly the case if a parent or teacher has used ideas of the Divine — probably supported by pictures of devils or of Hell — as threats to ensure our good behaviour. Through this a deep fear of the spiritual world has often survived into the unconsciousness of adult life. It may take a lifetime — or death — to undo some of the damage done to our spiritual growth by the manipulation of truths by adults in our childhood. Fear is an exceedingly strong motivation.

Although we are more impressionable in childhood, we still continue to be exposed to this outside source of knowledge in matters spiritual, but our adult mind has a different way of dealing with it — or perhaps of deliberately ignoring it. I recall that on one occasion when I was a small boy at my Preparatory School I was kneeling in the chapel before the Blessed Sacrament exposed in the monstrance. There appeared to me the "vision" of a shamrock on the white host. (We had been taught that the shamrock with its three leaves on one stalk was a symbol of the Blessed Trinity.) I learned later, to my great disappointment, that there was a "scientific" explanation for this: it was caused by the shadows formed by the spotlights. Nevertheless, the "spiritual" explanation of the experience held a message for me.

Our Intuition

The other channel of knowledge I call an inner source because it is spontaneous, unprovoked, and comes not through our senses and our rational mind sorting it out but from our intuition. Literally, intuition means tuition from within. It is defined in some dictionaries as "the quick perception of truth or knowledge without conscious attention or reasoning" or as "knowledge from within". Its coming is independent of our surroundings and is unprovoked. Some people are more attuned to it than others.

Applied to God-knowledge, it can be received by any person any time, irrespective of their background, education or culture; whereas outer God-knowledge is received and dealt with according to one's religious background and is therefore channelled most often through a religion, and consequently with that religion's interpretation. Every person, by virtue of their being human, whether of a particular religious persuasion or none, can be the recipient of intuition or, as we call it in a spiritual context, of divine inspiration. However, the way in which particular persons handle it and interpret it will depend on their religious mental baggage.

Knowledge from the outer source informs us *about* things. This is how we learn *about* God and what we learn about God — our earliest mental images — for instance, comes to us from the knowledge or understanding of other people about God, whether from a theologian or from our grandmother. So it is always second-hand and therefore coloured by *their* culture, education, experience, etc.

Intuitive knowledge, on the other hand, is direct — first-hand — and it is an experience.

Through intuitive knowledge we actually have a direct experiential encounter with the Divine, such that afterwards, when we try to express this in words or even rationalise about it in our own minds, we already begin to diminish it. We have encountered Truth. In rationalising about our experience we can only handle it partially, in a series of truths.

What I have been told: indirect knowledge *about* God coming from outside us.

Direct inspiration. An awareness *of* God coming from the deepest centre of our minds.

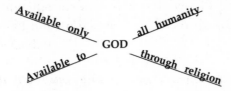

Encounter with God as Being in the depth of our being. Gives conviction: faith.

Provides us with images which convey a partial truth, e.g. God as Father, Dove, Good Shepherd, Trinity.

Our Knowing is Coloured by Our Culture

We might describe culture as the setting within which each of us lives out our lives. It includes everything from the moral values, laws and traditions by which we live, through what we call "good manners" (the way we hold our knife and fork) to what is "just not done". A more comprehensive definition might be:

> *Culture is a framework for life which gives identity to a certain people regarding their past, their wisdom, their activities, and their relationships to the created world, to each other and to the spiritual world.*

It is easy to understand, then, how the cultural framework in which we are brought up is the "material" out of which is created our knowledge about God and things spiritual and also our understanding of how we relate to these matters. Furthermore, as we said in our definition, it is the common culture that we share with a group which gives us our identity. I experience my belonging to the Christian community because we think about divine matters in (much) the same way, share the same Christian set of moral values, and relate to God in our worship in a similar way. When we come down to a particular Church or congregation, the sense of identity is much stronger because the similarities in each of these fields is much greater.

Even when we find members of some of the great world religions living together, as we do in many parts of the world today,
causing an apparent blending of the religious dimension of cultures, this can never give rise to one universal religion because
each of these religions was born within a particular culture, took
its first shape from that culture and still bears the marks of that
culture wherever it might be found among other cultures today.

One can never have a religion in the abstract, naked, as it
were, of a culture. It always lives and travels in cultural clothes.
Each religion is like a language: it expresses its meaning and its
spirit but it can never be exactly translated into another religion of
another culture. This is an important point as regards the Christian message coming to us from the pages of the New Testament.
We shall develop the point later. It means that in order to try to
understand the heart of this or that religion — or this or that way
of understanding the Divine — one has to try to distinguish between what is essential to that religion and what are the cultural
clothes it is wearing, either in the past or at present.

As the figure opposite seeks to illustrate, the meeting point of
the world's religions can only be at the mystical level of knowledge.

We Cannot Know God as God

We cannot know about God neat! We can only know about God
from what He shows us by His out-going energies, ranging from
the simplest created cell to the human person of Jesus.

If I were to be asked by a pollster in the High Street: "Do you
believe in God?" my instinctive answer would be Yes. But then
with equal truth I might answer No. I can really say no more than
that I believe in my own understanding of God. I have no way of
knowing what the pollster's image of God is or what was in the
mind of whoever wrote the question, and who would be inter-
preting my answer. To say either Yes or No might be to convey an

Levels of Knowledge

1. Superficial Level

Reason, Logic, Science, Technology

2. Religious Level
(To give meaning to 1.)

Christianity, Judaism, Islam, Hinduism, Buddhism, Bahai, etc.

Ritual, Laws, Structure, Hierarchy, Doctrine, Sacraments, etc

3. Mystical Level

UNITY
Experience of the Divine, of Reality
beyond thought or words

idea to the other which is quite the opposite of what I intend to say. If the question-writer, the pollster and myself were able to sit down and discuss what we all meant by the question, we might come to some agreed notion, but then it would only be *about* God. Our experience of God, which is the foundation of our belief in God, always remains personal to us and impossible to share.So there is another problem with the question which we shall have to tackle later. This is not only a question of how I perceive God but it is also a question about my faith in God. Does the questioner mean: "Do I believe the fact that there is a God?" or "Do I believe *in* God?" in the sense that I believe in goodness and justice?

This is all to say that we cannot comprehend God in totality. One cannot contain in the here and now that which is transcendent. Of necessity, we have to work with a partial idea of God, which we piece together from a number of elements: our upbringing, our education, our culture, our experience, our relationships — all very personal baggage. Once again: we create our God to our own image and likeness.

There is the God of our world, the God of our lives, the God whom we can relate to, the God whom we have to think of as Him or Her. We need God to be "human size" before we can relate to Her/Him. We can think of such a God as creating us — individually, specifically, because we are wanted as a part of His/Her loving plan — as protecting and guiding us. We can think of ourselves as loved personally by this God.

But when we put ourselves and our world in their cosmic setting, the cosy God–me relationship begins to be challenged. Our Sun is just one star among some hundred billion stars in our Milky Way and astronomers suggest that our Milky Way galaxy is only one of a hundred billion other galaxies about which we know next to nothing except that they are there. (Some scientists even suggest that there might be five billion other universes!)

How do we human beings cope with a Universe-sized God? Meister Eckhart, the German mystic of the thirteenth century, used to distinguish between God and the Godhead. "God" is the God of human proportions, the Divinity brought down to a size we can comprehend and relate to. But beyond this is the transcendent God we cannot grasp, the Godhead. He wrote:

> God and Godhead are as distinct as Heaven and
> Earth. Heaven stands a thousand miles above the
> Earth, and even so the Godhead is above God.

Similarly the Hindus speak of God manifest and God unmanifest. The former is God in human terms, while the latter can only be described in negative terms as God beyond our thought limitations: not this and not that. Within the Christian tradition too, we have a negative way of speaking of God, called the apophatic way, when we describe God as *in*finite, *in*visible, *im*mortal, *un*created, *in*corporeal, *in*divisible, *in*comprehensible, to indicate that he does not suffer our human limitations. St Dionysius wrote in the fifth century: "The most god-like knowledge of God is that which is knowledge by unknowing." Paul Tillich, the Protestant theologian, speaks of "the God above God". Perhaps we can most usefully speak of the God above God as "the Divine Mystery" and reserve the name "God" for our very limited human comprehension of this mystery.

A conversation on this subject might go like this:

"If you speak of God Unmanifest and of God Manifest are you not speaking of two gods?"

"No."

"Then at least two forms of God with different properties."

"No. The distinction is in us, not in God, in our way of comprehending — or rather, within the limitations of our way of comprehending. God Manifest is God in relationship to us."

"So if creation did not exist there would be no God Manifest?"

"Correct. And what is more, if creation existed but human beings did not, there would be no God Manifest because we alone in the whole of

creation (or at least on the whole of Planet Earth) are able to think about God and relate deliberately to God.

"The use of a Zen koan might help: What is the noise made by a tree falling in a forest if there is no living creature around to hear it? The tree falls, it causes the breaking of branches, the rush of wind, the tearing of the roots and all the other things that would be heard if there were any-one present. But can there be noise if nothing is heard by someone or something?

"God Unmanifest is always God but God is only God Manifest if there is a human being to observe, receive and interpret the manifesta-tion. If I did not exist, the problem of the existence of God would not ex-ist . . . for me."

Knowing God Partially

As a prism breaks up white light into its component colours — red, orange, yellow, green, blue, indigo, violet — so we can only think about the Divine Mystery through the prism of human con-sciousness, and deal with the component parts such as Love and Truth and Goodness and Beauty, as if they were separate entities, handling them one at a time (see figure below).

The Prism of Human Consciousness

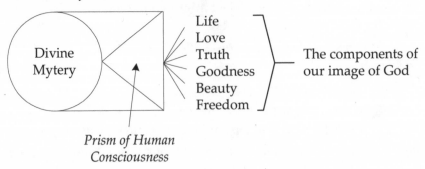

As far back as we are able to trace in our history — and still now we are observing the practice among the Aborigines of Australia and the Indians of America — the human being had an anthropomorphic attitude to animals: projecting human qualities upon them. And we continue to do so today. "Poor dog, he is missing his mistress." The dog, who lives entirely in the present, with no sense of past or future is surely aware that his mistress is not present but to say he is missing her is to say that he is reflecting, "I do hope she will come back safely", which of course is absurd.

While we project our mental abilities on to "lower" creatures, we have also done the same on to "higher" beings. Ever since our early ancestors became self-reflective and aware of otherness they created gods. God becomes an extension of ourselves. We expect God to have the same emotions as we have: to feel anger, sorrow, mercy, forgiveness . . . to be a loving father. Such anthropomorphism is only to be expected because it is the only way we can relate to pure spirit. This is how we "visualise" God manifest, how we can know *about* God with our rational, analytic mind. But with our intuitive mind we can comprehend reality, not in parts, but in a totality, and it is with our intuitive mind that we can have an experience, a glimpse, a taste of the Divine Mystery in its wholeness, God unmanifest.

Our two sources of knowledge complement each other. If the intuitive experience is to be of benefit to us, we need to apply our rational mind in order to interpret it. The knowledge coming from the outside source — tradition, culture, education — enables us to understand its relevance to our lives. On the other hand, the knowledge we receive from the outside source, second-hand, remains only a library of facts unless it is given life and soul by our inner experience, and thus made of value to our lives.

An analogy: A friend invited me to have a look at a house he was thinking of buying. He had made arrangements to look over it with the agent a couple of days later, but, knowing the owners were away, he was keen to take a first look immediately. We walked around the house, peering in each ground-floor window in turn. This way we could see just one room at a time and then only a part of each room. We could not see how the rooms related to one another, nor anything of the hall nor the staircase. And we certainly could not see upstairs. It was a very limited, partial and unsatisfactory viewing. Furthermore, what we did manage to see of each room was not our own conception of how the house might be, but the owners' — their furnishing, their carpeting, their decorating. Only when my friend was let in by the agent a couple of days later was he able to have an insider's perception of the whole and get the "feel" of it, and imagine the house as he would furnish and decorate it according to his tastes.

The first visit was like a perception of God from the outside looking in — partial, second-hand knowledge. The second visit was like the intuitive knowledge of God. It was from inside, from the centre. It was an inner experience, not just a peering in.

The Christian whose only knowledge of God is from without — only knowing facts *about* God — can have no more than an impoverished, dogma-directed, morality-ruled religious life. It lacks spirit, it lacks soul, it is lived only in exterior observance. As Aldous Huxley graphically expresses it in *The Perennial Philosophy*: "To suppose that people can be saved by studying and giving assent to formulae is like supposing one can get to Timbuctoo by poring over a map of Africa."

On the other hand, the person with no rational understanding of divine truths who undergoes a deep spiritual experience may be overwhelmed by it, but does not know how it can be of benefit for their spiritual growth and is not able to channel the experience into a life-enhancing form.

From Knowledge to Wisdom

The word "wisdom" can cover a range of meanings: enlightenment, the experience of the elderly, soundness of judgement in matters relating to life and conduct. We think of the proverbial wisdom of Solomon. One category of biblical books is known as the Wisdom literature: the *Book of Wisdom*, *Ecclesiasticus* (or *The*

Wisdom of Jesus Ben Sirach), *Job*, *The Proverbs*, *The Song of Songs*.
Here I distinguish wisdom from knowledge. The latter derives
from what I have previously called the outer sources of knowledge
— the senses — and is processed by the rational mind. The former
derives from the inner source of knowledge, from intuition, ma-
tured by experience. It is listed by St Paul among the Gifts of the
Holy Spirit. If we are to *know* God, we have to develop wisdom.

The first step is to be aware that we already possess wisdom,
as distinct from knowledge. Knowledge is like baggage: we pick it
up, carry it around, make use of it when required and, if our
memory does not serve us well, we discard it. It is an appendage
to life. Whereas wisdom is part of our being. While we speak of
people being knowledge*able* we speak of them as *being* wise. Wisdom is part of our essence as human beings, part of our spirit. As
we need to be reminded, we are not bodies that have a spirit but
spirits that have a body — for a time. As the Holy Spirit is the dynamic of life, we are, as it were, branches of this same Spirit.

Knowing is wisdom, knowing *about* is knowledge. Since
knowledge is on the surface of the mind, so to speak, it can be a
blockage to our cultivating wisdom. It is the concern of what has
come to be called "left-brain thinking". Too much of that (as pre-
dominates in western society) can prevent the development of
"right-brain thinking" — the domain of wisdom. Less technologically developed people in the developing areas of the world — the
Third World — show greater wisdom because they are more in
tune with the harmonies of nature, more aware of the spirit
world. They live more in the present than in the past or the future.

We have — some would say we are suffering from — an information explosion right now in the West. Information only becomes knowledge when we take it on board and make use of it.
But each of us can use only a limited amount of information due
to the lack of capacity of our mental computer. Sadly, our formal
education system is directed towards acquiring knowledge, not
towards developing wisdom.

Wisdom can be developed in two ways, what we might call vertically and horizontally. By vertically I mean that wisdom develops as our consciousness deepens. The most easily accessible "tool" for this is some regular practice of meditation, in the eastern meaning of that word, as for example with Transcendental Meditation. I will write no more about that here as I have dealt with the subject specifically in a previous book, *A Key to the Kingdom of Heaven: A Christian Understanding of Transcendental Meditation,* and we will be looking at it again when considering the Consciousness Factor.

When I speak of developing wisdom horizontally I refer to more deliberately living in the *now* moment. The *now* is the only reality. All other conscious creatures, animals, live only in the *now*. The only way we can commune with nature is in the present moment. We will be developing this understanding of the *now* moment in relation to past and future when we explore the Creation Factor.

We are not good at living in the present moment. Children do, and they give more attention to the future than to the past, while the elderly live more down "memory lane" than in the future (see figure opposite). Fear and worry are products of living in the past, arising from unhappy memories or of speculating about the future. Many years ago, while I was living in Zambia, I attended an introductory lecture on the "How to Succeed" course of Dale Carnegie. Just one item from it has always stuck in my memory and I have found it a useful rule: never worry about the things that might go wrong in the future. It is a waste of energy because nine times out of ten they never happen! Such negative future projection is a significant contributory factor to stress and ulcers. (Stress arises from our inability to handle an experience.)

Children	10%	50%	40%
	Past ⟷	*Now* ⟷	*Future*
Elderly	88%	2%	10%

Note: Figures are symbolic, not statistical

We need to develop the habit — and it has to be worked at — of living the present moment with the fullest possible attention. In Zen, the practice is called "mindfulness", becoming centred or one-pointed. As God is outside time, our only entry point into the Divine Mystery is in the *now* moment.

Conclusion

All that I have written in this chapter is written within the paradigm of a God "out there", a God beyond. It is based on a hierarchical understanding of God. But is there, perhaps, another paradigm that enables us to relate to the Divine Mystery in an entirely different way? I suggest that our new understanding of creation, learnt from what we term "the new physics", opens up another way of understanding our God–humanity relationship. It opens up a new way of moving from a God-out-there paradigm to a God-within paradigm.

However, before we come to see what our present-day scientific paradigm has to say about our understanding of God, we need to give some consideration to one of the tools we use: theology.

For further exploration:

Eckhart Tolle (2001), *The Power of NOW*, Hodder & Stoughton, London.

Donah Zohar and Ian Marshall (2001), *Spiritual Intelligence*, Bloomsbury Publishing, London.

Chapter 3

THE THEOLOGY FACTOR

Theology is the way we theorise about God. It is what we are doing now. It is the work of the rational mind dealing with religious experience. St Anselm described it as "Faith seeking understanding". It is head stuff. It is not the prerogative of professional people, whom we call theologians, but is something that we all do when we try to make sense of our world in a God perspective, and equally when we try to explore God in the perspective of our world. The simple people in the *barrios* of Latin America, meeting to share the words of Scripture together in order to make sense of their social condition and to try to understand to what they are being invited, are theologising. Professor Kosuke Koyama of Singapore coined the phrase "waterbuffalo theology" in explaining that his abstract theology only had value when it was able to be communicated in terms that had meaning for the humblest rice farmer working with his waterbuffalo. In fact, despite its continual claims, the Church no longer has the monopoly of theology. In this chapter I am concerned with the value and limitations of Christian theology as a tool for understanding the shift that is taking place in our concept of God.

We have already spoken briefly about Revelation. Until now it has been understood in the Christian Tradition as a special knowledge that we would not have if God did not inject it into human thinking. St Paul understood it in this way: "The gospel I preach is not a human message that I was given by man, it is something I learnt only through a revelation of Jesus Christ" (Galatians 1:11–12). This is what theologians refer to as Divine Revelation, as distinct from what they call Natural Revelation, which is that which the human mind can learn about the Divine Mystery from everyday experience. Preaching in Asia Minor, St Paul said: "[God] has always given evidence of his existence by the good things he does: he gives you rain from heaven and crops at the right times; he gives you food, and fills your hearts with happiness" (Acts 14:17). Such thinking is dualistic, contrasting the holy with the profane, supernatural knowledge with natural knowledge. All our knowledge of the Divine Mystery is a gift of God. Indeed all knowledge is a gift of God. Another way of expressing this is to say that human consciousness alone is the only source of knowledge of the Divine Mystery. In the last chapter we spelled out the idea that there is not a special department of the mind that deals with the Divine, nor is there a different way of experiencing what is divine from any other human experience.

Experience is the Midwife of Revelation

The figure opposite indicates how our "revealed" knowledge is born of our experience. Our experience is always interpreted through the two eyes of our collective history (our tribal story) and our culture. As with human eyes, these two work in conjunction. It is important to recognise that experience always comes first. The understanding that our rational minds construct out of that experience can only be based on the intellectual baggage we have already accumulated, after a process of selection, rejection and retention. Let us take, for an example, the experience of the Israelites after they had been liberated from the slavery of the Pharaohs in Egypt. Sitting under the starry night sky in the desert, around their scrub-wood fires, they would have exchanged opinions about what had happened to them and what their future might hold. One can imagine that with an abundance of time, with the silence and solitude of the desert, their reflection upon the events that brought about their liberation against all odds might easily lead them to the conviction that this could only have come about by the intervention of some outside, divine power: the power of their god. If their god was moving in these mysterious ways, favouring them so mightily, it could only be because he had a special destiny in store for them. They felt themselves to be set aside for a purpose, a people apart, a Chosen People.

Theology's Reliance on History and Culture

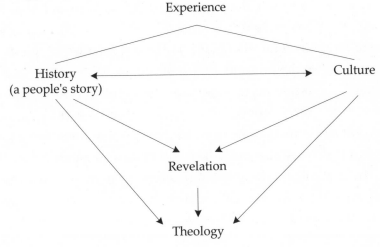

This reflection on their experience gave them a more developed understanding of their relationship to their god. But when we say it caused their understanding to develop, we are not saying that it approached nearer to the Truth, because we do not have an outside, objective knowledge of the Divine Mystery with which to measure it, enabling us to say that their understanding took another step in the right direction. But there are two things we can say about this development.

In the first place it was coloured by their past story, right back through their ancestors, to Abraham, and was a development of past understandings of the nature of divine power. This, coupled with their contemporary culture, caused them to make this particular interpretation — for it was no more than an interpretation — of their experience, and no other. It took them further along the road towards answering the fundamental questions that are continually, and are still today, asked within all cultures: Who are we? Why are we here? What is our origin? What is our value? What is there beyond death?

Myth is the Seed of Theology

As soon as our early ancestors became self-reflective, had arrived at a sense of their own identity, began to rationalise and to differentiate past from present from future — this was with the development of rudimentary language — these fundamental questions were asked. Myths arose to supply answers. Myth is the seed of theology. The origin myth is the most fundamental story of all societies. It has been defined as a sacred narrative explaining how the world or humans came to be in their present form and condition. But it also justifies the nature and culture of a particular society. The mythologist Joseph Campbell, who perhaps wrote more about mythology in his lifetime than anyone else, describes myth as an embodiment of Truth. He says:

> The comparative study of mythologies of the world compels
> us to view the cultural history of mankind as a unit.

He goes on to observe something particularly relevant to our study:

> We find that such themes as the fire-thief, the flood, a land
> of the dead, a virgin birth and a resurrection hero have a
> world-wide distribution — appearing everywhere in new
> combinations, while remaining, like the elements of a ka-
> leidoscope, only a few and always the same.

Secondly, we can call the Israelite's myth a development because, just as there is continuity in the human story, so there is continuity in the interpretation of spiritual experience. As the Exodus event led to a clarification about the nature of the Divine and the awareness of a special God–Israelites relationship, so it became another step towards a further developed understanding. Our Judeo-Christian theology is built on the edifice of the Israelites' understanding of themselves as a Chosen People, and also, as we shall see later, on their world view, their cosmology.

In his book *The Chosen Peoples*, missiologist Walbert Buhlmann makes the point that tribes and societies, the world over, have considered themselves to be "chosen", to be favoured in a special way by their supreme deity who defends them against their neighbouring tribes. In the Judeo-Christian tradition, it is believed that it is through the myth of the Hebrew people and their understanding of the Divine Mystery that God "chose" to make himself known more truly. This was not because they alone were to receive God's blessings but because they were chosen to be a sign to the rest of humanity of God's plan for all creation. In their Scriptures they are reminded by God, through the mouth of the prophet Amos:

> People of Israel, are not you and the Cushites [Ethiopians] all the same to me? Did not I, who brought Israel out of the land of Egypt, bring the Philistines from Caphtor and the Aramaeans from Kir? (Amos 9:7)

Understanding the Jesus Event

We have another example of this process of experience-reflection-understanding in the Jesus event. From the beginning of Jesus' going public he called together a small band of men, his disciples, whom he hoped would be his co-workers in the renewal movement he was launching. Since, in its essence, the movement was to be about a new way of living based upon a new and revolutionary value system — Jesus named it the Kingdom of God — he called around him not the intellectuals or the religious leaders, but Mr Averageman. The new way was not something to be philosophised about but experienced by living it. He needed people who would make this new way of living a reality by actually living it.

(Incidentally, before the growing number of followers were named Christians, they were called the people of "The Way". It is recorded in the Acts of the Apostles (5:20) that when an angel released the apostles from prison the instruction they received was: "Go and stand in the Temple, and tell the people all about this new Life." It was not a doctrine that was to be promulgated but a way of living.)

In the account of the apostles' final parting from the risen Jesus, the event we name the Ascension, we see how little Jesus' message had penetrated their minds. They were still thinking of his announcement about the advent of God's Kingdom in political terms: "Lord, will you at this time give the Kingdom back to Israel?" (Acts 1:6). It was only after they had retreated to the safety of a hideaway (because they feared they would be the next victims of the purge and be executed like their Master) and had time to reflect together upon what the Jesus experience had meant to them over the past three years, that their minds were expanded and they arrived at a deeper level of understanding of what Jesus' presence among them was all about; how the values by which he lived and about which he spoke were based upon an entirely new God–humanity relationship. It was a move from a people relating to a tribal God, with whom a tribal covenant had been made, to an understanding that there can be a personal God–humanity relationship, so personal that God might be addressed by each one as Father, or, to use Jesus' own Aramaic word "Abba" — "Dad". And the demanding consequence of this was that, having a common father, every woman and man was to treat others as their sisters and brothers.

The most traumatic experience this little band of disciples suffered was seeing their hero's life cut short while it was still in its ascendancy, and cut short so brutally, by his being left to die on a cross — a punishment meted out to criminals. With the belief that this brutal and unexpected death must have a purpose in the divine plan, a meaning had to be found to explain it; indeed, to enable them to come to terms with it themselves. Drawing on their cultural-religious background, a cultic, priestly theory of atonement soon developed. Jesus' "sacrifice on Calvary" became the central, indeed, the unique location of his saving action. Only a physical sacrifice by such a person as Jesus could pay the price to win God's forgiveness for humanity's sin. Yet in his teaching, reconciliation is brought about, not by a price being paid but by healing a severed relationship (Luke 11:4; 15:11-32). (We will develop this more in the chapter on the Atonement Factor.) So it was not to Jesus' own teaching that the early Christians looked for an understanding of their traumatic experience; instead they drew on their religious culture.

To return to the figure on page 31, we see from these examples that the theologising done by the Israelites in the desert and later by Jesus' disciples resulted in their gaining a new and deeper understanding of the Divine Mystery, a new "revelation". While it developed out of their own history and was expressed in terms of their own culture, in turn it was absorbed into and enriched that culture and paved the way for the next enlightenment. This is the process that in Church circles is known as Tradition: the faith experience that is always living and developing.

From a Christian perspective, a Christian theology, the death of Jesus reveals God's love. In Jewish theology, from a Jewish cultural perspective, the death of Jesus is not recognised as revealing anything about God. We base our theology on a claim of Revelation, but actually it is because of our culturally determined theology that we recognise what is and what is not Revelation.

Cultural Limitations

It is important to note that the record of each step is always expressed — can only be expressed — within the limitations of that particular culture at that particular moment of its history. In other words, its recording for posterity, its communication, suffers from the limitations of language and cultural values. That in itself is a handicap when trying to communicate what belongs to the spiritual realm. But there is the further handicap present when trying to communicate with another culture and with another age. Each human language is an expression of a particular culture. We are never likely to arrive at a universal language which would have the advantage both of being known by everyone in the world and having the same cultural value everywhere. One only has to look at the different cultural interpretations found in Britain and the United States, of such words as "suspenders", "vest", "car", "dough" in our own time. Over centuries the problem is magnified because words so easily change their meaning, as I soon discovered upon returning to England after fifteen years in Zambia when I described someone as "gay"!

The point being made here is that one cannot take literally and interpret with today's vocabulary a verbal expression (of necessity a limited expression) of a spiritual experience formulated in another age and another culture. We shall have more to say about this in the chapter on the Revelation Factor.

Theology is a Living Study

So, theology is a living study, not a once-and-for-all formulation. It is always growing out of people's lived experience which, in turn, is interpreted according to their history and their culture. This is why one cannot speak of *the* Christian Theology. There are always many theologies abroad — Scholastic, Reformation, Systematic, Contextual, Liberation, etc. — but we can speak of them as being Christian when they are a particular expression of an understanding of the Divine which has its roots in the Judeo-Christian tradition.

Just as there is no one, universal, culture-free language, so there is no culture-free, world-wide theology. Theologies differ because they are seeking to answer different questions in different cultures in different ages. No theology can ever be naked, divested of cultural and historical clothes, in a pure form. We will see in the chapter on the New Paradigm Factor how our Christian theology has up to now been within the hierarchical paradigm (God above and outside his creation) of Jewish theology, despite Jesus' attempt to give us an alternative paradigm two thousand years ago.

The fact of theology being a living study is illustrated in the figure below.

How Theology Developed through External Influence

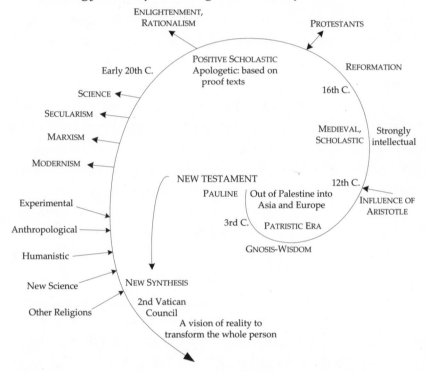

This figure illustrates how culture and philosophy in different periods of history have influenced each era's way of reflecting upon its experience of the Divine and giving it an interpretation. The arrows pointing outwards indicate the way theology was defending itself against new cultural threats, while the inward-pointing arrows show what cultural and scientific factors have influenced theological thinking. The very fact that traditional Christian theology felt itself to be under attack (from such influences as Rationalism, Secularism, Modernism) caused a reaction which in itself has been a growth point.

With the period known as the Enlightenment in the sixteenth century, when rationalism began to dominate the search for knowledge, three hitherto intertwined strands began to emerge as separate and independent avenues leading to the expansion of knowledge. These were Mysticism, Theology and Science. By Mysticism we mean the experience of a direct contact with the Ultimate, or Divine reality in its unity. By Science we mean the study of measurable facts which provide us with a rational explanation of causes and effects. Science, as we understand it today, only began to develop with an identity of its own in the late seventeenth century.

For the last three centuries, the three strands followed their separate paths, each often in conflict with the other two. In the post-Reformation era (since the sixteenth century) theologians were on the defensive, on the one hand suspicious of science and on the other belittling the value of the direct religious experience of mysticism. At the same time science was liberating itself from the control of the Church which still regarded questions about the nature of the universe to be religious issues for which theology alone could hold the answers. Having parted company, science and theology became two parallel systems of intellectual exploration. And science also had little time for mysticism. While science is concerned with the factual world outside the scientist, mysticism turns to the laws which govern the seeker herself/himself. The methodology of the scientist is the verification of facts which seem to explain the mystery of being: the methodology of the mystic is meditation, seeking a direct experience of being.

One of the major characteristics of the late twentieth century — often referred to as the New Era of Consciousness — is that these three strands of knowledge — the mystical, the theological and the scientific — are drawing together again, each realising that there exists a unity and an interconnectedness of all being, to the understanding of which each strand has a unique contribution to make.

Contemporary Developments

Over the last half of the twentieth century, a fundamental shift took place in theology which has given rise to a number of new approaches. Since the causes of this shift are the same as those which compel us to re-think our perception of the Divine Mystery, they will be dealt with in some detail as related factors in the ensuing chapters. However, it might be useful to mention them briefly here.

The most fundamental theological shift is from a top-down direction to a bottom-up direction. Until the twentieth century, theology began with God, from our knowledge of whom we drew an understanding of creation, its origin, its meaning and its destiny. Today, however, theologians start from human experience to see what they can discover about God and creation. Two contrasting syllogisms about the nature of Jesus will illustrate this. With a top-down approach we would argue:

God is like this and this.
Jesus is God.
Therefore Jesus is like this and this.

The contemporary bottom-up approach argues:

Jesus is like this and this.
Jesus is the icon of God.
Therefore God must be like this and this.

This new orientation, coupled with other religious-cultural shifts of our day (from individualistic religious observance to a communitarian spirituality, from a "pieces and parts" to a holistic world view, from a "next life" to a present world understanding of the Gospel message) have given rise to some new forms of theology. In brief, some of these are:

- **Liberation Theology.** This developed out of the experience of oppression in the Latin American countries and an understanding that Redemption was about integral human development (of body, mind and spirit) in the here and now and not about "pie in the sky when you die".

- **Contextual Theology,** popular in southern Africa, reads the "signs of the times" in order to inculturate the Gospel into the contemporary life of people. Its basis is the belief that God continues to speak to us through current events.

- **Feminist Theology** of the western world emphasises the feminine (not to be confused with the gender word "female") qualities of intuition, creativity and the holistic in opposition to the over-emphasis on the rational, the analytical and the patriarchal.

- **Creation Theology** which arises from a sense of awe at the recent astronomical discoveries and the current concern for the health of Planet Earth. It no longer perceives the human person as being the centre and pinnacle of creation but as one element in the total picture and it parts from the traditional view of the world as tainted with evil and to be despised. It recovers our role as co-creators with God.

Let us now explore some of the most influential factors which are causing us to think anew about the significance of the word "God".

For further exploration:

Bede Griffiths (1989), *A New Vision of Reality: Western Science, Eastern Mysticism and Christian Faith*, Collins, London.

Sallie McFague (1987), *Models of God: Theology for an Ecological, Nuclear Age*, SCM Press, London.

Monika K. Hellwig (1992), *What are the Theologians Saying Now?* Gill and Macmillan, Dublin.

Denis Edwards (1992), *Creation, Humanity, Community: Building a New Theology*, Gill and Macmillan, Dublin.

Chapter 4

THE SCIENCE FACTOR

A ll religions are founded on some form of experience of the Divine Presence. This might be the experience of the tribe, considering itself to be especially favoured by its gods, demonstrated by its success in conquest following sacrifices or rituals performed in their honour, or the experience of an individual — be it a vision or enlightenment — such as Buddha, Jesus, Mohammed, Simon Kimbangu (founder of the Kimbangist Church in former Zaire) — around whom a group of followers gathered.

Expressing Experience

Direct mystical experience, however, is always experienced individually and seldom collectively, so some way has to be found of sharing this experience with those who are drawn to participate in the fruits of it. And even if a number of people in a group have a mystical experience it is never the same or at the same depth for all. Therefore the experience has to be externalised in some form that can be communicated. This is where, as we said in a previous chapter, the intuitive knowledge has to be handled by the rational mind if it is to have any application to or benefit our way of living. For example, the children who believed they had seen an apparition of the Virgin Mary at Fatima in Portugal in 1916 had to translate their experience into concepts before they could communicate it to others.

Because mystical experience touches the profundities of life it relates to our deepest search for meaning. It touches the fundamental questions to which humanity has always been seeking answers: what is our origin? What keeps our Universe ticking? Where is it all going? The religious answers to these questions — the answers which give expression to the mystical experience — are always in the idiom of the philosophy and the cosmology (the world view) of the time, the place, the culture. In other words, they are influenced by the "science" of their day. What every religion does is to offer its adherents a picture of the world and of each one's place in it which matches and makes sense of their experience.

For instance, the ancient Greeks, experiencing their impotence in the face of natural forces — winds, thunderbolts, earthquakes — deified these forces and regarded themselves as playthings of these gods and goddesses. The concern of the Jewish religion was law and social order and this was brought about by a faithfulness to a set of commands which came from a god exterior to their world, thus producing the dualism between earthly matter and the spiritual of heaven. The Buddhists, by contrast, with their background of Vedic culture, understood the source of power with which to live a more perfect life as being within consciousness; the path to nirvana was for individuals to be so stripped of longings that they could realise their innermost nature as fundamental consciousness. The early cosmology of the Christians and of the Muslims was that of the transcendent God of the Jews because these two religions are branches of the Jewish stock.

The Birth of Science

But let us concern ourselves here with the religion and cosmology with which we are most familiar, that of the western world. The theologians of the early Church — the Fathers of the Church — living in a world in which the Greek science of Plato and Aristotle was the backdrop, explained the belief of Christians in their "scientific" terms. However, they rejected Aristotle's notion of a Universe that had always existed, because it was not compatible with the biblical account of creation. In fact, such was the influence of the Church on western society that it was the current biblical interpretation of how things spiritual and material interrelated which shaped "scientific" thinking right up until the seventeenth century. The monks were the scholars in the Middle Ages and there was no question of their allowing rival theories abroad. We all know what happened to free-thinking men like Copernicus in the sixteenth century, and to Galileo, the mathematician who was condemned in 1630 for teaching the Copernican thesis that the Earth revolves round the Sun. The former's writings were placed on the papal Index of forbidden books. The latter was condemned by the "Supreme and Universal Inquisition" in these words:

> It is our pleasure that you be absolved, provided that with a sincere heart and unfeigned faith, in Our presence, you abjure, curse and detest the said error and heresies, and every other error and heresy contrary to the Catholic and Apostolic Church of Rome . . .

Their condemnatory document had previously stated two such heresies:

1. The proposition that the Sun is in the centre of the world and immovable from its place is absurd, philosophically false and formally heretical because it is expressly contrary to Holy Scriptures.

2. The proposition that the Earth is not the centre of the world, nor immovable, but that it moves, and also with a diurnal action, is also absurd, philosophically false and, theologically considered, at least erroneous in faith.

Science as an accepted discipline has appeared only very recently in our history. We could say it really only came into its own in the seventeenth century. With its acceptance as a distinct channel of knowledge grew the profession of "scientist". The very word "scientist" was only invented in the nineteenth century. So recent is this profession, and so fast is this discipline's development, that it is said that 90 per cent of all the scientists who ever lived are alive today. And each of science's main concerns is constantly splitting into more and more specialist fields.

The New Science

But now we are speaking of what has come to be termed the "New Science". It is new in that it is a shift from one foundation for science to another: from the "classical" model to the "quantum" model.

Although the shift started to take place — in so far as one can put dates to new ideas — with the publishing of Albert Einstein's *Special Theory of Relativity* in 1905, the first crack in the neatly elaborated classical physics was made by Max Planck in 1900 when he discovered that if matter is made red hot it absorbs and emits energy, not smoothly as was thought, but in packets. Planck called these packets of energy "quanta". But the development of the new physics really only began a quarter of a century later when Einstein and an international group of physicists (including Planck) formulated their "Quantum Field Theory".

Before proceeding, it is interesting to go back and look at some of the major steps in the explanation of our Universe that have led up to this point. In early religious writings — the only source we have for knowing how creation was understood 2,000 and more years ago — we perceive an all-embracing unity, a unity of the divine with creation and of the human being with creation. This began to break down with the Greek philosophers — with Plato, for instance, who introduced a distinction between the world of experience and the realm of ideas. It was the beginning of humanity's sense of alienation from the rest of creation which gave birth to our feeling that we are strangers in the Universe. The notion of alienation was further fuelled by the development of Christian theology and spirituality which set the soul in opposition to the body.

The next major step came with René Descartes (1596–1650), a key figure in the emergence of later philosophical and scientific thinking. He wrote a general account of scientific knowledge that was strongly influenced by mathematical models. One could say he introduced doubt as a scientific method. He would only accept as true that of which he could be certain by objective proof. (From which arose his famous affirmation, "I think, therefore I am".) His philosophy set the human being apart from the rest of creation. We were entering that period of European history known as the Enlightenment when human reason was given supremacy over all other forms of knowledge. He had been helped by Copernicus, who had put an end to the worldview held by the medieval theologians that our Earth, and consequently the human being, was at the physical centre of God's creation, by suggesting that our planetary system was not Earth-centred but Sun-centred (the solar system).

Classical Physics

Perhaps the name which most readily comes to mind of a proponent of classical physics is Sir Isaac Newton. When he published his great volume *Principia Mathematica Philosophiae Naturalis* (The Mathematical Principles of Natural Philosophy) in 1687, he presented us with a worldview that was entirely mechanistic: everything was governed by discoverable and unchanging physical laws. This presumed that everything was made up of tiny pieces of matter, the smallest being the atom, which was indestructible. In his work *Opticks* (1704) Newton sums up his picture of the Universe:

> It seems probable to me that God in the beginning formed matter in solid, massy, hard, impenetrable, moveable particles, of such sizes and figures and with such other properties and in such proportion to space, as most conduced to the end for which he formed them.

The relation of one thing to another was fixed and determined by physical laws. No room for the mystic here, or even for the possibility of indeterminate forces at work. Such classical physics dominated the development of science until the early years of the last century, and to this day his model survives in popular culture.

Although Quantum Field Theory has been with us now for a hundred years and is the foundation of today's science, most of us, as we go about our everyday life, still think of our world in terms of the Newtonian picture. It is easier. We can understand how everything fits together. It is predictable. Many people who reject God today are in fact rejecting the Newtonian understanding of God and his theory of the way in which God created and sustains the Universe, a theory no longer acceptable to scientists. But be not alarmed! We do not need to pursue an understanding of Quantum Physics: it is not that simple. The scientist Neils Bohr has said: "Those who are not shocked when they first come across Quantum Physics cannot possibly have understood it."

Quantum Physics

From the point of view of our study here, Quantum Field Theory has re-linked us with the throbbing life of the Universe. The heart of the theory is that the Universe is not composed of tiny building blocks but rather that at the sub-atomic level all being can be described equally well as particles or as waves, as matter or as energy. All being is *both* wave-like and particle-like; only one is available at any given observation. But which one? This is unpredictable. (A sub-atomic particle should not be thought of as a "thing", as we used to think of an atom, but as a set of relationships.) Quantum Field Theory gives us a new appreciation of creation: a holistic understanding of it, since with this theory everything becomes inter-connected, is alive. There are not inorganic bits of matter but a web of energies.

What takes us even further from the immutable laws of Newton is the discovery that sub-atomic particles act not according to laws but only according to probabilities. One cannot know, at any instant, both the position and the momentum of a quantum particle. In 1926 the German scientist Werner Heisenberg coined the phrase "the Uncertainty Principle" as the most satisfactory way of coming to terms with how "things" happen.

Where does this lead us in our attempt to "re-cognise" the mystery we call God? It contributes to our understanding in three ways.

Continuing Creation

In the first place, it has been customary to think of God as having created the whole cosmos a few billion years ago as a one-time act, albeit as a developing, evolving entity, not as static. (We are leaving aside the theory of Deism, according to which God, having created the Universe, leaves it to run itself. Newton's world-view supported this theory: God simply set up the whole machine with the laws that would enable it to run on. This was refuted in the nineteenth century by the First Vatican Council, which stated that "God, by his providence, protects all that he has created", that is, he preserves it from relapsing into nothingness.) However, understanding creation's infrastructure as being energy, not matter, it becomes easier to conceive how the creative act is an ongoing act by which the Divine force is doing more than keeping a once-created entity in existence (keeping the fly-wheel from running down, so to speak), and to envisage our Universe in a state of continual creation in every "now" moment. The creative power is no less necessary for our survival at the very second you read these words than it was at the instant of the Big Bang.

A Self-Creating Universe

The Uncertainty Principle poses a second challenge to our traditional ideas. It leads us to question whether every event has a cause. One of the traditional proofs of the existence of God, espoused by that theological colossus of the Middle Ages, St Thomas Aquinas, has been based on the cause–effect chain. Namely, that every effect has a cause and that this cause in turn is the effect of a previous (in time) cause, and so back and back along the chain until we arrived at the very first effect (the Big Bang?) and that too must have been caused by something or Someone, since only a power outside and "before" creation could have caused creation. There had to be a "prime mover" as it is called. And that, of course, must be God. For centuries this has been a very neat and acceptable proof that God exists.

The major premise of this argument is challenged today, for the notion of causation is itself a temporal concept. Any knowledge we have of a law of cause-and-effect is from our experience within the Universe. We cannot presume the same law applies beyond the Universe. Causation only applies to an existing thing producing another thing, not to existence itself. There was no "before" the Big Bang. We have discovered that on the sub-atomic scale events occur without well-defined causes. This phenomenon is known as "quantum uncertainty" and one of its consequences is that matter can appear from nowhere in certain high-energy processes. So we find scientists today speaking of the "self-creating" Universe. This leads physicist Paul Davies to state, "We may say that God is not so much a cause of the Universe as an explanation" (*God and the New Physics*). In what sense an explanation? Scientists can offer us explanations and provide us with evidence as to *when* the Universe came into being and even offer mathematical models for *what* occurred. But it is to theologians and mystics that we have to turn if we are looking for an answer as to *why* it came into being. This belongs to the realm of the Divine Consciousness or the "Will of God". Stephen Hawking ends his bestselling *A Brief History of Time* with the words:

> If we find the answer to that it would be the ultimate triumph of human reason — for then we would know the mind of God.

But to know the mind of God is to *be* God! We will develop these ideas further when we consider the Creation Factor.

The Universe is Alive

Thirdly, quantum physics enables us to appreciate how everything in the Universe is alive. We can no longer think of our Earth, for instance, as composed of living beings (plants, animals) and non-living beings (rocks). Everything is a collection of energies (as particle/waves), their distinction being the way in which groups of them are clustered together to form "things". At the microscopic level there is no difference between you, the reader of this book, and the book you are reading. It is just that the clusters of energies take a different form. As Sir James Jeans, the physicist, had already remarked in 1931, you and I and everything around us are composed of nothing more than the ash left over from the long-dead stars. Even our Ash Wednesday liturgy reminds us that we are the fallout of the stars: "Remember you are dust and to dust you will return." It is we, with our human intelligence, who differentiate between things and give them names.

The sense of the aliveness of everything, and the belief that all life issues from one source which we name God, can easily lead to the belief that therefore all creation is God and that God is all creation — that God and creation are precisely identical. This belief is found in some eastern religions. The idea bears a Greek name "pantheism". It has always been the Christian tradition, however, to distinguish the Creator from the creature. (Pantheism was actually declared heretical by the First Vatican Council in the nineteenth century.) Today the sense that we and all creation are alive with the life-force of the Divine is being expressed by theologians with the word "panentheism", meaning that God is *in* all things and all things are *in* God. *The Oxford Dictionary of the Christian Church* defines panentheism as:

> The belief that the Being of God includes and penetrates the whole Universe, so that every part of it exists in him, but (as against pantheism) that his Being is more than and is not exhausted by the Universe.

Thus, creation and Creator retain their separate identities: God is more than His creation. Not that this idea is new. We find the English mystic Julian of Norwich (c.1342–1416) expressing a Christ-panentheism when she writes that Christ is the one "in whom we are all enclosed and he is in us". (She is distinguishing here between the Christ and the historical Jesus.) And the German mystic, Mechtild of Magdeburg (1210–1280), even earlier wrote of her enlightenment: "The day of my spiritual awakening was the day I saw and knew I saw all things in God and God in all things." Her words were echoed two centuries later by another German mystic and philosopher, Nicholas of Cusa (1400–1464):

> Divinity is the enfolding and unfolding of everything that is. Divinity is in all things in such a way that all things are in Divinity.

Panentheism sits happily between two unacceptable philosophies: Deism, by which God is only transcendent, and Pantheism by which God is only immanent.

So far we have seen the contribution the new science is making to our current understanding of the Divine Mystery in so far as the quantum theory has enabled us to explore the microcosm: the world within the atom.

From Micro to Macro

At the other end of creation's scale, into the macrocosm, the sciences of astronomy and astrophysics have also, in recent decades, made their contribution to changing our perception of God.

Even after Copernicus and Galileo between them had shifted the Earth from being the geographical centre, the pivotal point of our stellar system, and thus moved humanity from centre stage, the Catholic Church continues in its official documents to speak of the human being as "the only creature on Earth willed for itself" (*Gaudium et Spes*, 1965, N. 24), as if every other being and lifeform on Earth since the beginning of time was of no more value than as a step towards what God *really* wanted, a human being. When we consider that it is estimated that there are some thirty million species in existence of which only about five per cent have been named, it surely gives us a sense of creation being for its own sake and not entirely for the benefit of humanity! Perhaps this is the next Copernican conversion the Church will be called upon to make! It would certainly have wide theological implications for ecclesiastical attitudes towards the environment.

If we accept that our own Universe commenced with a Big Bang then we can speak of this happening some 15 billion years ago and on so vast a scale that it is beyond our imagining. Our telescopes are able to detect a faint spot in the constellation we have named Hydra as being so far away that this spot of light has taken two billion years to reach us — with light travelling at the fastest speed we are able to measure, 186,000 miles per second. (A light year is the distance that light travels in a year, equal to 5.880 million million miles.) Was all this a necessary prelude to creating the human species? Our own planet Earth is reckoned to be four billion years old and has been through a great many evolutionary stages before human beings evolved. Ninety-nine per cent of all species that have ever lived are now extinct, as we can learn only by finding their fossils — dinosaurs and all! Were all these previous forms of life no more than a necessary prelude because all the Creator really wanted in the end were human beings? This is surely the supreme arrogance!

Other Intelligent Beings?

Do some or any galaxies contain other forms of life recognisable to us as human life? Might such "humans" be less developed than us . . . or more developed? Do they experience evil? Has a Christ appeared among them? Have they been redeemed? Are we humans on this tiny planet Earth really so special? May we think of ourselves as unique in creation? Do we really believe, as Church documents and liturgical texts would have us believe, that we human beings are "the crown of creation"?

As I write, Mars robots are discovering the existence of water, the essential requirement for life, on that planet. A decade ago, the Jesuit Director of the Vatican Observatory, on the Canary Islands, announced that they had discovered planetary systems, outside the Earth's solar system, with conditions conducive to the evolution of life forms similar to our own. While admitting that the existence of the right conditions for life elsewhere does not mean that it has necessarily evolved, it would be dangerous to believe that the only intelligent beings in the Universe were on Earth. Incidentally, discoveries of conscious life elsewhere would pose enormous questions for theologians! (Not, presumably, with regard to evangelising them since to send such beings any message would take millions of years and their response would take further millions of years. Rather a difficult situation for meaningful dialogue!)

"We know, of course, that we are made in the likeness
of God....but what if there are other worlds.....
other beings?...."

Cartoon by John Ryan, reproduced by courtesy of the Catholic Herald

All these discoveries cause us to adjust our view of God, especially of God the creator and of how each of us personally relates
to Him. So long as we retain the dichotomy between supernatural
revelation and natural revelation, with the implication that the
former is of greater value than the latter, we underrate the value
of the latter as contributing to our total picture of the Divine Mystery. Or else we say that the former is the preserve of Christians
while the latter is for the non-elect: adherents of other religions or
of none. This is a most arrogant assertion of the supremacy of
Christianity!

If we hold this view we will give so much importance to the revelation of the "Book of the Word" (Scripture), as interpreted by Christian Tradition, as to belittle or even ignore the revelation of the "Book of the World". As Thomas Berry, the American cultural historian and theologian, says in *The Dream of the Earth*:

> The Universe itself, but especially the planet Earth, needs to be experienced as the primary mode of divine presence.

And elsewhere he calls the created Universe "the primary religious reality, the primary revelation of the Divine". He is only echoing what St Paul wrote in his letter to Christians in Rome:

> Ever since God created the world, his invisible qualities, both his eternal power and his divine nature, have been clearly seen; they are perceived in the things that God has made. (1:20)

From this can be inferred that the evolutionary process is from the beginning a spiritual as well as a physical process. Many scientists today are awakening to the numinous quality of the Universe and approaching it with a sense of wonder. This is the moment when scientists and mystics draw closer together.

The Search for Truth

The respective paths of the scientist and the theologian, on the other hand, still tend to run in parallel. What they have in common is that both are searching for a rationally motivated belief about the way things are. As the late Donald Mackay, Professor of Neuroscience at Keele University, argued, scientific and biblical statements can both be true, but they are expressing truth in different terms. Each represents complementary aspects of the same reality. For instance, I could describe an ice cream quite objectively in terms of its chemical components or I could describe it in terms of its look and taste as it has meaning to me as a food. To a scientist, an object is impersonal; in a religious context, an object is personal because religion is concerned with relationships. Both the scientist and the theologian are pursuing absolute Truth which is beyond their grasp and not directly observable, so both have to make use of models and metaphors. Both are pursuing their goal within a community which has a tradition. What keeps them apart, however, is that while the secular scientific community is concerned with creative energies and views the world in a positive light, the theological community is occupied with redemptive energies, concerned to heal a flawed world.

As each draws nearer to the Truth, their paths must converge. The good will is there. When, in 1992, 359 years after the Vatican Holy Office condemned Galileo, Pope John Paul II formally retracted the sentence, he said that from the beginning of the Age of Enlightenment to the present day, the Galileo case had been a symbol of the Church's supposed rejection of scientific progress.

> A tragic mutual incomprehension has been interpreted as the reflection of a fundamental opposition between science and faith . . . this sad misunderstanding now belongs to the past.

He went on to add that it was the duty of theologians to keep themselves regularly informed of scientific advances in order to examine, if necessary, whether or not there were reasons for introducing changes in their teaching. In this he was reflecting what Einstein had said long before: "Religion without science is blind. Science without religion is lame."

Since the turn of the century scientists have been discovering such amazing things about the Universe, in both micro and macro directions, that they have not only contributed to the revelation of God, but cause us human beings, who are part of this mystery, to re-adjust our relationship to our environment. Can we any longer retain our self-awarded status as the dominators of the Earth, putting ourselves at the top of the pyramid of creation?

For further exploration:

F. Capra and D. Steindl-Rast (1991), *Belonging to the Universe: Explorations on the Frontiers of Science and Spirituality*, Harper, San Francisco.

J. Templeton and R. Herrmann (1989), *The God who would be Known: Revelations of the Divine in Contemporary Science*, Harper & Row, San Francisco.

Paul Davies (1984), *God and the New Physics*, Penguin Books, Harmondsworth.

Gary Zukav (1980), *The Dancing Wu Li Masters: An Overview of the New Physics*, Fontana/Collins, London.

Diarmuid O'Murchu (1997), *Quantum Theology: Spiritual Implications of the New Physics*, Crossroad Publishing, New York.

Peter Russell (2000), *From Science to God*, Peter Russell Publishing, Sausalito, CA, USA.

Michael Talbot (1981), *Mysticism and the New Physics*, Routledge & Kegan Paul, London.

Stephen J. Hawking (1988), *A Brief History of Time*, Bantam Press, London.

Thomas Berry (1988), *The Dream of the Earth*, Sierra Club Book, San Francisco.

Chapter 5

THE RELATEDNESS FACTOR

At the heart of Christian belief is the doctrine of the Trinity: "there are three persons in one God". However, we do not find any of the great biblical prophets, not even Jesus himself, making an explicit statement about or giving us a definition of the Trinity. In fact, the word "Trinity" is found nowhere in the Bible, not even in the New Testament. We might call the idea of the Trinity a working hypothesis, giving us a way of understanding that relationships are at the heart of the Godhead. The notion of the Godhead as a trinity has been deduced from Jesus' own sayings about God, about God as his father, about the Spirit; and only became a doctrinal formulation in the fourth century.

A God in Relationship

We will say more about God as a triune God when we deal with the Paradigm Factor. Let it just be said here that the Christian understanding of the Trinity enables us to conceive of God as a "God in relationship". That is to say, a relationship between God unmanifest as the Ultimate Reality and the Christ as the manifestation of God in creation (manifested supremely in the person of Jesus), and the Holy Spirit who is the dynamic force in the God–Christ relationship, the creative power, the source of love.

Understanding relationship as being at the centre of the Divine Mystery, it comes as no surprise to learn that relationship is also of the essence of all created things. If evidence were needed, we have only to reflect on our own humanity, on how we arrived on this Earth, how we discover our identity, grow (and indeed survive): all through relating to others — and in its most perfect form, through love. All relationships are exchanges of energy: love is the highest form of energy.

What is less evident is that relatedness is the glue which keeps the whole of creation together, and for our coming to realise this, we have the new physics to thank. In the previous chapter, we saw how current scientific thinking proposes that physical reality is essentially non-substantial. According to Quantum Field Theory only "fields" are reality. They, and not matter, are the substance of the Universe. Particles of matter are no more than the momentary manifestations of interacting fields.

Fields

What do we mean by "fields" in this context? A field is an area of influence. We speak of a person's field of influence, the extent of their power. Or of our field of vision, meaning everything within range of our eyesight. Every form of physical force or power has a limited range. Usually the closer the source, the greater the force felt.

We speak of a magnet having a field of attraction. If we sprinkle iron filings on a sheet of paper and put a magnet underneath, the filings will align themselves with the magnetic force so that we can actually see the magnet's field of influence.

We are all familiar with the means of finding our bearings with a compass. It points towards — is attracted by — the magnetic field at the North Pole. Biologists show us how various life forms such as bacteria, birds and fish use the Earth's magnetic field to find their direction.

Some fields are much more forceful than others. The force of gravity, for instance, covers the whole Earth and causes all things on or near the surface of the Earth to be drawn towards the Earth.

It is so great and so all-pervasive that we do not even stop to think about it, yet it influences every movement we make and all objects around us. It gives things weight and causes things to fall. The moon moves around the Earth because of the Earth's gravitational field. The gravitational pull of the moon causes the tides in our seas, while the gravitational field of the Sun causes the Earth and the other planets to revolve around it.

Electro-magnetic fields are all around us. Without them our electric motors would not work. They are the carriers of all sorts of rays. Some, such as light rays, we can see with our eyes. Most are not perceptible through our five senses. Some we can tune into with our radio and television sets. These fields enable objects to act upon one another even when they are not in material contact.

Unlike material objects, fields have a holistic quality. They are not diminished by being divided up. For instance, a magnet has two poles: one end attracts and the other repels, while the middle part is neutral. If one cuts it in the middle one has two complete magnets, each with an attracting and a repelling pole, each with a complete magnetic field. It is the force of fields which causes everything in the Universe to relate to everything else and to have an effect on everything else.

While many people today are in tune with this new vision of the unity underlying all reality — even if they have not heard about the scientific Field Theory — the fact remains, however, that all our major institutions, be they political, social, ecclesiastical, economic, still operate as if everything existed independently of the separate parts comprising it. They are still immersed in the old "mechanical" consciousness. They still attempt to dominate, manipulate and control the world by controlling different sections and parts in isolation from the others.

The relationship that exists between First World and Third World countries is a good example of this. The problem of the poverty suffered in the Third World is not solved simply by the First World sending its surplus riches to the poorer nations. It is not an isolated economic problem. The problem will only be solved with any permanence by those whose thinking is based on the understanding that all people on this Earth share one humanity, that all the fruits of this Earth are for the benefit of that one humanity. A solution has to be reached, not by decisions made from the superior position of one party but through dialogue between all concerned. Then the problem will be seen to embrace many aspects of human life, all of which must be treated with respect and as interrelated: customs, human history, political ambitions, religious beliefs, levels of education, human expectations, the forms of family and clan life. If this seems to be a digression, it is to make the point that nothing exists in isolation. Only through coexistence in interdependence does everything make sense.

Western Science

We have already seen that that which today we call science had a distinctly spiritual and holistic flavour from the period of the early Greeks into the Middle Ages. In the West, this characteristic was lost with the Enlightenment and the introduction of Reductionism (the reducing of complex patterns and data into less complex constituents in the belief that anything can be completely understood in terms of its simpler components) as a scientific method.

Eastern science, on the other hand, drawing on the ancient Vedic philosophy of India, has retained its spiritual holism right up to our present time.

Today a new creative synthesis of eastern and western science is becoming possible. It has not yet taken place — many people do not even recognise it — but it is imminent within the next ten to twenty years!

The search by western scientists for the ultimate building blocks has recently taken a strange detour. It looked very promising in the early 1970s as scientists matched the bits and pieces of the quark jigsaw. (Quarks are the most recent sub-atomic particles to be discovered.) But they were in for something of a shock. The end result was not the isolated physical objects that scientists had hoped for, the vital clue as to what our Universe is made of. They were confronted, not by stable physical objects, but by mobile energy patterns which only made sense in relationship to one another. (Carbon, for instance, has the same chemical composition whether it is found as graphite or diamond. To understand the structure of each — why one is only graphite while the other a priceless diamond — it is necessary to know the relational ordering of each, their specific field.)

This discovery was so contrary to all expectations that few scientists could accept it and most still do not. Life is about wholeness, not isolated bits, and within the whole everything is interconnected, interdependent, interrelated. So many western scientists continue to search for the fundamental building blocks, almost daily uncovering some new and fascinating pattern, yet rigidly and blindly rejecting the holistic basis that is staring them in the face. And, of course, there are none so blind as those who choose not to see!

What has remained unnoticed is the long western mystical tradition which has uncovered these holistic truths on many different occasions, but even the Churches have never taken the mystics seriously.

For example, there are the great "creation" mystics — so-called because they recognise the beauty and goodness and unity underlying all creation — of the twelfth and thirteenth centuries: Hildegarde of Bingen (1098–1179), Mechtild of Magdeburg (1210–1280) and particularly Meister Eckhart (1260–1329), who were disowned by the Church in their own day, and only in recent times have been viewed in a more favourable light. Many know of the Jesuit palaeontologist, Teilhard de Chardin, whose written works were suppressed until after his death in 1959. Despite a much more amenable attitude in recent times, the Christian Church continues to distrust the contribution of mystics.

Eastern Science

Vedic science is a holistic understanding of creation, based on the age-old knowledge of the Vedas, a group of Indian/Aryan poetic and philosophical writings, compiled between 1500 and 700 BCE. Veda means "knowledge", and the many insights and intuitions of Vedic seers and sages from the Himalayas are known collectively as Vedic science.

In general, the eastern worldview is a great deal more holistic than the western one and this is strongly reflected in its scientific pursuit. Vedic science begins with the cognition that a unified field of pure consciousness underpins all material reality. All the laws of nature — the energy that creates and co-creates in so many external forms — arises from within this field of pure energy, which may also be described as pure spirit or creative intelligence.

Radiation

Let us return to what we were saying about fields and look at some everyday manifestations of their influence. Another word for this is radiation. We hear much more about the effects of radiation today than we did twenty years ago and it mostly has a negative connotation. Investigation is currently going on — and indeed litigation being brought — into the high incidence of leukaemia related to people's proximity to a nuclear power station. It is also observed that both leukaemia and other cancers are being found in people, in a higher proportion than the national average, who are exposed to high intensity magnetic fields, for instance among children whose homes lie beneath or near high-voltage power lines.

Though most of us are unaware of the fact, in the last fifty years, we in the West have become victims of a bombardment by electro-magnetic waves. Apart from the more obvious waves beamed by radio, TV, telecommunications, spy satellites, radar and navigation beacons which are continually crisscrossing our planet, we are being bombarded by microwaves from such household objects as mobile phones, metal detectors, anti-theft devices, remote controls and ovens. Research is showing that the density around us of these human-made waves is now 200 million times the natural level reaching us from the sun. These are humanly created fields of radiation. But vibrations in the Earth's magnetic field also have an effect on many forms of life, including human life. The building block of our nervous system is the neuron. Acting like an aerial, it picks up the vibrations of the Earth's field and is stimulated by electrical impulses from outside. Since a changing magnetic field generates a corresponding electrical field, such changes are picked up by our nervous system. The magnetic field of the Earth is linked to the magnetic fluctuations of the sun by way of the solar wind. (The solar wind is a constant stream of sub-atomic particles flowing from the sun's corona.) Our relatedness to the sun is much more subtle than that of its being our source of light and warmth. The inter-stellar magnetic fields are hypothesised to be the basis of astrology as a science.

Such fields are in the physical order. They are measurable. But there is also the whole range of fields of consciousness.

Fields of Consciousness

When discussing the Consciousness Factor we will be looking at "distance healing" and the effects of petitionary or intercessory prayer — both examples of psychic energy working through fields — and also how these energies can be located by dowsing.

There are other instances which reveal that one person's consciousness can exercise a power over others through fields of consciousness. Perhaps the best known form is that of transpersonal imagery: an image being transmitted, not always intentionally, from one mind to another. It can happen in a number of ways, the most widely experienced being that of a person feeling a sudden physical pain at the very moment someone dear to them, spouse, child, parent, or especially twin, undergoes an accident. There is also the sudden awareness that a close relative has died. To give a personally known example, I was at school during the Second World War. One day a group of us were running down to the rugby field when one of the boys suddenly stopped in his tracks and, to our embarrassment and bewilderment, burst out in tears and declared that his father had been killed. A telegram next day announced just that, and later it was confirmed that his death had occurred at the very time the boy had had the experience.

All forms of telepathy, or mental communication, can be understood as happening through fields of consciousness which know boundaries of neither space nor time. But just *how* they happen we cannot yet explain because we have not yet explored the realm beyond the measurements of physics. I mention such occurrences briefly — they can be read about in all their variety in any book by Lyall Watson — because they take us beyond the realms of science. We are cosmic creatures, with a relatedness to all dimensions of creation.

Einstein's theories are not the last word in understanding our Universe, although they may be the last word within the parameters of physics. They are confined to a particular parameter, the edge of which is the speed of light, beyond which time is not measurable. Relativity cannot cross this without having to acknowledge that messages could be received without any time gap. What relativity theory is unable to cope with is any form of existence in frequencies which are different from the observable. Here we are into the realm of the paranormal, the world of spirits which physicists cannot take on board because they are prepared to accept as reality only that which can be "measured" according to their own rules.

Beyond Science

Scientists are limited to dealing with what they experience through their five senses. But our senses are only channels. We do not in fact see with our eyes or hear with our ears or taste with our tongue. We "see", "hear", "taste" with our mind. How often have we heard a voice or footsteps and would have been convinced it was that of someone we knew well, had we not already known that she was abroad at that moment? It was our mind that sorted out the sound and identified it. Music is only music because the mind interprets the harmonies that exist amidst the vibrations our ears take in. If several people hear the same piece of music, some will delight in it as pleasurable, others will find it discordant and disagreeable. Our mind has made a judgement about the sounds and decided how to react to them. We see a picture on our TV screen and our mind tells us we are seeing a dog. A dog watching the same picture will not necessarily identify what it sees as being another dog but simply a mishmash of colours. As we have already said in considering the Knowledge Factor, we edit our experiences to fit preconceived ideas. This is illustrated by the figure below. This is known as a Kanizsa triangle, after the Italian psychologist Gaetano Kanizsa. We "see" a large white triangle that appears to stand in front of the three black discs. The triangle is only real to us because we have edited our visual experience and superimposed the extra lines out of our consciousness.

We are surrounded by many forms of existence which in the usual course of a day we are unaware of because they exist on a different wavelength from our own. To be unaware of them through the senses is not to deny their existence. They are as real as we are and in continual relatedness to us. Because we call "natural" those experiences which come to us through the senses, which we can evaluate empirically and test scientifically, we regard as preternatural or supernatural those rare occasions when there is a breakthrough to another wavelength. We tend to regard their cause as either divine or diabolic, whereas they are as much part of the totality of creation as we are. They are simply in a different wavelength. Once again, this is a case of our belief system providing us with an interpretation.

Where do the spirits of departed people go after death? Do they actually "go" anywhere? Or do they simply move into another wavelength "here"? If imaginings of a Heaven "up there" were still lingering in anyone's mind a few decades ago, the idea has been dealt a death-blow by our explorations into space and our awareness of its immensity . . . and emptiness. Today, hundreds of different messages can be sent down the same telegraphic cable at the same time without their interfering with one another because they are sent at different frequencies. They are, so to speak, existing in the same space but quite "unaware" of each other's existence. Why can this not be equally applicable in the totality of creation . . . and just as real? Perhaps we have to hyphenate the location of Heaven from *nowhere* to *now-here*!

There have always been "visionaries" in human history. In our own times we are aware of children receiving visions of Mary the mother of Jesus at Lourdes, Fatima and Medjugorje. In fact, in recent years, Mary seems to have been appearing in so many places: in Latin America, in the United States of America, in several countries of Africa. Perhaps what is happening is that the senses of these recipients are given, however briefly, the ability to tune into a higher wavelength. It is noteworthy that after the Resurrection the resurrected body of Jesus was not visible to everyone as his pre-death body had been. He "appeared" only to those who had previously had faith in him, and even these (e.g. Peter, Mary Magdalene, the couple walking to Emmaus) did not recognise the apparition they saw until he made himself known.

We too easily forget that we are surrounded, indeed bombarded, by a whole range of frequencies of energy above and beneath the frequencies which impinge upon our senses. White light, for instance, passing through a prism splits up into its constituent colours, from red to violet. We are familiar with this sight in the rainbow. Each colour represents a different wavelength of electromagnetic radiation. We see these colours because they are within the range of our eyesight. Beyond the red light, at longer wavelengths, are infra-red radiation, microwaves and radio waves. At shorter wavelengths than violet are ultra-violet radiation, X-rays and gamma rays. There is but one energy but it is manifest at different frequencies, with different wavelengths. In the figure below I illustrate how there is a relatedness of all creation through the energy spectrum.

The Energy Spectrum

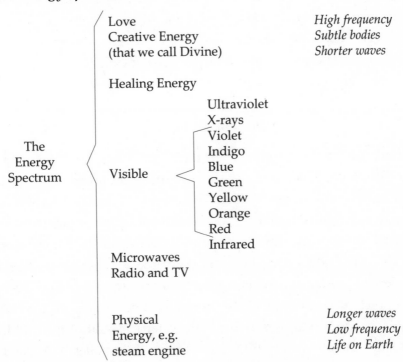

A whole area of spiritual healing is based upon the belief that there is more to our body than what is physical. Healers speak of the Etheric (bioplasmic) body formed by the energies which radiate from our physical bodies, and outside that the Astral (emotional) body. Kirlian photography reveals the energy level surrounding a living object, the hand, for instance. For centuries, statues and paintings of saintly people have been given haloes. This symbolism can only have arisen from an experience that we each have an aura, the energy field that surrounds us. Many healers today operate, not by direct physical touch, but by healing the aura: bringing greater harmony into the psychic energies which envelop us.

The planet Earth itself has an energy body with energy flowlines criss-crossing it. They have been called Ley Lines and the Curry Grid. Dowsers are able to trace their direction and to discern whether they are negative or positive energies, just as an acupuncturist works on the energy meridians within the human body. Negative energies are misdirected energies and these cause suffering. Suffering is alleviated by rebalancing the energies so that they are all in harmony.

The Vortex Theory

David Ash and Peter Hewitt, in their fascinating book *Science of the Gods*, have developed a theory originally proposed by the Belfast-born physicist, Sir William Thomson — later Lord Kelvin — who was knighted for having pioneered the laying of the first successful transatlantic cable in the middle of the nineteenth century. In 1867 he made a discovery and delivered a paper to the Royal Society of Edinburgh on his vortex theory of atoms. We find many examples of vortices in nature: tornadoes, hurricanes and whirlpools, or the way in which our bath water runs out of the tub! In his time, the atom was still believed to be the smallest particle. It was also believed that waves — light waves, for instance — travelled through ether, an invisible substance supposed to fill space.

Today, with our work in the sub-atomic area and the disproval of the ether theory, Ash and Hewitt have applied the vortex theory to energy. They propose that while energy is not some stuff or fluid that flows, but nevertheless requires form, the vortex is its form. "It is not that energy forms the vortex or wave", they declare, but "the vortex is energy". Just as we know now that light waves do not require ether to wave in, "so matter is not a vortex in anything: it is pure energy with no material moving". As an atom consists of sub-atomic particles, so each of these in turn is a vortex of energy.

It is interesting that "the Buddha describes forms of matter as whirlpools in a busy stream". Does this theory bridge the experiences of the mystic and the scientist by taking them both into the realm of super-energy? We said in the previous chapter that for the scientist, the fastest speed is that of light, but that this applies only in the physical world. Does this apply to movement which underlies energy itself? In fact, we find in the realm of consciousness that information *does* travel faster than light. There is no before or after: it is instantaneous; it happens in the *now*. This is the world of what scientists call the paranormal: the realm of super-energy. Invisible worlds can exist in frequencies which differ from our own. Is Heaven the biblical name for realms of super-energy existing beyond the speed of light?

Understanding the inter-relatedness of all creation in terms of fields of energy throws a new light on what, until recently, we have attributed to divine power or divine intervention. This is another instance of how our mental parameter is diminished by our defining all reality simply in terms of the natural and the supernatural.

For further exploration:

D. Ash and P. Hewitt (1990), *Science of the Gods*, Gateway Books, Bath. Republished as *The Vortex: Key to Future Science*.

Lyall Watson (1979), *Lifetide*, Hodder and Stoughton, London.

Chapter 6

THE CONSCIOUSNESS FACTOR

Throughout our lives we human beings are absorbing experiences at the conscious or subconscious level which cause us to change from moment to moment. We are not the persons we were yesterday on account of the experiences we have had in the last twenty-four hours. These experiences can be at the physical level or at the psychic level or at the spiritual level.

Varieties of Experience

At the physical level, it might be some pain we suffer. This could be a wound inflicted on us from a mosquito bite or from someone sticking a knife into us. Or it might be caused internally, for example, a headache. How we deal with it in our consciousness decides whether it is simply pain or whether it is suffering. Unlike animals, we human beings reflect upon the pain, wondering what caused it, wondering if it is going to last long or how it will impair our activity. This is what we mean by suffering the pain. Suffering is what our consciousness does with pain. We can control the extent to which we allow it to debilitate us. If we have a headache we might find the pain diminishes if we concentrate all our awareness upon it. Those with a developed facility for healing can bring this power to bear on their own pain until it diminishes to the point of leaving them altogether. They have healed themselves.

At the psychological level, we can experience the hate someone has for us, or their love. These hate and love energies are intangible, immaterial, but nevertheless we can experience their flow as realities. We can come into a group and experience the mood of the group — whether it is happy or sad, united or divided. We can say there is a happy spirit there. We speak of a school spirit or of a team spirit. It is quite beyond the ability of any one of our five senses of smell, taste, touch, hearing or sight to recognise, yet we are aware of it as a reality, and it affects us.

At the spiritual level we can experience being blessed — "the gods are smiling on us", "it is my lucky day" — or that everything is going against us, and these experiences have a very real effect on our attitudes. More deeply, it may be a sudden and quite unexpected experience, a peak moment, an instant of complete and unaccountable bliss that has a lasting effect on our lives. Researchers in Britain have found that as many as 60 per cent of the population has had some such deep spiritual experience, so profound that they have been unable or unwilling to tell of it to anyone, not even to their partners or closest friends, because it was so "out of this world" that they feared they might be considered odd or mentally deranged if they revealed it. This experience comes to people irrespective of their religious beliefs, and as much to people who have no religious beliefs at all. In 1975, the National Opinion Research Corporation in the USA reported that more than 40 per cent of the adults polled believed that they had had at least one genuine mystical experience.

These experiences are not indications of a divine intervention in our lives: they come to us in our natural condition as human beings. In themselves they are neutral. What effect they may have upon us depends upon our interpretation of their meaning, and that will be influenced largely by what we believe is their source or cause. We may interpret them at the very least as a glimpse into a higher realm of being.

Interpreting Experiences

Our interpretation of their meaning and our belief in their source derive from a number of factors. One is the memory of past experiences because each of these has had an effect in making us the person we are today. Such a memory can make us suspicious or worried or joyful. It can cause us to block it out of our lives or to embrace it fully as a point of growth. Another factor is our education, by which is meant the facts we have learnt from others — other people, books, etc — and the moral values we have acquired from sources that have contributed to building up our personal value system. A third factor is our culture. Some cultures are much more receptive to and understanding of — even welcoming — spiritual experiences than others which are more materially or scientifically oriented, such as ours in the West. The latter may be the more technologically advanced; the former cultures will be those who live nearer the earth and are more influenced by the cycles and moods of nature. A fourth factor is our faith, by which is meant our fundamental belief system that gives purpose to our lives. This may or may not be based on an acceptance of what we understand by a Divine Revelation. This factor belongs to the spiritual dimension of our lives — that which calls us beyond ourselves — as distinct from a religious dimension which boxes the spiritual in a particular system of belief, a creed.

Supernatural or Natural?

On the basis of the above understanding, we can see why it is that some people regard certain happenings as being divine or supernatural interventions while others find a natural, human explanation. The experience is the same for everyone because it is a product of our humanity, though the degree will differ, but it is the explanation of its cause, its meaning and even of its purpose which varies from one person to another. Let us take a number of examples to illustrate this.

From time to time great disasters befall us, be they purely natural, like an earthquake, or caused by human deficiency like the Chernobyl nuclear disaster, or humanly spread such as the AIDS epidemic. While some people will explain the cause entirely in scientific terms and attribute no meaning to them, others will claim that they are caused by God or the gods and are sent as a punishment, or to warn us that we have deviated from a divinely appointed path. Others again, while acknowledging a scientific cause, will nevertheless account for the place and time of occurrence as being under divine direction and try to interpret the meaning of such an intervention. The experience of the event is the same for everyone: the interpretation of the experience is what gives it a personal value.

Another example. Increasingly these days people are experiencing other people's healing powers. Most healers draw on a power extraneous to themselves. In a Church context, healers will say they are channels for the healing power of Jesus or for the creative power of the Holy Spirit and the recipients of such healing will regard it as a God-given blessing and maybe as a sign of divine favour and an answer to prayer. Thus the healing miracles at the shrine of Mary in Lourdes, France, are attributed to the intercession of the Blessed Virgin. Officially, medically acknowledged healing miracles at Lourdes are far less common than is generally supposed. In its 130 years as a healing centre, over 2,000 acclaimed cures have been investigated by the Lourdes Medical Bureau, of which only 65 have been acknowledged by the Catholic Church as miraculous. To the recipients of such favours, they are supernatural occurrences. Other healers will draw on a cosmic power, perhaps attributed to Mother Earth or to the healing rays of the Sun, while others will invoke the power of the spirit world. It would appear that healing on a one-to-one basis, for example as practised by the National Federation of Spiritual Healers in Britain, often brings about more lasting healing than that arrived at through a religious charismatic healer on the occasion of a great rally. Maybe the latter draws on a lower level of energy — mass hysteria, possibly — than does the one-to-one healer. (It is noteworthy that all the Sacraments of the Catholic Church, each with its dimension of healing, are administered on a one-to-one basis.)

Does healing depend upon the recipient believing that it will work? An experiment was carried out in 1995 in which 44 people, having had a small laceration made on their arm, were told to insert their arm through a hole in a screen behind which, so they were told, was a new piece of equipment which was to be tested. In fact there was no such instrument. Each of the first 22 held their arm there for five minutes and then withdrew it. The next 22, unbeknown to them, had their arm subjected to the power of a healer, without being touched. The scars of the latter group were found to heal more quickly. The expectation of healing was present in none of the candidates, which shows that on this occasion the effect was produced by the power of the healer and not by any wishful thinking or faith-healing on the part of the recipients. On the other hand, healing effects can be brought about purely by the power of the mind over the body, when the results are expected or desired strongly enough. While helping in a mission clinic in Africa where the variety of medicines was exceedingly limited, I have often had to give a plain aspirin to patients whose expectations of its effect was such as to bring about a cure which bore no scientific relation to the medical properties of the aspirin. This result is known as the placebo effect.

In each case, the healing occurs as a human phenomenon. The physical effect is the same. But depending on their interpretation of its cause, for some it is a purely natural event while for others it is a supernatural event. It is their interpretation that bestows a value upon it.

Dr Larry Dossey MD, a former president of the Isthmus Institute of Dallas, an organisation dedicated to exploring the possible convergence of science and religious thought, puts the different forms of healing on the following scale:

Paradoxical Healing, *in which being has a priority over doing*
Miracles
Prayer
Placebo Effect
Biofeedback
Psychological Counselling
Medication
Irradiation
Surgery
Rational Healing, *in which doing has a priority over being.*

The spiritual cause a person ascribes to healing is related to their understanding of the God–world relationship. A person who thinks of God as outside, beyond the world, governing it by external laws, explains healing as God intervening in His creation, from outside, to put right something that is not going according to plan. The event is a miracle: it is contrary to the laws of nature set by God for all time. A person who thinks of God as being within creation (a panentheist) believes she can draw on the creative powers already and always present in order to make the un-whole whole.

Petitionary Prayer

Let us take a look at the power of petitionary prayer. A great deal of praying is done to implore healing, of oneself or of another. In the case of the latter it is what healers would call "action at a distance". Whatever form our prayer takes, what we are actually doing is sending out love and positive thought towards the person for whom we are interceding. This in itself has a positive effect, as was shown in an experiment conducted by a Baptist heart specialist in a San Francisco hospital. He divided his cardiac patients into two groups. He had prayer cells all over the city praying for one of the groups, without being told from what the patients were suffering, so consequently without knowing what they were praying for, except for the patients' recovery. The group that was being prayed for became distinctly better than the other group. Neither group knew about these prayers, so there was no placebo effect. An institute in Salem, Oregon, USA, has been making a similar experiment on the prayer effect on batches of seeds. Those that were prayed over — sent love and wishes for growth — produced more abundant fruit. The same effect is said to be achieved by those who talk to plants.

When I was stationed in a "bush" mission in northern Zambia in the 1960s, it was the custom for the women, at planting time, to place their bowls of seeds on the altar rails in church with the expectation that when Mass was over I would come and bless them. The women, however, withdrew from the church to have a smoke outside, leaving me to get on with it! I used to call them back, explaining that the purpose of the blessing was to assist them to plant their seeds in an attitude of asking God to make them fruitful: the blessing was not going to do anything "magical" to the seeds themselves. I now wonder if I would give the same explanation!

A large enough group of people praying fervently for something to happen, or to be saved from some disaster or to bring about peace, or to call for rain during a drought, may well have their wishes fulfilled. Has there been a direct cause and effect? Have they channelled some power to bring about their wishes? Explanations will differ. Some will say it is by direct intervention of God, especially if their concept of God is of a caring, protecting father who is there ("up there") to be called upon whenever an emergency arises which is beyond our technical skills to deal with. Others will say it is not the power of prayer but sheer chance; while the more scientific will attribute the effect to the power of the collective human consciousness which, when concentrated upon a single need, will cause that to come about, perhaps through morphic resonance.

Let me illustrate this with a case of the power of mind over matter. In Naples each year thousands of Catholics gather to pray on the feast of St Januarius (19 September) who was martyred in

Naples in the year 305, for the blood of this saint to liquefy. If it does, they claim, it is a sign that that year they will be spared the effects of the eruptions of nearby Mount Vesuvius. If it does not, they take it as a divine warning that they can expect a calamity. The last time the powdery blood failed to flow was in 1980, just three months before an earthquake in Naples which left 3,000 dead and 13,000 homeless. Is their collective prayer actually influencing God to decide whether to cause the mountain to erupt or not, as they believe? Or is the power of their collective consciousness, their intense desire for the blood to liquefy, such that it causes that physical phenomenon to happen?

It is only in these last decades that we are learning more about the effects of waves sent out by the human mind. Our great-grandfathers knew nothing about radio waves until an inventor named Marconi demonstrated a way in which the human voice could be sent from one box, the transmitter, to another, the receiver, beyond the natural range of the voice. The transmission was wire-less! Nowadays every household makes use of this discovery in its use of radio, television and satellite dish, without any sense of amazement.

Our brains are like radio transmitters and receivers and, as with these instruments, the more finely the mind can be tuned, by passing into deeper states of consciousness, the greater the potential for having an effect on the surroundings.

The Power of Group Meditation

The power of group meditation is another example of consciousness affecting the environment. I refer to the different meditation techniques such as Zen, Yoga, Transcendental Meditation, which came from the East to the western world in the 1950s. Each is understood by its practitioners in the East as a human exercise in order to gain a higher than usual state of consciousness — the fourth state, as I explain later. The practice, which goes back four or five thousand years, long before the birth of the great eastern religions, is given several names, for instance the Sanskrit word *dhyana* or the word *samadhi*, which has been defined as "complete absorption and concentration of the mind in itself: the free working of no-mind transcending action and quietude". No mention of anything religious there. Unfortunately, there is no equivalent word in western languages to describe that experience: the best that can be found is *meditation* and this, today, is used most commonly in a religious context. It is not surprising, therefore, to find in the West thousands of Christians using these techniques as a form of prayer. Again, their benefit to the individual will depend upon the value bestowed on them. For some the practice is a purely human exercise to become a more enlightened human being, for others it is a means of entering into a very deep dialogue with God — in an exercise of active passivity — whom they believe they encounter in the depth of their being, at their centre point. For both, the psychological experience is the same: transcendence. As Daniel Goleman says in *The Meditative Mind*, "A meditator's beliefs determine how he interprets and labels his meditation experiences".

The practitioners of Transcendental Meditation claim, as a result of innumerable case studies, that the mental coherence brought about by a group of people meditating together will cause the level of stress in that geographical locality to decrease with such consequent effects as a drop in the number of accidents and traffic fatalities, a fall in the number of hospital admissions, a lowering of the crime rate and less violence. Studies of this effect in a number of cities throughout the world over the last couple of decades have shown that one per cent of the population practising Transcendental Meditation will bring about these effects in their area. The practice is believed to influence the field of consciousness in that locality on account of the meditators producing brain waves of the same frequency, causing maximum coherence.

On a world scale, a body based in Texas called the Planetary Commission for Global Healing attempted, in 1986, to reach "the critical mass of human consciousness" by enlisting 500 million people in 77 countries to spend an hour in "healing meditation" at 12 noon local time on December 31st so that there would be a 24-hour period of meditation being undertaken by 10 per cent of the world's population. The number reached 800 million in 1987. During the following year we saw peace "breaking out" in more places than we have seen in recent decades. A coincidence? This is not an isolated attempt to bring about a global effect. There was the Festival of Harmonic Convergence on 17 August 1987, the Million Minutes of Peace devised by Raja Yoga students and the widely distributed "Prayer for Peace" and "Great Invocation". Every spring I receive a leaflet from Operation Planet Love, based in Mexico, naming twelve specific dates, related to the Equinoxes, Solstices, Easter, Wesax and certain conjunctions of planets, upon which all the recipients are asked to meditate or pray for at least 21 minutes, to spread love all over the planet.

What is true of good must, on the same basis, be true of evil. In biblical times, natural disasters were attributed to human misdeeds on a tribal scale, interpreted as an act of a punishing God. As I write we are continually hearing news bulletins about bloodshed, tribal factions, international wars, racial pogroms and ethnic battles the length and breadth of the African continent. Is it entirely fanciful to suppose that there might be a connection between so much violence, bloodshed, hate and negativity in the human consciousness of millions of people and the climatic changes, the droughts — what we might call cosmic violence?

The twentieth century saw some great developments in the study of human consciousness, of its effects on the individual and on what has come to be called the collective or global consciousness. This inevitably influences our concepts of the God–humanity relationship. Reciprocally, the minds of individuals are influenced by the global consciousness. Before examining this phenomenon further, we need to clarify some ideas about the word "consciousness".

Consciousness

Human beings normally exercise three states of consciousness and, apart from exceptional moments, pass the whole of life in these three. They are the state of deep sleep, when the body and the mind are fully at rest, so deeply in fact that we are unaware that we are in this state at the time and only realise we have been in it when we wake from it. Secondly, there is the twilight state, the dream state, when the body is at rest and the mind is relaxed and not under conscious control, but when nevertheless we are aware of all sorts of disconnected thoughts passing through the mind. It usually precedes or follows deep sleep. The third is the wakeful, alert state in which we spend most of our daylight hours, when both body and mind are active and influencing each other.

Beyond this is a fourth or higher state which transcends the other three in that the mind transcends the ordinary rational thinking processes and is consciously in contact with the "centre" of our mind, the very source of thought itself. All of us have had fleeting moments of this experience or at least of its effects, as when we have had what we would call a sudden inspiration or an intuitive impulse: a thought arising to our consciousness from the depth of our unconscious. Contact with the transcendent mind can be cultivated, and in the West is being cultivated, by increasing numbers of people, with some of the meditation techniques mentioned above. Such practices, although originating prior to the emergence of the great religions of the Middle and Far East, have been incorporated into them.

Many authors describe this fourth state as having four levels — making seven states of consciousness altogether — but clearly, the higher the states the more difficult it is to differentiate between them. One is attempting to analyse a right-brain phenomenon with left-brain categories! These four transcendental states are:

- **Transcendental Consciousness:** A temporary state of pure awareness marked by inner peace and harmony. The rational thinking processes are transcended.

- **Cosmic Consciousness:** A permanent state of transcendence in which pure awareness and ordinary relative awareness are experienced simultaneously. The Absolute is experienced even at a subjective level.

- **God Consciousness:** *(Not* the consciousness *of* God) Everything is perceived as being filled with the Divine. The Universe comes alive with godliness.

- **Unity Consciousness:** This is the highest state which the human being is capable of reaching, one of perfect harmony and mystical union between the person and divinity.

Within Christianity, the great mystics, such as Eckhart, Hildegaard, Teresa of Avila, John of the Cross, or the unknown author of *The Cloud of Unknowing*, have written about their transcendent experiences in terms that are more poetic and symbolic than scientific. Being absorbed in the Christian tradition, they have spoken of their experience as being a special gift of God and referred to it as a form of prayer. They call it contemplation. Although traditionally we have named those receiving this divine gift as saintly, the experience itself is no indication of the depth of a person's relationship with God, their holiness, since it can be experienced equally by the godly and the ungodly, the believer and the unbeliever.

The Christian understanding of sanctity is about a person's relationship with God and this is measured by one's love of God — expressed by one's willingness to do what is understood to be the Will of God — and by our love of our neighbour. In the case of the Christian mystics, their transcendent experience has been the cause of their deepening their relationship with God because they understood their mystical experience to be an unsolicited gift of God. The experience of transcendence is the same for all humanity because it is a condition of the mind. Our thought processes are inseparable from the electrical and chemical activity in the brain and nervous system. As human beings we are all alike in our nervous systems. The interpretation of the experience and its value to each of us, however, is coloured by the paradigm out of which we operate. The extent to which we regard it as a God-given gift is dependent on how we think of God. Conversely, our notion of God is formed by how we understand our experiences, our spiritual experiences especially.

Two people may experience the same event: for one it is traumatic and causes her to change the direction of her life, for the other it is without consequence. The different effect is determined by the interpretation each gives to the experience. And that interpretation will arise from their respective belief systems. Two people receive identical Christmas cards from Africa picturing a young village woman with her baby. To one recipient it is a tropical African scene and not much to do with Christmas; to the other it is an African symbol of Mary and Jesus. The value we give to our experiences depends upon what we believe.

The rainbow has been in the sky for as long as rain fell on Planet Earth while the sun was shining, but in the Noah myth it was understood as a sign: it was given religious significance.

> As a sign of this everlasting covenant which I am making with you and with all living beings, I am putting my bow in the clouds. It will be the sign of my covenant with the world. (Genesis 9:12–13)

Global Consciousness

Increasingly today, consciousness is being understood, not as something simply possessed by each individual, but as an energy

field into which we tune our minds. We speak of Global Consciousness: a field of energy wrapped around the world. The Jesuit palaeontologist, Pierre Teilhard de Chardin, in the 1940s used
the word *noosphere* (from the Greek *noos*, "mind") to describe the
interconnectedness of all human minds right around the globe
and their cumulative effect. He pictured the Earth as enwrapped
in a human, reflective, planetary layer of consciousness daily becoming more and more complete. It is one form of the total sheath
of energy in which the whole cosmos is wrapped. We are aware of
such energy when we tune into the different wave-bands of radio,
television, radar. They are unbounded and all-pervading but we
need an instrument to attune to them. Otherwise, like our great-
grandparents, we would be quite unaware of their existence.

We do not need instruments to be aware of the sun's energy,
without which there would be no life on Earth. The source of almost all the energy we use is the sun. It can be put to good use by
us (solar heating, sun-bathing) or we can allow ourselves to be
damaged by it through over-exposure, thus burning our skin, giving us sun-stroke or damaging our eyesight. Our ancestors of long
ago worshipped the sun. Appreciating its power, they treated it as
divine. Today, with our increased understanding, we treat it scientifically. Just as electricity can be experienced as light, heat, motive-
force (causing electric motors to rotate), so energy is experienced as
electricity, as magnetic force, as healing power, as wind and in so
many more forms. For all its uses, who can tell what energy is? Its
definition is beyond the ken of science. In fact the general concept
of energy only appeared in the science of physics in the middle of
the nineteenth century. It cannot be seen or touched. The notion
was originally introduced as a purely theoretical quantity.

There is also energy to be experienced which is not measurable by science. I have already mentioned the mental energy emit-
ted by a group of meditators and its effect on their surroundings.
Love too is an energy. A dowser can demonstrate lines of energy.
Plucking a leaf from a plant and placing it a few feet away, the

dowser can reveal the line of energy between the plant and its leaf: his rods will cross as they pass between the two. But they will also cross when he passes them at the far side of the leaf at the point where the latter is in line with the plant. Is the energy flowing all the way round the Earth from the plant, through the leaf, back to the plant?

While all energy is one and had its birth in the Big Bang, we put different labels on it — Spiritual, Psychic and Physical — according to the level at which it is experienced. Healing, as we have said, is a channelling and harmonising of energy and it can be effective at any or all of the three levels.

The Global Memory

Each individual conscious mind contributes to the collective consciousness as the collective consciousness contributes to each individual mind. Rupert Sheldrake, a biochemist, proponent of the theory of Morphic Resonance (which he defines as the transmission of formative causal influences through both space and time), describes the memory as working in the same way. He postulates that memories are no more stored in the brain than television programmes are stored in the TV set, but the brain is like a receiver which is tuned into the collective human memory. This might be one explanation of how a person can recall a previous human life with the exact details of place and events — a phenomenon which is more often attributed to reincarnation.

Some people, known as "sensitives", are more sensitive to the energies of consciousness than most people. Their consciousness is more finely tuned. Again, these are all levels of human experience for which a variety of explanations is offered. Their meaning for each of us depends on our particular paradigm. The degree to which we veer towards a spiritual or a scientific interpretation of phenomena will indicate the depth or otherwise of our belief in the existence of a Divine consciousness: God. The Christian believes that all phenomena reveal such an existence. What differs among Christians is whether they attribute the cause to direct intervention or to the overall creative energy of God. So our level of consciousness is another factor affecting our concept of God. Is the creative consciousness emanating from within creation or received from outside it? This leads us to consider our next factor.

For further exploration:

Serena Roney-Dougal (1993), *When Science and Magic Meet*, Element Books, Dorset.

Larry Dossey (1993), *Healing Words*, Harper, San Francisco.

Ervin Laszlo and Peter Russell (1999), *The Consciousness Revolution*, Element Books, Dorset.

Daniel Goleman (1989), *The Meditative Mind: The Varieties of Meditative Experience*, Crucible, Thorsons Publishing Group, Wellingborough, UK.

Rupert Sheldrake (1984), *A New Science of Life*, Paladin Books, Granada Publishing Ltd., London.

Chapter 7

THE CREATION FACTOR

We find the word "cosmology" appearing in many recent books on theology and spirituality. The authors use the word to mean the big story of the Universe into which our lives fit.

As a branch of science, cosmology is a comparative newcomer. As the science which deals with how the Universe came to exist and how it will end, it began to be taken seriously only in the 1920s. This was largely due to a discovery made by Edwin Hubble, who found that the Universe is perpetually expanding. This obviously led to the assertion that it must have had a beginning with a sudden gigantic explosion, to which has been given the name the Big Bang. Hurray! Scientists — some at least — now hold what has been the belief of all traditional peoples worldwide from their earliest days: that the Universe had a beginning! One of the earliest accounts we know of is that in the Babylonian epic poem *Enuma Elish* (pre-1100 BCE), which describes the origin of the Universe as a victory of the gods over chaos, not unlike our Genesis account.

However, it would be prudent to add that not all scientists are convinced about the Big Bang. It is a model upon which a theory is built. Although widely accepted, at least as the best model we have at present, there are dissenting voices. Sir Fred Hoyle, who coined the name "Big Bang" during a BBC radio programme, is one of its most vehement critics. He supports what is known as the Steady State Theory, proposing that the Universe has no beginning and no end. Such scientists accept the notion of continual expansion but instead of projecting this backwards to a starting point, they account for it with a theory that atoms are created individually and continuously. This keeps the density of the Universe constant as it expands. Here, we will continue to presume on the Big Bang, not only because it is the majority view but because it equates with traditional Christian teaching about a Prime Mover.

It should also be acknowledged that there still exists a small handful of Christians who believe God created the world on 23 October 4004 BCE. This calculation was made in the early 1600s by James Ussher, Archbishop of Armagh. (It was improved upon by the Vice-Chancellor of Cambridge University, Dr Lightfoot, who claimed, in 1642, that creation actually took place at 9.00 am on that date!)

The Theories of Science

As we have said in an earlier chapter, scientists can now tell us *when* the Universe began and even *how* it began but they cannot tell us *why* it began. Nor can theologians, on the other hand, provide us with a scientific answer to that question; they can only offer us their interpretation of biblical accounts. Most of us have been fed on pious explanations. Living in a scientific era as we do we are inclined to give too much weight to scientific theories and to attribute too much to scientific knowledge. In fact, the knowledge of scientists is only a small part of knowledge. It deals with facts which can be verified by repeatable experiments. A great deal of their knowledge has to be based on theoretical premises, as for example during the last two centuries physics was based on the Newtonian mechanics — viewing the world as a great big clockwork machine (which is not surprising, for in Newton's time, the late seventeenth century, the most sophisticated machines were clocks) — which in this century was greatly modified by Einstein's theory of relativity. The mechanistic picture was turned upside-down by atomic and sub-atomic physics, explained by the Quantum Theory which in turn was extended to the Quantum Theory of Fields and more recently of Superstrings. Theories are no more than partial models of the real world. So the scientist's concern is with only one aspect of reality. It has nothing to say about love or hate or morality and cannot even adequately answer the question, "What is life?" Physics, of which cosmology is a part, treats only those aspects of reality which can be measured — such as size, shape, motion, position, weight, electronic charge — but has nothing to say about the subjective experience of smells, colours or feelings.

The Limitation of Imagination

A great handicap from which we human beings suffer in endeavouring to understand reality is that we rely so much on our imaginations, on creating mental pictures. Yet the greater part of reality cannot be understood in this way. Reality, like love and beauty, is one of the absolute values which are beyond our ability to comprehend in entirety. We can only know our experience of what we call reality. Today scientists have had to go beyond images and symbols and have had to theorise on realities that can be based on no more than mathematics.

We Christians suffer the same handicap in our attempt to relate to God. It is extremely difficult to make abstraction of those early images that were created in our minds during childhood. The dove still hovers around when we try to think about the Holy Spirit! A mental picture is created when we address God as Father. These may be helpful, at some stage of our growth, but they are not adequate as we mature. No amount of mental agility is sufficient when a human being tries to grasp the concept of God. We end by saying "God is a mystery", and leave it at that. But should we leave it at that? Hindus, as we have already said, tackle the problem by referring to God manifest and God unmanifest. The former is that of

God which we can cope with mentally and relate to as God: the
God who relates to creation. In this chapter we are attempting to
discover what we mean by the expression "God the Creator". And
to do so we have to leave our mental pictures behind.

Even when we say, as Christian theology has been saying for
centuries, that God created the Universe "out of nothing" our
imagination plays tricks and we picture God with a lump of
"nothing". When theologians speak of God creating *ex nihilo* they
do not mean "out of nothing" but rather "from no thing". The Jerusalem Bible translates 2 Macabees 7:28 in this way:

> I implore you, my child, observe heaven and earth,
> consider all that is in them, and acknowledge that God
> made them out of what did not exist, and that mankind
> comes into being in the same way.

No *thing* changed at the moment of the Big Bang since before that
moment there was no *thing* to change. This differs from the pagan
creation myths which presume not only the pre-existence of the
gods but also of material stuff upon which they worked. The Bible
too presumes that God created the Universe from something. We
simply cannot *imagine* how things were, or what was, *before* creation because there was no "before" creation. "Before" is a time
word and as St Augustine said already in the fifth century, the
world was created "with time and not in time". Scientists refer to
time as the fourth dimension, but they do not mean it is a fourth
dimension of space. Time is physically distinct from space, so they
speak about the creation of space-time. Time and space were created, like matter, in the Big Bang. There was no "outside" space in
which the explosion occurred.

The Length of Time

There is no way we can ever know objectively who or what "preceded" the Big Bang. But even within (created) time we are faced
with such astronomical figures that our imagination is of no help.

Scientists put the development of the Universe on the following time scale, using our measure of a year:

- 15 billion years ago, the Big Bang (after a million years clusters of galaxies grew up in the Universe.)

- 13 billion years ago our galaxy, the Milky Way, appeared.

- 4 billion years ago, the planet Earth came into being.

- 3.8 billion years ago we find the earliest recorded fossils of the most elementary life forms (it has taken 4 billion years for Earth life to evolve from primitive micro-organisms.)

- 0.5 billion years ago there were still no living beings on land.

- 300 million years ago the first dinosaurs appeared.

- 200 million years ago mammals entered Earth's story.

- 1.6 million years ago *Homo Erectus* (upright man) appeared.

Supposing we were to put the whole creation process, from Big Bang till now, in the time scale of one year, we would have to say that human beings are very recent arrivals, in the last few seconds, so to speak. It is only in the sense that we are the latest arrivals that it can be said that we are "the crown of creation". What might evolve in the next few billion years?

Edwin Hubble, we said, discovered that the Universe is perpetually expanding. However, the expansion rate is slowing. One possibility predicted by Einstein's General Theory of Relativity is that gravity will one day overcome the force of expansion and that will halt the growth of the size of the Universe. At that point, there will begin a process of collapse until ultimately the Universe decreases to so small a volume that it disappears altogether. This moment is popularly referred to as the Big Crunch. (The thought need not give us sleepless nights: it is not likely to happen for trillions of trillions of years!) An alternative possibility is that there is not enough matter in the Universe to cause this to happen, and that the Universe will go on and on expanding, becoming colder and colder, and eventually become lifeless, full of dead stars.

The Expanse of Space

When we come to space, figures are even more astronomic. We can only measure space in terms of light-years — the time it takes for light to travel between, for example, ourselves and the stars when light travels at the speed of 186,000 miles per second, the fastest speed we are able to measure. A light-year is shorthand for 5,880,000,000,000 miles! Just as a plane travelling at supersonic speed leaves its sound-wave behind it, so if we were to travel faster than light the electromagnetic fields which hold our atoms together would be left behind us and we would disintegrate. One of the more extraordinary possibilities apparently offered by Einstein's Special Theory of Relativity is that anything which can travel faster than light is also able to travel backwards in time.

Our Earth is just one planet in our solar system, and the nearest star to us, *Proxima Centauri* (after the sun, which is only 92,955,800 miles away), is four light years away (23.52 million million miles). Our Milky Way galaxy measures 100,000 light years across. It is only one of a cluster of galaxies, each cluster being part of a super-cluster of many thousands of galaxies. Some scientists suggest as many as a hundred billion. (The mind boggles!) Our Milky Way galaxy consists of some 100 billion stars, or suns, arranged in a flat disc, each of which could be accompanied by planets similar to Earth. This is within the scope of what we know. We simply cannot know about — nor ever will — the regions of the Universe further than 15 billion light years away because the light from such regions has not yet had time to reach Earth since the Big Bang!

The Law of Nature

A further point for our consideration in the Creator–creature relationship is who or what controls the Universe, for order is certainly apparent. Simply to quote God as the answer does not address the question "how?". All science is based on the assumption that the physical world is ordered. We speak of the laws of physics, but nobody knows where these laws originate. The old mechanistic physics of Newton spoke of "eternal" laws, as if they were in existence "before" creation. This equated with seventeenth-century theology, which took a more literal view of the biblical account of creation in the first two chapters of the Book of Genesis. Namely, that the laws governing all creation were fixed in the mind of God from the moment the Word, or Logos, of God created the whole Universe as it is today, and these immutable laws have persisted ever since. While modern cosmology has departed from the notion of a once-for-all creation and regards it as being an evolutionary process, the theological notion of eternal laws — even if not regarded as God-given — still persists as the metaphysical basis of this science. Stephen Hawking, in *A Brief History of Time*, assumes the timelessness of the laws of nature while he pursues, with so many other physicists, the "Theory of Everything", the fundamental law from which all others can be explained. This, they believe, is the key to understanding the whole Universe.

The question arises: if all creation is evolving, if the Universe is continually expanding, do not the laws governing creation have to evolve along with it? Just as the human laws which govern societies are not, nor can be, immutable but are constantly being adjusted to social and economic changes in society: they evolve. I suggest a "yes, but" answer to this. As each species evolves, laws governing that species are activated. In other words, they are eternally in the mind of God, and only come into operation within created time as each new need arises. However, that is only a possible answer. In trying to understand by what power our Universe is ordered, we are faced with a profound mystery.

God of the Now

Since we are only able to think of existence within a timescale, we have to find an appropriate way of relating this to a God whom we believe to be eternal. Rather than trying to think of God as existing outside time — whether before time or after time (for which we use the word "eternity") or both — it is more helpful to think of God at the centre of time: existing in the *now* moment. In fact, the only reality is the *now*. In the language of physics, there is no such thing as the past or the future as self-existing realities. One can only think of that which has preceded *now* as past — a past sequence of events — and that which might follow as future to the present. History has no existence except that it has been recorded in the past. To think of time flowing from the past, through the present and on to the future is an illusion, not unlike the illusion of believing that the train in which you are sitting is moving when it is actually standing still in a station: an illusion caused by your seeing the train next to you, which you suppose is stationary, beginning to move. The German mathematician Hermann Weyl stated cryptically: "The world does not happen, it simply is." We can say the same of God.

It is said of people that in their imagination they are living in the past or in the future. In reality, we can only live in the present. What is past is no more than a memory, be it a memory preserved in the mind, in books, in recordings, on film, in buildings. But we remember it, recognise it, let it influence us, only in the present. The future is no more than a speculation, a possible projection. We feel time is flowing, but in fact the *now* moment is the only reality. Only in the *now* are we in contact with God — if you like, in the eternal *now*. To help the mind grasp this concept the illustration of the wheel is often used. We feel time moving as if we were rotating on the rim of the wheel. Like spokes we are always at the same distance from the centre point, which represents God. To the eye, the centre also appears to be rotating, but mathematically the very centre is a still point with movement neither forwards nor backwards in relation to the rim. Yet, without the "the still point of the turning world", as T.S. Eliot put it, the wheel cannot turn!

Why this Particular Universe?

If physicists cannot answer the question of *why* God created the Universe, they are struggling with the question why this particular Universe exists rather than one of billions of possible alternatives. For some, the answer confirms their belief in a creative designer who chose to create the best possible Universe to produce and sustain life. For others, for whom God plays no part, the question is in terms of humanity, and so their theory is known as "The Anthropic Principle". Their argument runs that this particular Universe is the only kind that can produce intelligent life. Since we humans actually do exist as intelligent creatures able to think about our Universe, then its properties must be just such as to be consistent with our own evolution and present existence. The principle has been expressed thus: "There exists only one possible Universe designed with the goal of generating and sustaining observers. And this is it."* One cannot help but think that the advocates of the Anthropic Principle are struggling to maintain humanity's position at the summit of the evolutionary tree: we human beings are the ultimate reason for all else. (We will say

---

* We could say that St Paul, writing to the Colossians, stated the Christian Anthropic Principle: "He [Jesus the Christ] is the image of the unseen God and the first-born of all creation, for in him were created all things in heaven and on Earth, everything visible and invisible, Thrones, Dominations, Sovereignties, Powers — all things were created through him. Before anything was created, he existed, and he holds all things in unity" (1:15–17).

more about this when looking at the Paradigm Factor.) To subscribe to this explanation is to admit there is a purpose in creation
(which many scientists do not admit) and that simply throws us
back to the question of *why* did God create. The theologian may
speculate about that question but only the mystic can understand
it, because the answer cannot be obtained from reason, which de-
termines what is and what is not Divine Revelation, nor from
mathematics, but from the seventh state of consciousness, as we
explained it in the previous chapter. The belief that creation has
an end purpose marks one of the great differences between the
rational monotheist religions of the West and the mystical religions of the East. In fact, it is a characteristic of the western mind to
be obsessed with questions about our origin and our future because for us time is linear. It is not of much concern to eastern philosophers, for whom time is cyclic.

We can speak of the whole of creation being structured in layers. Starting from the gross level and moving to greater refine-
ment, we have first the surface level, as can be experienced by the
five senses and which appears to consist of solids, liquids and va-
pours. Next come molecules and after that atoms. The notion of
atoms is older than we might imagine. The Greek philosopher
Democritus in the fifth century BCE hypothesised that the basic
building block of all matter was a tiny invisible and indestructible
particle which he called "a-tom", meaning that which cannot be
cut. In recent times we have delved deeper to discover the sub-
atomic levels of electrons, protons and quarks. At a finer level still
are the quantum fields, non-localised waves. These fields have
now been reduced to four, known as the Gravitational Field, the
Strong Nuclear Force, the Weak Nuclear Force and the Electro-
magnetic Field. (Physicists now believe the Electromagnetic Field
and the Weak Nuclear Force are simply two facets of the same
force, the Electroweak Force, thus reducing the fields to three.) In
the splittest of split seconds after the Big Bang, they are thought to
have emerged from the Unified Field.

The Unified Field

Scientists today are in the process of trying to perfect a Theory of the Unified Field. In discovering that, they claim, they will have discovered the Soul of the World, the origin of all existence. This, however, is not a physical field. It is the most subtle, refined field of all. It is a field of consciousness. The power of creation is consciousness. It is that which generates time, space, energy. When we speak of the Unified Field are we, then, speaking of God? No, not of God but rather of the Will of God.

It would seem that in the whole creative process there exists a unifying power drawing us ever more rapidly forwards: towards the Omega Point, as Teilhard de Chardin calls it. Just as the physical gravitational field acts upon matter through space, so there is a spiritual gravity acting on consciousness through time, drawing us forward as conscious beings, drawing us perhaps into the next evolutionary stage of consciousness. For Teilhard, the ultimate growth of individual consciousness into cosmic consciousness is equivalent to the Biblical vision of the Kingdom of God.

Because of God's involvement in the continuing creative process we are able to say that as God influences us so we, in mutual reciprocity, have an influence on God (manifest). We have only to instance the way in which we have seized creative power from God. Before 6 August 1945 (the day we dropped the atomic bomb on Hiroshima) we had understood God to be the sole creator and sustainer of human life and implicit in that was the belief that He was the sole terminator of life as a whole. We have now assumed this power for ourselves. When the first atomic bomb was exploded in the desert of New Mexico the official report sent to President Truman contained these words:

> Then came the strong, sustained, awesome roar which warned of doomsday and made us feel that we puny things were blasphemous to dare to tamper with the forces heretofore reserved to the Almighty.

For the first time in the millions of years of human history we have "progressed" from the ever-present reality of homicide to the possibility of omnicide. We now share with God the mastery over the life of our planet. We co-create with God by allowing Him to continue His creative act. God is no longer uniquely "Almighty God" as far as Planet Earth is concerned.

But further, with our adventures into the field of genetic engineering we have given ourselves the power to reshape all life forms. We have taken "creation" into our own hands. It makes all our former attempts at "playing God" look puny.

We often hear people giving a warning with the words: "We are playing God." The warning is given as if there was a department of life that God allows us to play with but that there are frontiers beyond which is God's area of control. But who is to say where that frontier lies? Such warnings assume a God who would rather we were not creators, despite His having given us the intelligence so to act. Are we not so ready to declare that we are "made in the image of God"? But God is a creating God!

In the eternal *now*, God's plan for creation is already accomplished. But for its working out within created time, God depends upon our co-operation. How soon his dream of what Jesus called "The Kingdom of God" will come about depends upon the degree to which we are prepared to go along with it. I have a feeling it is going to take a few centuries yet!

God, Creation and Us

The way in which we understand the God–Universe relationship — as Deists or Theists — will dictate our attitude to creation and to our place as human beings within it.

Up to this point I have been using the word "creation" in its traditional meaning. Now I want to make a plea to use the word "origins" when speaking of *how* the Universe came into being — the realm of scientists — and to use "creation" to mean the continuing act of God holding everything in existence in the *now* moment — the realm of theologians. The theology of creation has very little to do with origins but almost everything to do with our Universe's continual dependence upon God.

If we hold that God, having once created it, left the world to its own devices, then God is so transcendent and aloof from creation that it is not ruled by his goodness but, as we might conjecture from our everyday experience, by evil forces. This belief was prevalent in Christianity for many centuries due to the influence of the Gnostics, for whom all in the world was evil, as a consequence of "The Fall", and the only goodness was in the human soul: a spark of the Divine. So the world was hostile to us. This notion, particularly influenced by Manichaeism, reinforced the Greek dualistic notion that we are made up of body (evil) and soul (good). With such a paradigm, creation — and even our very bodies — are enemy number one.

Such a view is quite contrary to the Biblical attitude to creation, which is very positive. Right from the Book of Genesis, we read that as God took each step in the creating process he "saw that it was good". Psalm 104 is a hymn in praise of the Creator and of His creation. What is interesting is that all the elements of creation are seen to be good in their own right, and not because they are good for or useful to humanity.

A third attitude towards creation, however, dominates our world today: it sees it as neither evil nor good but neutral. In our secular society this is understandable. The world is there for our use, to be pillaged, raped — it is just raw material for economic growth, technological development, scientific discovery. Nature, though not evil, is there to be conquered and dominated so that we human beings may evolve independently towards our own perfection. Surprisingly, this attitude is not the child of eighteenth-century rationalism but could be said to have originated from Thomas Aquinas in the thirteenth century. Anxious to move from the earlier Gnostic negative view of the world and of the human body, he taught that the world is not just neutral but good. However, it is good, not on its own account, but only because it serves our human needs. The body is good only in so far as it is at the service of the soul.

One of the most influential writings on western spirituality, originating in the sixteenth century but claiming increasing popularity today, is the *Spiritual Exercises of St Ignatius*. In it we read:

> Man has been created to praise, reverence and serve our Lord God, thereby saving his soul. Everything else on Earth has been created for man's sake, to help him to achieve the purpose for which he has been created. So it follows that man has to use them as far as they help and abstain from them where they hinder his purpose.

There is a growing reaction to this stance today in the expression of environmental and ecological concerns, and in the increased awareness of the interdependence of all elements of creation, including human beings. This is largely being forced upon us for purely scientific and even selfish reasons by the threatened long-term effects of some of our human activities: pollution of sky and sea with industrial waste, the greed with which we devour Earth's mineral and vegetative resources; the extermination of so many species — all in the interests of "progress". Such manipulation of our delicately balanced Earth threatens us with raising the terrestrial temperature, destroying the ozone layer, melting the ice caps, raising the level of the oceans, causing skin cancer, producing acid rain and so on and on to our final achievement: the development of nuclear energy without adequate means to control it.

Within the Christian tradition, there is a growing awareness of the sacredness of creation in our materialist West, thanks to the resurgence of Celtic Spirituality and the inspiration of Creation Theology. A deeper understanding of the meaning of the Cosmic Christ, so beloved of Teilhard de Chardin, and an appreciation that God is in all creation (panentheism) are contributing to more people seeing the spiritual dimension present in all being. If we live in partnership with the Earth, the Earth will live in partnership with us — supplying all our needs but not our extravagances. As more people are coming to realise today, the problem of world hunger is not a problem of lack of resources but lack of good will and desire to share on the part of those who control the resources. It is not a resource problem but a consciousness problem!

Each of us is a part, though a minuscule part, of the totality of creation, and our contribution matters. David Wilkinson, in his book *God, the Big Bang and Stephen Hawking*, tells the story of a former President of the United States who, before retiring to bed, would go outside the White House to search for the constellation Pegasus and say to himself: "One of those lights is the spiral galaxy of Andromeda. It contains one hundred billion stars each the size of our own Sun. It is but one of one hundred billion galaxies in the Universe, each as large as our own Milky Way galaxy." Then after a pause he would add, "Now I feel small enough, I can go to bed!" This is a graphic way of stating what Dostoevsky said: "Man needs the unfathomable and the infinite just as much as he does the small planet which he inhabits."

It is from our appreciation of creation that we learn to appreciate the Creator.

For further exploration:

Brian Swimme and Thomas Berry (1994), *The Universe Story*, Harper San Francisco.

David Wilkinson (1993), *God, the Big Bang and Stephen Hawking: An Explanation into Origins*, Monarch, Tunbridge Wells.

Fritjof Capra (2003), *The Hidden Connections*, Harper Collins, London.

Chapter 8

THE NEW PARADIGM FACTOR

The Meaning of Paradigm

There is a great deal being said today in many quarters about the fact that humanity is currently undergoing a "paradigm shift". In this context the word "paradigm" is used to mean a mental pattern or framework within which our mind operates. Unless we have such a framework, we simply cannot come to grips with the world around us. It provides us with mental pegs upon which to hang new experiences so that they fit into the overall understanding we have of our world. It gives us a structure by which we interpret our reality. Our paradigm may be a scientific world view or a religion or an ideology. It is the home of prejudices: we pre-judge people or events according to how they fit in with (or do not fit in with) our conceptual framework. It tells us what ought to be, what to expect. An illustration will make this clearer. In the pre-Second World War years, the Swiss were the unchallenged masters of watchmaking. All watches at that time were mechanical, operated by a collection of cogwheels powered by a spring. In the decades following the war, the digital electronic watch began to flood the market and Japan and other East Asian countries took over from the Swiss as the world's suppliers of watches. What many people do not know is that the digital watch was invented by a Swiss. However, the Swiss mind was so stuck in its particular watch paradigm that it simply could not accept an entirely new form of watch. So the inventor went East where minds were more open.

Paradigm Shifts

The term "paradigm shift" was coined by Thomas Kuhn in his book *The Structure of Scientific Revolutions* in 1962, in which he defined a paradigm as "the entire constellation of beliefs, values, techniques and so on shared by the members of a given community", although it is said that in the course of the book he himself uses the word in 21 different senses! By a paradigm shift is meant a fundamental break with a preceding mental parameter — as illustrated in the case of the watches. Again, the watch story exemplifies what Kuhn also says about a new paradigm: that it is not only incompatible with but often actually incommensurable with that which has gone before.

Two examples of such paradigm shifts were given in the chapter on the Science Factor: the shift from the rationalist, Enlightenment paradigm, which was the generally accepted framework in western culture (not only for science but for all disciplines including theology), to the present quantum, holistic, interrelatedness paradigm; and obviously, before that, the shift to a Copernican view of the Universe.

We all know that while change is welcomed and often brought about by the few, it is resisted by the majority. Never is this more evident than when the change involves the mental parameters from which we make sense of our world. The drawbridges are raised and the protagonists of the old paradigm immunise themselves against the arguments of the new. It is the human defensive mechanism at work, a sign of our insecurity. In our present times we see this happening in the swing to conservatism — in both religion and politics — and, at the extreme of the spectrum, in the rise of religious fundamentalism, as much in Islam as in Christianity.

Whereas in science a new paradigm replaces an older one irreversibly because the two are incompatible — after Newton it was no longer possible to understand the Universe with the framework of Copernicus, let alone of Ptolemy, as it is now not possible after Einstein to understand it as Newton proposed — in theology previous paradigms can live on in ecclesial pockets. Hans Küng points out that the Greek paradigm of the Patristic period still lives on in parts of the Orthodox Churches, that the medieval Roman Catholic paradigm continues in contemporary Roman Catholic traditionalism, while the Protestant Reformation paradigm lives on in Protestant confessionalism. Do we not find in nearly all Christian denominations layers of fundamentalists, conservatives, moderates, liberals and radicals? Which reminds us that our theologies are partial, culturally and socially based projections of one or other aspect of Truth.

Revelation can only be expressed in the thought-forms and transmitted in the paradigm of the recipient. So all revelation is limited by culture and time. It is received and transmitted in terms of the world view of that society. Let us see how this applies to the origin of Christian Revelation.

World View Paradigm of Biblical Times

What did Jesus mean when he spoke of Heaven as God's home? His language was Aramaic and Aramaic is a very "earthy" language. "Heaven" in Aramaic is not a metaphysical concept but presents the image of "light and sound shining through all creation", according to one Aramaic scholar. However, the cosmology of Jesus' culture rested on a belief that the Earth was flat, that Earth was mid-way between a Heaven above and a Hades or Hell beneath.

In this paradigm "he came down from Heaven" in the act of incarnation, "he descended into Hell" after his death and eventually "ascended into Heaven" above us, as we declare in the Creed.

The Greeks also thought of their gods as residing "up there", but for them the "up there" was the top of Mount Olympus!

If science today has informed us that there is no "down there" because the Earth is round, and that there is only molten matter at the centre; and it has discovered that "above" us is an immense galaxy of 100 billion stars with 100 billion other galaxies beyond, we are released from thinking of the location paradigm employed by the Bible.

Consequently we are released from thinking that there are but two possibilities after death: a Heaven or a Hell. There is no reason to prevent us thinking of life, after journeying through death, as passing into a series of higher-consciousness lives, passing from level to level so to speak; or passing to ever-higher wavelengths, as we mentioned when considering the Relatedness Factor. "In my Father's house there are many rooms", to quote Jesus (John 14:2). The first level we pass into after death is that which assists our purification, enabling us to complete all that unfinished business of which people having a near-death experience are so aware: the level that Catholic theology refers to as Purgatory.

Being only one remove from Earth wavelengths, people at this level are occasionally able to communicate between wavelengths in the form of ghosts, poltergeists, apparitions, channelled voices, etc.

The "departed" are no longer in the time-space dimension so the question of how much time they spend in each level being purified for the next just does not arise. That is an Earth-bound question.

True, about this we can do no more than speculate, but eschatology — the doctrines about Death, Judgement, Heaven and Hell — is the least developed area of theology. In fact, the conservative theologian of great stature, the late Hans Urs von Balthasar, said of the treatise on "The Last Things" that it "is closed for repairs"! How we think of what lies ahead of us after death will depend upon our (probably religious) paradigm.

Our paradigm is formed by our culture, as illustrated below.

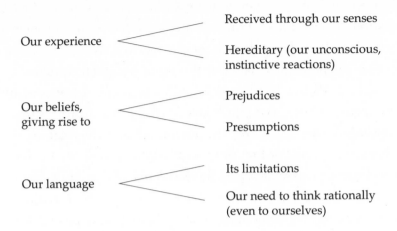

Our experience
— Received through our senses
— Hereditary (our unconscious, instinctive reactions)

Our beliefs, giving rise to
— Prejudices
— Presumptions

Our language
— Its limitations
— Our need to think rationally (even to ourselves)

Today's Paradigm Shift

We opened this chapter by saying that it is now widely recognised that our present times are marked by a shift of paradigm. Why now, at this particular moment in history? One might be forgiven for asking. Because at this period of human history there just happens to be a concatenation of events, of discoveries, of insights, each of which is feeding the other ingredients, not one of which would have been a sufficient cause on its own. The present paradigm shift is best described as a shift in the level of human consciousness and is being brought about by a number of factors, many among them providing this book with its chapter titles. One consequence of a shift in consciousness is a need to re-think what we mean by God — to make a God shift! — since that small word is no more than a symbol of our perception of Ultimate Reality. "God" is the name we give to the Reality that cannot be named.

When we look at what is labelled by the mass media as "The New Age" we will be asking (when we look at the New Spirituality Factor) whether it is new or not, and "why now?" However, let me just mention one factor at this point which I believe is contributing to our assuming a new world view. It is the fact that we have recently entered a new millennium. A first reaction to this suggestion might well be: but that is only a convention. It is no more than a calculation — a miscalculation, actually — based on the supposed date of the birth of Jesus. It so happens that we are following the Gregorian calendar (a revision of the Julian calendar, established in Rome in 46 BCE, which was revised in 1582 and introduced by Pope Gregory XIIIth). We might just as likely, had history turned out differently, be following the Revolutionary calendar of the First French Republic or that proposed by Hitler. Besides, the Jews have a different calendar, as do the Moslems, and so do a further fifth of the world's population, the Chinese. All that accepted, there is, nevertheless, something special about having passed what we designated as the year 2000, and it is not just that our western calendar happens to be the most established worldwide for purposes of trade, communication and travel.

An event so special is accompanied by a great sense of expectancy. There must be something new about it: things will surely get better. When perhaps a large majority of the world population has these expectations, its very consciousness generates something new. (We spoke of the power and results of collective prayer or wishing in an earlier chapter.) Despite expectations at the time having been dashed for many by events of the last few years, there is still a considerable body of people in the west who are aware of signs of a shift taking place in human consciousness. There is something deep within the human psyche that looks for something new, a chance to begin again. The ubiquity of flood myths, found in societies on every continent, testifies to a universal longing to reach a turning point where an unsatisfactory past can be put behind us and a new beginning embraced.

The Hierarchy Paradigm

If I have dwelt at length on the notion of a paradigm shift, it is in order to stress just how fundamental, how radical, such a shift is to our outlook on all aspects of life.

In this chapter I want to enlarge upon one particular element of the current paradigm shift to a new consciousness. It is not one that is immediately evident, yet it is very influential in our changing perception of the Divine-human relationship. This is a shift from a hierarchical to a centred relational framework.

As far back as we can trace, human beings have related to each other and to the cosmos in a hierarchical paradigm. An obvious example of this is in our common view of the order of creation, as illustrated below.

and in the spiritual order:

In each of these paradigms, the presumption is that what is at the top is best, holiest. So many phrases in our everyday language reveal just how innate this pyramidical paradigm is: "the ascent to God", "the ladder of perfection", "higher states of consciousness", "upwardly mobile", "low achievers", "upper, middle and lower classes", "at the bottom of the pack", "our lower nature", "seeking promotion", "the top of the table", "one-upmanship", "head teacher", "peak performance".

In nature there are no hierarchies, no above or below. To view some creatures as superior to others is a human projection. In nature there are only networks by which all of nature is mutually related. The fact that lions kill wild dogs, which kill rabbits — and so on down the line — for food, is simply a segment of the ecosystem. It is the human mind that classifies them into an order of superiority, a superiority of power.

The hierarchical paradigm is a power structure. Absolute power is at the pinnacle and percolates downwards, the powerless being at "the bottom of the stack". It demands obedience to the level above and assumes domination over the level below. It is a structure of control. We teach our children that this is the way our world is ordered and operates and the experience of it begins in the parent–child relationship. It is only in recent years that we are coming to recognise that children too have rights as human beings; that their parents and their "elders and betters" (to use a Victorian phrase) do not have absolute power over children. This framework, it is true, provides a form of security. We know our place in society; we acknowledge the "pecking order". But it also preserves the parent–child relationship into adulthood, which enables those at the top to manipulate those at the bottom: "Father knows best."

Despite this being a non-Gospel paradigm, as I shall explain below, it is still very evident in the Church today, and has been ever since Church structure modelled itself on the Roman Empire. In fact, the very word "hier-archy" was coined by Dionysius the Areopagite, a sixth century monk in Syria, to denote the totality of ruling persons in the Church. Hier-archy means Sacred Government, just as Mon-archy means government by one person, a king.

In the Church context hierarchy looks like this:

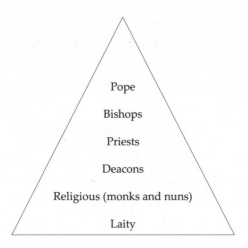

The laity, forming 99.9 per cent of Church members, are at the bottom. Instructions, doctrines, precepts filter down from top to bottom. We even refer to Bishops as "the Hierarchy". All decisions too are made at the top for the benefit of those at the bottom, despite the fact that in the 2,000 years of Church history any major change has always been initiated at the grassroots and never from the top. The current worldwide popularity of the Basic Christian Community movement, which all indications show will be the future structure of the Church, is an example of this. The pattern has arisen from a felt need of Christians, not because of any instruction from the Vatican. There must, of course, be the exercise of authority in the Church, but authority as leadership, as unifier, not as control. Authentic leadership needs to be continually adjusting to different shapes to meet differing situations.

Hierarchy is also a structure of achievement, when achievement is brought about by competition. One climbs to a higher position — to more power, to more authority — by trampling down the less powerful, the less able. There is the presumption that we strive to rise to the level above that in which we are at present. Sadly, our position on the ladder is also the measure of our self-worth, our "success", our dignity. Our worth is measured by our value to society, which in turn is measured by our achievement. The role of women in the home has no value by this measure, which can cause many housewives to have little self-esteem. How often their self-esteem depends upon the position of their husband. "I would like you to meet Mrs Jones. She is the wife of the Managing Director."

Origins of Hierarchy

What gave birth to the hierarchy paradigm? This is not easy to establish. Is it possible that it arose from the human experience of gravity? It takes effort to rise — the more power, the higher we can go — whereas without power we drop, we fall. We use the gravity experience to describe our mood. We speak of lightness of heart, heaviness of spirit, of feeling low, feeling down or of being on a high, of walking on air.

Wherever we human beings live in relationship to each other, we form a social structure. This ranges from the family unit — whether nuclear or extended — to the village, town, state, nation and beyond. Each is a search for the perfect way to share life in friendship. But because of our inability to share life fully, openly — because we dare not take the risk of that — our communication is restrained by fear. We overcome our fear by dominating. So our social structures, instead of being such as to be life-enhancing for everyone, become structures of oppression. Instead of giving a fuller life to others, we take life and freedom from others "to keep them in their place". We have only to look around the world to-day to be reminded of how domination gives birth to violence, whether it be the collective violence of a suppressed racial minority or the violence of frustrated individuals deprived of security, of a job prospect, of an opening to improve themselves. Our whole world economy is based upon the few dominating the many. As Rosemary Haughton wrote in her book *Love*, "A serious outbreak of love in the world would bring the [stock] markets crashing down." It would also bridge the First World/Third World gap.

Maybe the origin of hierarchy in our human society is due to our failure to be fully human: our failure to love unreservedly.

How far back can we trace the repressive hierarchy paradigm in our history? Looking at the designs found in many ancient cultures to symbolise their creation myth, we notice that one thing all these myths have in common is a belief in three worlds: Earth is the middle world, *above* Earth is the Heaven of the Divine Beings and holy spirits, while *below* is an Underworld, the place of evil spirits. From this model we receive our Biblical "placing" of Heaven, Earth and Hell, that we mentioned above.

And yet we notice that almost all these creation myth designs, with the exception of the Tree of Life, are circular, resembling a mandala. In the myth of the Pawnee North American Indians, the first human beings built their camp in a circle to resemble the map of the heavens. In the legend of King Arthur, he and his knights sat at the *Round* Table.

As a power and achievement structure, the hierarchy paradigm appeared upon the European stage more recently than we might suppose, as the research of Riane Eisler persuades us. In her widely acclaimed book *The Chalice and the Blade,* her thesis is that in the Neolithic period our ancestors worshipped the creator as a goddess and not as a male god. (We are speaking of the period between 10,000 and 4,000 BCE when humanity moved from being gatherers and hunters and settled down in communities, having developed skills in agriculture and animal husbandry.) Consequent upon such worship, the feminine values of creativity and nurturing were uppermost over the male values of domination and rule by fear or threat. Riane Eisler presents plenty of evidence that during this period people lived in a non-male-dominated, non-hierarchical society. Nor was it female-dominated, although it was a matrilineal society in which descent and inheritance were traced through the mother. It was an egalitarian society in which women played key roles in all aspects of life. Furthermore, it was a

peace-loving society, indicated by the absence of heavy fortifica-
tions and throwing weapons.

What changed all that? There were three major waves of invaders (between 4,300 and 2,800 BCE) who were nomadic cattle
herders of Indo-European or Aryan-language-speaking stock who
swept down into Europe from the Asiatic and European north-
east. Ruled by powerful priests and warriors, they brought with
them their male gods of war and mountains. But there were other
nomadic invaders as well, among them the Semitic people (the
Hebrews) who invaded Canaan (Palestine) from the South. They
were ruled by a tribe of warrior-priests — the Levites — and
brought with them a male god of war: Jehovah or Yahweh. Chapter 21 of the Book of Numbers describes Yahweh's instructions to
Moses for a war of revenge against the Midianites. Yahweh gives
clear instructions about the distribution of booty between the sol-
diers, the priests and the community: sheep and goats, cattle,
donkeys and virgins (in that order)! Eisler writes:

> The one thing they [the invaders] all had in common was a
> dominator model of social organisation: a social system in
> which male dominance, male violence and a generally
> hierarchic and authoritarian social structure was the norm.

However, she offers no explanation as to how such male values
came to predominate among these nomadic herdsmen in the first
place, or who put a higher value on the power that takes rather
than the power that gives life.

Power at the Top

It is sometimes argued that the hierarchy paradigm is of divine
origin because the source of all power is God, and God is "above"
creation. But then we have to ask, what is the origin of that belief?
Which came first, the notion that God is "above" and outside creation, which gave rise to the idea of perfection and power being at
the pyramid's peak, or did the human working structure of hierar-

chy cause human beings to think of a God who *must* be at the top? A parallel question may throw light on this. Did the Israelites institute a rhythm of six working days to be followed by a day of rest, based on the account of God creating in six days and resting on the seventh, or did the post-exile author of this version of the myth of creation explain God's timetable in this way because the Israelites were already living this pattern of life, having found from experience that it suited the human rhythm? (The Israelites had just returned from captivity in Babylon and would have known of the great Babylonian epic *Enuma Elish* which also speaks of creation happening over six days with the seventh being a day of rest.)

The accounts of human origins in the scriptures of the Hebrew people were written only a few hundred years before Jesus, by which time the Chosen People had already experienced being structured into a hierarchical society with a king at the top — a king of divine choice. Within this context of power at the top, the earliest chapters of Genesis were written, and in Chapter 1, verse 26, we read:

> Then God said: "And now we will make human beings; they will be like us and resemble us. They will have *power* over the fish, the birds and all animals, domestic and wild, large and small".

And in verse 28 God is saying, "Be fruitful, multiply, fill the Earth and *conquer* it". Upon this biblical basis arose the authority we human beings have given ourselves to dominate, to use for our benefit, to destroy even, all the rest of creation at our whim. This is echoed — again in hierarchical form — in Psalm 8:

> What is man that you are mindful of him? You have made him inferior only to yourself [some translations say: You have made him a little less than a god], you crowned him with glory and honour. You appointed him ruler over everything you made: you placed him over all creation.

Here is the cosmic pyramid of command and domination. We still speak of "the conquest of nature". In the Judeo-Christian tradition (and in most other cultures) men are above women and children are beneath adults, with adults owning and controlling children. This was the measure of their worth! There are still societies today in which the man is regarded as owning his wives, his children and livestock, with power of life and death over them. Little wonder that in the West God has been traditionally thought of as male!

Perhaps the first person to write about hierarchy as a specific structure was Aristotle (384–322 BCE), as he did in his treatise *Physics*. He wrote of a hierarchy of existences with the Unmoved Mover (creator) at the top. Each "layer" of existence gave form to the one below and the emanations grew weaker the further down the pyramid they went.

Curiously, in our present-day scientific understanding we speak of the antithesis of this: matter evolves "upwards" from the simple cell to the increasingly more complex.

It is logical that a people who believe their God to be outside their cosmos, dominating them, should in turn see themselves, believed to be made in the image of God, as above nature with the role of dominating it. This was the paradigm out of which the early chapters of Genesis and the Psalms were written. Why has humanity created such a gap between itself and the rest of creation?

The most common presentation that one sees of the theory of evolution in natural history museums is in the form of a tree — a variation of the pyramid — with the human being at the very top, of course. We place ourselves at the pinnacle because our consciousness gives us our identity as individuals, beings who are separate from others. This sense of selfhood makes us feel special and so separate from and "above" the rest of nature which is not self-reflective. Christians express this as being created individually by God. There may have been evolution of the species, some theologians begrudgingly admit, but each human soul is a special creation. No wonder we have created a gulf! Thomas Henry Huxley wrote of "the vastness of the gulf between . . . man and the brutes" and his grandson, Julian Huxley, saw the gulf as so vast that he suggested *Homo Sapiens* be classified as a totally new sector, the Psycho-social, "as against the entire non-human biological sector".

Rather than an evolutionary tree, it has been suggested that a hedgerow would be a more appropriate model, with its dips and rises at certain points — at places it is thick and healthy, at others it is scraggy and with some dead patches. Evolution is a process, not a climb. And there have certainly been dead patches. In the Earth's history there have been five mass extinctions, during which the majority of species disappeared. The fifth, the Cretaceous, is the best known — 65 million years ago — because that was the occasion of the dinosaurs becoming extinct (along with 60-80 per cent of other terrestrial species), probably due to a large asteroid or comet colliding with the Earth and raising a fatal dust cloud. It is recorded that more than 99 per cent of all species that have ever lived are now extinct and some environmentalists estimate that the way we human beings are treating our planet today, as much as 50 per cent of the present species in the world will become extinct within three decades. So much for "dominion over the Earth"! But we are slowly beginning to learn our lesson.

Three Great Shifts

We learn by shifting our paradigm. The first shift to "put us in our place" was in the sixteenth century when Copernicus dislodged the Earth, and therefore ourselves, from our central position in the Universe to that of one small planet among others circling a small sun. The next jolt by which we were "put down" was provided by Darwin and his theory, now generally accepted, that we humans are just another species that happened to emerge as part of an evolving process. As if this were not enough to rid us of our arrogance, the discovery by astronomers in recent decades of the vastness of the

Universe with its galaxies upon galaxies will surely convince us
how very minute human beings are within the total creation picture.

But surely, a Christian will respond, what makes us special is
that we are made "in the image and likeness of God". But isn't
everything a reflection of the Divine? I well remember how it
came across to me as a blasphemy when someone pointed to the
cat in the room and remarked that the cat too is made "in the image and likeness of God". Having got over the shock of the remark, I could only agree. The cat is a divine manifestation although manifesting less of the divine than we humans do. It is not
simply our souls, nor even just our intelligence and ability to love
that mirror the Divine. If we believe that God creates everything
then He can only create according to His own design: everything
that exists reflects some qualities of God. There can be no other
model. To put it another way, all we can ever know about God
can only be known through His creation, which is a reflection of
the Divine Mystery. Contrary to the hierarchical model, our God-
knowledge does not come down from above to us below — from
Heaven to Earth — but from the bottom up. Any concept we have
of Heaven can only come from Earth. We can only visualise
Heaven in terms of our experience of Earth. Similarly, any concept
we can have of God can only come from our understanding of
ourselves. We human beings claim for ourselves more God-like
qualities than any other species we know of . . . but that is according to our assessment.

Why should not geese say to themselves (are we so sure that
geese are not self-reflective in their own goosy way?): "We are the
pinnacle of creation, the most perfect of all creatures. We can fly in
the air, we can swim on water and we can walk on land. When we
migrate we navigate for thousands of miles without any of the instruments humans need. We know all about aerodynamics: we fly
at a height and in a formation that gives us maximum benefit. As
we fly our leadership changes — the best goose for the present task
leads. This is decided, not by argument and vote but by the consent

of our common consciousness. Certainly we are God's most favoured creation!" Geese comprehend creation in terms of geese.

When we meet these ideas for the first time they can be very
threatening. They undermine our sense of importance, our feeling
of power. We are not the reason why everything else exists. We
are not necessarily the end of the evolutionary process; we may be
just another stage on the way to a further species beyond the human. It is this sort of thinking that is bringing about what I believe
to be the most radical, the most all-encompassing paradigm shift:
the mark of our entering into an era of new consciousness.

From Hierarchical Model to Centred Model

It is the shift from the hierarchical model to the centred model. I
call it "centred" because from understanding ourselves as "above"
nature, we are learning that we are within nature. We are part of
the diversity of nature, all of which is a reflection of the Divine. As
we come to appreciate more that the Divine Reality is present in
everything and everyone (panentheism) we must surely become
more loath to destroy anything around us or to torture and maim
other human beings. In such destruction and killing we are killing
something of God. That "something" is the manifestation of the
Spirit, for as the ancient wisdom of the Bhagavad Gita reminds us:

> Interwoven in his creation, the Spirit is beyond destruction.
> No one can bring to an end the Spirit which is everlasting
> (2:17).

Commenting on this verse, Dom Bede Griffiths wrote:

> In every particle of matter, in every living thing, in every
> human being, in every human situation, the one eternal
> Spirit is always present. (*River of Compassion*)

Where we have been mistaken in the past is to give rank to diverse persons and objects rather than to appreciate the richness of

diversity. The value of each species, including the human, lies in its particular, indeed unique, contribution to the whole. Rather than feeling threatened by another person's difference or belittled because we recognise their talents as "superior" to our own, we can rejoice because we can benefit from them: they add a richness to our life. Ranking people and objects causes us to ask the wrong questions such as: Which is better, man or woman? A black person or a white person? A human being or a tree? It is sometimes argued that the higher a species is up the evolutionary tree, the more complex it is; the more complex it is, the more useful, the more functional it is. But useful for what?

The astonishing fact is that Jesus was saying all this 2,000 years ago but, as with so much of his "Good News", we have taken so long to mature in consciousness that we have simply not understood the depth, the radicalness, of his message. Nowhere in the Gospel account do we find Jesus approving the hierarchical model; quite the contrary, as we see in the instruction he gave to those who were to be the leaders in his new community:

> You know that the men who are considered rulers of the heathen have power over them, and the leaders have complete authority. This, however, is not the way it is among you. If one of you wants to be great, he must be the servant of the rest; and if one of you wants to be first, he must be the slave of all. For even the Son of Man did not come to be served; he came to serve. (Mark 10:42–45)

This was said to them after they had been prospecting for positions of dignity in the Kingdom of glory. The only occasion upon which Jesus allowed the crowd to acclaim him as a king was immediately preceding his being tortured and put to death. They cheered and waved palm branches as he entered Jerusalem. And even then he did not ride triumphantly on a horse like a conquering king, but on a donkey, the peasants' beast of burden. Matthew (21:5) tells us that in this he was fulfilling a prophecy (Zechariah 9:9): "Look, your king is coming to you! He is humble and rides on a donkey."

Christians accept the model Jesus gave us of God as a loving Father. This is easy to accept: a father figure answers our needs, is protective, gives us a sense of security. But we have not yet learned the corollary to this: that we have to accept all other human beings as our brothers and sisters, children of a common father. In this paradigm the primary relationship of any one of us to any other is that of brother and sister. The relationships that exist on account of our roles (parent–child, teacher–pupil, policeman–citizen, Pope–layperson, judge–plaintiff, etc) are only secondary. Jesus' primary relationship to us is as brother. When Joseph Campbell, the mythologist, was asked if he believed Jesus Christ was the Son of God, he replied, "Not unless all of us are."

Our Personal Value or Our Role Value

Hierarchy values us for what we have, or for what we can contribute from what we have — our role, our ability, our power, our honours and titles, our class or caste. In this paradigm, we are what we are only by being measured against others. Our worth depends upon how others regard us. This breeds the ethos of competition. But the centred paradigm values us for what we are. It is non-competitive. Our worth comes from our being of value to and beloved by God, because there is that of God in us. We are accepted because we are a brother or sister of the same Father.

When mothers brought children to Jesus, his bodyguard "scolded" them, as much as to say, "Jesus has more important people to bless and heal than mere children." But we are told that Jesus was angry with his disciples and what he said about the Kingdom of God being as much for children as for adults reveals that he did not judge a person's worth by their place in society (Mark 10:13-16). Contrary to the custom prevailing, he did not treat women as being in any way inferior to men. He had special concern for the outcasts, for lepers, for the public sinners, for tax-collectors. Roles played no part in the way he valued people.

One of the ways in which we notice our hierarchical paradigm at work is when we look for the "authority" by which someone speaks or writes. (Who is this Adrian Smith writing this book? What is his academic background, his position in the Church, his experience of life?!) So often Jesus was asked by what authority he said the outrageous things people heard him say. It is interesting to notice that he never replied directly to that question. The authenticity of what he said gave it its own authority. Did it match with their experience? Did it ring true, as we say? This is how we should make our judgement about opinions and pronouncements in the centred paradigm. Who says what is less important than judging the rightness of what is said by its inner value.

The top-down approach is also a feature which emphasises the divide between religion and science. Religion is concerned with truths that come from on high, with their formulation in revelation and authority. It presents a unified vision of truths which are universally and eternally valid and presented as a ready-made set of doctrines. Their unity is imposed on a diversity of experience.

Science, on the contrary, is from the centre outwards. It grapples with facts that emerge from observation and experiment which is essentially pluralistic. It uses models which are partial because it does not claim to have the totality. Science is always seeking fuller clarification and accepts to work "at the frontier", always open-ended, testing its assumptions and re-writing its theories.

The New Values of Our Time

Why, 2,000 years after the time of Jesus, is this shift taking place only in our own day? The explanation lies in the new values that are emerging at this time: regaining the value of the feminine, the holistic vision — the new paradigm. These are the seed-bed of other values, for example the increasing preference for all that is life-giving, for the non-competitive.

A recent initiative founded on the belief that all work is of equal value, whether cleaning the office or managing it, because the value lies in the person doing it and not in the product, is the birth of the world-wide LETS scheme (Local Exchange Trading System) whereby the time spent on a service for others, whatever its nature, can be bartered for someone else's service for one's own benefit.

Becoming more apparent also is the understanding of "authority" as being given, not to dominate, but to facilitate, to enable people to be creative, to accomplish, to grow, underlying which is the holistic view that my talents are not for my glory but for the benefit of all. It is because each person's talents are respected that leadership is able to rotate round the group, community or organisation. No one person is good at everything all the time! When creativity is shared, new ideas are not a threat.

Another current trend today is towards "networking" at all levels of society, which is another form of collaboration. By networking, power is exercised horizontally: it facilitates communication between like-minded people which is not only supportive and enriching for these people but, on account of the co-operation it engenders, is a powerful force for creating a new society. In her bestselling book *The Aquarian Conspiracy*, Marilyn Ferguson succinctly states this shift in paradigm: "Power is changing hands, from dying hierarchies to living networks."

God at the Centre

Moving from the hierarchical paradigm to the centred paradigm — which we should call the true Christian paradigm — we move from the God-out-there, separate from, beyond creation, to the God at the centre. One of the first theologians to popularise this shift was the Anglican Bishop John Robinson when he published his book

Honest to God in 1963. In it God is described by such phrases as "the uncreated depth dimension of human life", "the centre of our being". Many theologians today are using the Greek word *panentheism*, of which we spoken in the chapter on the Science Factor, as the most suitable way of describing the God–creation relationship — God in everything, everything in God — while keeping distinct the separate identities of creator and creation.

The idea that God is to be *experienced* as a centred God, and not as an out-there God, has a long tradition in Jewish history, despite their Heaven-Earth-Hell cosmology. In the first recorded message of Yahweh through the mouth of Isaiah, the people of Judah are reproved in very strong language because their externalised religion of sacrifices and feasts was to a God whom it was supposed they could only meet externally.

> Do you think I want all these sacrifices you keep offering to me? I have had more than enough of the sheep you burn as sacrifices and of the fat of your fine animals. I am tired of the blood of bulls and sheep and goats. Who asked you to bring me all this when you come to worship me? Who asked you to do all this tramping about in my Temple? It is useless to bring your offerings. I am disgusted with the smell of the incense you burn. I cannot stand your New Moon Festivals, your Sabbaths, and your religious gatherings; they are all corrupted by your sins. . . . When you lift your hands in prayer, I will not look at you. No matter how much you pray I will not listen, for your hands are covered with blood. Wash yourselves clean. Stop all this evil that I see you doing. Yes, stop doing evil and learn to do right. See that justice is done — help those who are oppressed, give orphans their rights and defend widows. (Isaiah 1:11-17)

Instead, their relationship to Yahweh should have been through other people, through exercising justice and mercy because they recognised the presence of God in other people. Their religion had to be interiorised. Justice is, in fact, one of the most emphasised subjects in the Bible. For both the minor prophets Amos and Hosea, an interiorising of religion was their main theme as they preached the message during the same period in the Northern Kingdom of Israel. Yahweh declares through Amos:

> I hate your religious festivals; I cannot stand them! When you bring me burnt-offerings and grain-offerings, I will not accept them; I will not accept the animals you have fattened to bring me as offerings. Stop your noisy songs; I do not want to listen to your harps. Instead, let justice flow like a stream, and righteousness like a river that never goes dry. (Amos 5:21–24)

The message of Hosea (quoted by Jesus: Matthew 9:13) is similar:

> I want your constant love, not your animal sacrifices. I would rather have my people know me than burn offerings to me. (Hosea 6:6)

The "know" here is not a philosophical knowing but the Hebrew *daath*, which comes from the verb *yada*, which is a knowing from the heart, a relationship, sexual even, as "Adam *knew* his wife Eve" (Genesis 4:1). It is within and through our relationship with creation — not outside it — and through our co-operation with the creative flow, bringing creation to its perfection as desired by the creator, that we encounter God.

It is sad that liturgical worship still uses hierarchical titles to denote God in prayers, which put God outside and above us (Lord, Judge, King, Almighty, Creator) rather than other Scriptural titles: Truth, Wisdom, Love, Life, which relate to the deepest dimension of our lives. Elizabeth Johnson reminds us of just how many images are used in the Bible to speak to us of God: potter, fisherman, farmer, builder, merchant, physician, metalworker, teacher, writer, artist as well as through images found in nature: lion, rock, light, cloud, fire and water.

Even today, in all the major religions, the majority of "religious" people prefer to restrict their relating to God to their times of worship in church or temple or synagogue or mosque: to keep God apart from life. It is much more demanding to relate to the centred God; this requires that we recognise His presence within us and all around us and "act justly".

We find a pleasing expression of God's closeness to us in the Qur'an: God is closer to us than our jugular vein.

The Trinity

The paradigm shift from a hierarchical model to a centred model must cause us to reflect on the traditional understanding of the Trinity. It is as well that its "definition" is referred to as the "Mystery of the Trinity", thus acknowledging that the last word has not been said . . . nor ever will be.

It was inevitable that the symbol of the Trinity should be a triangle or pyramid with the Father on top. How much more meaningful if it had been a circle, for the very essence of God as triune is relatedness. If God is Love there must be (projecting on to God our human reasoning) a Lover, a Beloved, and the act of loving. The concept of God as Trinity is unique to Christianity among the three monotheistic religions issuing from Abraham. In fact, the very idea that there might be three aspects of God is anathema to both Jews and Muslims. And yet we find in Hinduism a similar expression of Trinity. There is a trilogy of deities: Brahman (the power which sustains everything), Shiva (the deity of both good and evil, the creator and destroyer) and Vishnu, the playful god who shows himself to humanity in different incarnations or avatars, the best known being that of Krishna. In the Vedas, the poetic and philosophical writings of ancient India, pre-dating Hinduism, we find another trinitarian formula to explain the balance of forces in nature: Satva (creation), Tamas (destruction) and Rajas (maintainer). Again, the Hindu understanding of creative energy is that it is pure knowledge which develops in a tripartite dynamic of the Knower (Rishi), the act of knowing (Devata) and the object Known (Chhandas) (see below). This is not dissimilar to the model favoured by St Augustine: the Father is the Knower, the Son is the Known and the Spirit is the relationship between them: the bliss of knowing.

The Tripartite Dynamic

In Vedic Science, the three aspects of Knower, Knowing and Known are referred to as *Rishi*, *Devata* and *Chhandas*.

Rishi is that aspect of the whole known as the Self or the Knower, the fully developed understanding of the scientist as the agent, whose perception can actually influence the outcome of any experimental situation as Relativity Theory confirms. (Although they never named it, Eastern scientists have known Einstein's Relativity Theory for some 3,000 years.)

Devata refers to the process of knowing, including the various modes of description, rigorous methodologies, use of intelligence and learning skills. In this aspect, the Knower is interacting with the environment, entering into its "mind": in a sense, becoming part of the object or reality it is striving to understand.

Chhandas refers to the subject matter being perceived and analysed, not as a cold, inert, distant object, but as an aspect of life with which a "relationship" can be established.

The underlying wholeness that unifies all life and holds it in being is referred to as *Samhita*, a Sanscrit/Pali word, which we can translate as "that which is put together" or "that which is united within its source".

In ecstasy one reaches the highest form of the love of God — an immediate spiritual intuition — by which the Knower, the act of Knowing and the Known are experienced as one.

The catechism "definition" of the Holy Trinity — "three persons in one God" — can appear to most Christians as no more than a dry theological-mathematical formula, hardly designed to enable us to draw closer to the God who is at the centre of our being, the object of our experience of ecstatic union!

While this "explanation" may have served the purposes of former times and has much to be said for it, it is less helpful in our present emerging age of new consciousness, which sees things more as wholes.

This "definition" of the Godhead is a product of the Greek mind expressing analytically what is found expressed holistically in Scripture. Jesus in his preaching never mentioned the word "Trinity" but from the way he spoke about God it became apparent that he was aware of a diversity in God's unity. Even to use the word "person" of God is to employ an analogy because the only form of person we know is a human person. In fact such a "definition" of the mystery of God has even less meaning now than it had at the time of the Church Council of Nicaea in the year 325, which expressed the Trinity as "three persons in one God". With the development of our present day psychology, the word "person" has a much richer content than it had in the fourth century. The value of the word has changed.

Today, theologians are proposing other expressions to give meaning to our belief in a triune God. For example, thinking of God as Being (not as "a" being nor even as "the" being), John Macquarrie proposes "movements" of Being or "modes" of Being. The Father may be called "primordial" Being, the Son "expressive" Being and the Spirit "unitive" Being. Others propose that the Biblical Father, Son and Spirit can be understood as different modes of God's action, or rather, as three distinguishable ways in which the one God is experienced as acting in relation to us: as Creator, as Redeemer, as Inspirer. What is common to all these expressions is that in the Godhead there is both unity and diversity. God is relationship as well as consciousness.

Unity through Relating and Transcending

The two deepest and most pervading dynamics in the human person are inward towards transcending and outwards towards relating. The first draws us irresistibly towards the source of all consciousness, all being, all energy, out of our egos, towards the Greater. The second attracts us towards building up relationships: towards unity of person with person, of person with nature, of person with the cosmos.

In God the relating and transcending are not so much fully balanced as fully developed. In the relationships of the Trinity all "persons" are equal in terms of autonomy and intimacy. Because of the perfect harmony and acceptance, each finds perfect autonomy. The relationships within the Trinity defy and supersede all human ideas, concepts and explanations. Because of its fullness, the trinitarian relationship transcends all we can say or imagine about it. Yet we are fascinated by it, because in the depth of our own being, we too intuitively know that this is our destiny; that already on this Earth, we share in something of this profound mystery.

In these concerns — because human language is so limited — there is a tendency towards dualism, contrasting transcending and relating. In the Godhead there are no dualisms: all is one. It may be more appropriate, therefore, to say that the transcending takes place through the relationships rather than alongside them. And this helps to explain another conviction, shared by all the religions (although variously expressed) that we come to know and love God to the extent that we really love (relate deeply with) one another.

The journey of our created Universe is one of mutual interdependence, of loving and respectful relating. God is the loving energy that draws all things towards that fullness of life which we attribute to the Trinity. In the different religious traditions that fullness is given various names: the Promised Land in the Hebrew testament, the Kingdom of God in the Christian testament, the State of Nirvana in the great Eastern religions.

The unity within the Godhead encompasses all that is fragmented and incomplete in our world. And yet, God does not absorb the world into himself. This is one of the great paradoxes which we can only appreciate in our ability to transcend, in our capacity to think holistically rather than fragmentarily or dualistically. In the Trinity all "persons" are free and autonomous; so is creation in its journey to wholeness. Creation is neither determined nor predestined, but carries within its womb the seeds of imperishable life that guarantee its final unity and realisation in the all-knowing mind of God.

For further exploration:

Diarmuid Ó Murchú (1992), *Our World in Transition*, Temple House Books, Lewes.

Peter Russell (1992), *The White Hole in Time*, Aquarian/Thorsons.

Riane Eisler (1988), *The Chalice and the Blade: Our History, Our Future*, Harper Collins.

Donah Zohar and Ian Marshall (1994), *The Quantum Society*, Flamingo: Harper Collins.

Hilary Wakeman (2003), *Saving Christianity: New Thinking for Old Beliefs*, The Liffey Press, Dublin.

Chapter 9

THE REVELATION FACTOR

The Divine Revelation that is probably best known to the reader is the collection of revelations called the Bible. The Christian Bible has two major sections: the Hebrew Scriptures which we Christians call the Old Testament — or the writings of the Old Covenant — and the post-Jesus writings which we call the New Testament, the revelations of the New Covenant. Here are the opening verses of one of the latter, the Letter to the Hebrews.

> In the past, God spoke to our ancestors many times and in many ways through the prophets, but in these last days he has spoken to us through his Son.

This is both a factual statement and a faith statement. That the prophets spoke and that Jesus had a message is a statement of fact. (We are not concerned here with the historical exactitude of the fact.) That the message of the prophets to their people and the message of Jesus to the crowds was in fact God speaking to us through them is a statement of faith. Faith allows us to make a value judgement. With faith one can say, "Indeed, I believe this message is of God and in it God is revealing something of Himself to us." (We will be considering the Faith Factor in a later chapter.) But here we attempt to see what we mean when we speak of this or that as being Divine Revelation. We need to keep in mind, however, that nowhere in the Bible do we find anything about Ultimate Reality, God unmanifest: the writings are a cultural interpretation of God manifest. To say, as the Bible does, that God spoke to Joseph in a dream is to say that Joseph dreamt that God spoke to him.

It is of the very nature of humanity to pursue Truth. From the persistent "Why, Mummy?" of the small child to the probing wisdom of the mature mind, our lives are a pilgrimage towards Truth. As we have said already, Truth is one of those absolute values which is always beyond our grasp because it is found in its fullness only in the Divine. Our search for Truth, therefore, has an other-worldly dimension: it is more than the gathering of facts and information. These are no more than pieces enabling us to build up the fuller picture. This reaching out to Something beyond us is of the very nature of the human mind and is seen to be present from the earliest days of *Homo Sapiens* — who might also be called *Homo Religiosus*.

Because of this other-worldly element, we need, indeed we expect, a revelation of aspects of Truth that are beyond our mental ability to acquire at the level of reasoning. We look for an intuitive level of knowledge — what we might call Divine Inspiration — to raise our consciousness in order to be more fully human, to feed that in us which is spiritual.

So we might say there are two poles to Divine Revelation: us and the Divine. God, who alone can fulfil our total humanity, reveals Himself to us and in turn we respond by allowing this revelation to have a bearing on our lives, on our search. We seek Truth in order to become more whole.

This is why one of the marks of a developed religion is that it contains a body of revealed truth and consequently why those who choose to follow the path of that religion are required to adhere to a set of beliefs, a creed, which provides signposts along that particular religion's path. Yes, revealed truths are no more than signposts, especially because they have to be expressed in some sort of limiting formula. They point towards a reality; they do not contain the reality. This is because Reality, like Truth, is an absolute, not a relative value. That reality upon which we base our lives is no more than our understanding of what we believe Reality to be.

All religions offer a way towards understanding Reality, a way that they claim can only be known by Divine Revelation which has been given to either an individual — usually the founder, as in the case of Mohammed and Buddha — or to a community, as in the case of Judaism and Christianity.

Two Meanings of Revelation

A clarification needs to be made at this point. In Christian theology, the word "revelation" is used in two different senses. It is used to describe the collection of truths that have been made known to us and which are beyond our normal powers of reasoning or deduction to know. This has been the uppermost meaning in Catholic theology from the Middle Ages until recently. It is the framework of systematic (or Scholastic) theology. Since the middle of this century there has been a revival of biblical theology and this has caused the emphasis to swing from the knowledge to the way of knowing. In this latter understanding the word revelation refers to the process continuing throughout history by which God makes Himself known to his creation.

Both Judaism and Christianity (now) understand that revelation comes to us through events, through God's action in our history, and will continue to do so. Revelation, in this sense, is not about a lot of facts but is a self-gift of God to humanity which is experienced in events. The meaning of the events are interpreted under the guidance — or inspiration — of the Divine Spirit. In the chapter on the Theology Factor we saw how this applied to the Hebrews experiencing their escape from Egyptian slavery and to the community of the first Christians after their experience of the Jesus-event.

I began writing this book while I was staying in Sweden. One day my host took me to visit a church belonging to the (Lutheran)

Church of Sweden, in Saltsjö-Baden near Stockholm. It was named
the Church of Revelation. I was intrigued to find four large murals
inside giving equal honour to four great pre-Christian channels of
knowledge: Plato, Socrates, Elijah and Isaiah. This was an acknowledgement that God does not differentiate between what we
would label secular or sacred channels for making Himself known.

So often it is thought, by Christians at least, that revelation
consists, in the first place, of certain truths being handed down
directly to the Church (meaning Church leaders) by God and then
passed down to us by Church authority. This is not so. The truths
which have been formulated are first of all the fruit of an experience. A community, for instance, experiences God relating to the
community and then endeavours to express that experience in
appropriate (though inadequate) language.

Moreover, the individual members of that community must
also have had some experience of relating to a Divine Being or they
would not be disposed to accepting the revelation; they would not
be disposed to belief in it — disposed to faith, as we say.

The Limitations of Revelation

To return to that understanding of revelation as the "deposit of
faith" or the expression of truths in doctrinal formulation, we have
to appreciate the limitations that abound here. The initial experience or revelation comes to a person or community of a particular
culture and so can only be comprehended in terms of that culture.
Christians believe that it took all of two thousand years for the Hebrew people to be prepared, step by step, for the revelation which
would come to the world through the person of Jesus of Nazareth.
Had he lived centuries earlier his message would have been quite
incomprehensible because the ground would not have been prepared. Indeed, as it was, there were very few able to accept it and
we have to admit in honesty that even today, two thousand years
later, very few so-called Christians really grasp and are able to

accept into their lives, to the point of being transformed by it, the radical nature of what Jesus revealed about being fully human.

Added to this is the limitation of language when trying to express an experience. We have all suffered from being unable to share with others some wonderful experience we have had, when words are our only means to communicate it. We need not repeat here what we developed in an earlier chapter, namely, the limitations imposed upon communication by culture and language. However, it is important to remember, in the present context, that a revealed truth stated in a doctrinal formula in one century within one culture cannot be understood literally in another age and another culture if one is to be faithful to the original revelation. This applies as much to our understanding of the Bible (as we shall see below) as to the Church "definitions", that is, definitive dogmatic statements. One has to be aware of the particular circumstances that caused that statement or definition or condemnation to be made in the first place. In the words of the veteran theologian of the Second Vatican Council, Edward Schillebeeckx: "What theologians openly apply to Scripture, which is inspired, they must just as openly venture to apply to conciliar statements."

For instance, any non-Christian, seeking to learn what Christianity teaches, who picked up the Catechism issued after the Council of Trent (in 1546) would not find an overall teaching with truths of greater importance being given more attention than those of lesser importance. Such a searcher would need to know the reasons for its publication, namely, to counteract the theological opinions arising from the Reformation. Consequently, a disproportionate amount of attention is given to these. Unless one knows this, one would receive a very unbalanced picture of what the Catholic Church teaches.

When I arrived in the North of Zambia as a missionary, I learned that in the early days of the missionaries' presence some of the local African Evangelists (village teachers with a rudimentary education whose task it was to evangelise their fellow villag-

ers) who had been taught and employed by the missionaries of
the Free Church of Scotland found themselves in an area of the
country more recently occupied by Catholic missionaries. Knowing which side their bread was buttered, so to speak, they
changed their allegiance and offered themselves as Catholic Catechists. They already knew the fundamental Christian beliefs but
had to be "topped up" with those which were specifically Catholic. Imagine the astonishment of the Catholic missionary visiting
the villages some months later upon discovering that the only
subjects the catechists were teaching were the Assumption of the
Virgin Mary, the Sacrament of Penance, Indulgences, the role of
the Pope, etc. They had understood that this was the totality of
Catholic doctrine, replacing the Protestant teaching they had
learned earlier! They had no idea there was such a thing as a hierarchy of truths: that some truths have more weight than others.

Because God is the great unknown, whatever we are able to say
about his revelation to us is going to be partial. Again, Edward
Schillebeeckx has said, "Dogmas are correct, but not exhaustive,
statements about Revelation" and, we could add: only relatively
correct. I recall the words of Archbishop William Temple:

> There is no such thing as revealed Truth. There are truths of
> revelation, that is to say, propositions which express the re-
> sults of correct thinking concerning revelation; but they are
> not themselves directly revealed. (*Nature, Man and God*)

It is consoling to read the words of the (Church) Council of Orange in the sixth century, assuring us that whenever we say anything about God we are as much wrong as right!

Three Ways of Knowing

Let us remind ourselves about the three different ways of knowing. The first is that of science. This way deals with facts, facts that
are outside human life: the world of things. This knowledge is

expressed in a scientific, objective language. Even if its object of study is human beings, they are treated as things. This knowledge enables us to control things. Its being objective can mean that we can understand something in a way contrary to our experience of it. For example, it is quite clear from our everyday experience that the sun rises in the east and sets in the west. Ask any tribal person anywhere in the world and he will vouch that this is so. The scientist will correct him by explaining that the sun neither rises nor sets but that our Earth is revolving in relation to the sun.

So our experience is another and different way of knowing. This happens when the knowledge touches me personally, subjectively. William Blake wrote of the sunrise in these words:

> When the Sun rises, we do not see just a round disk of fire like a golden guinea; oh no, we see an innumerable company of the heavenly host crying, Holy, Holy is the Lord God Almighty.

This kind of knowledge illuminates our whole being. We say our hearts are touched. For this we do not use the bald language of the scientist but we are extravagant, metaphoric; we hint at a vision of reality rather than trying to define it. This is closer to the language we use in speaking about revelation and religion.

Then, thirdly, in this context, there is revealed knowledge. This is knowing something or somebody rather than the knowledge *about* them that we spoke of in an earlier chapter. This is far removed from the statistics and general laws of the scientist. This kind of knowledge cannot be "proved" by one person to another so as to remove all doubt. There is a willingness necessary to take this truth on board, within one's paradigm. It is knowledge of something beyond ourselves, of a higher order: something that we allow to possess us. We decide to surrender to it. Such a knowledge is expressed in the prayer of Dag Hammarskjold, "I do not know you but I am yours." It is the knowledge of the mystic. It is the way in which we experience mystery. All religions show this is an authentic, even the most authentic, way of knowing. It is the most profound way in which we can experience Reality in its wholeness. The figure below gives some examples of the three ways of knowing.

Three Ways of Knowing

Science	Personal Experience	Christian Revelation
The Universe is governed by scientific laws.	There is a purpose in my life.	There is purpose in all creation.
There is an economic and psychological interdependence of all things.	I need to relate to others to be fully human.	We are all children of the same Divine Parent. We have to act as brothers and sisters.
Our Universe began with a Big Bang.	I live in time, with a beginning and an end.	God's design: The fulfilment of his Kingdom.
All can be explained by the Theory of the Unified Field.	There are powers at work beyond my understanding.	There is a spiritual dimension to life. God partners us in shaping history.
We are destroying our Earth and each other.	What is anti-growth can only bring me suffering.	We must live in harmony with God's creative purpose or we perish.

Different Forms of Revelation

Theologians make a distinction between two forms of Divine Revelation. The first they call Transcendental Revelation, by which they mean the manner in which God makes Himself known, in secret and silent ways, to the hearts of all people, even if this is never explicitly realised by the recipients. It is transcendental in the sense that it is different from the other form, "Historical Revelation", because it is outside historical events or formulations. The latter is the form of revelation we have been describing above: given to a certain people at a particular historic moment and experienced and interpreted by them.

The recognition of Transcendental or, as it is sometimes called, Universal Revelation, provides the theological basis for Christians to accept the revelatory value of other religions.

Public Revelation

Another distinction made by theologians is between public revelation and private revelation. The former is that which is given for the benefit of all humanity and is authenticated by the Church, which understands that it has received its teaching authority from Jesus. According to this view, public revelation ended with Jesus (or more precisely, with the death of the last of the Apostles, who were the immediate disseminators of Jesus' message). This is because the historical Jesus of Nazareth is regarded as the one who most fully reveals to us in a visible and concrete way what God is like and what God is doing in every human life. Jesus cannot be said to be the revelation of God's totality; he is the fullest expression within the limitations of his humanity. Jesus is sometimes referred to as the ultimate revelation of God. If that be the case, how can we say, as we have above, that God continues to reveal Himself in the experiences of human history? All of us who regularly read the Bible have had the experience of one day reading a passage which we have read many times before and suddenly discovering a new depth of meaning in it which had never struck us previously. In saying that Jesus is the ultimate revelation of God to humanity we are not saying that now "we know it all". The Truth which has been revealed invites us to endless exploration. We are not going to learn any more "facts" — these have all been given us — but we are always discovering a deeper meaning. A story will illustrate this.

A man who could only describe his past as "having lived a filthy life" lay dying. He realised in his last moments that all his pursuits of pleasure — drugs, alcohol, womanising, gambling — had been unsatisfying. He had missed out on what he had really been searching for. In his dying agony he called his five-year-old son to his bedside. "Promise your old Dad this," he said, "don't follow your Dad's example. I have lived a filthy life and it has brought me nothing but unhappiness. Promise me you will always live a clean life." His mystified son nodded consent. With that the old man closed his eyes and died. From that day on, for the next five years, that boy washed himself thoroughly from head to foot. Only at the age of ten did he come to the sudden realisation that that was not really what his Dad had meant. At the age of ten the boy had not received any more information, no more facts had been revealed to him; but he came to a deeper insight of the real meaning of the original message.

This is what we mean when we say the Church develops doctrine. The Church, like us individually, is always arriving at a deeper meaning behind the recorded message of Jesus the Christ.

Perhaps the clearest example of this development lies in the doctrine of the Trinity. Although this belief is at the very heart of Christianity it took hundreds of years for the doctrine to be formulated. As one theologian has said: the doctrine of the Trinity is simply the attempt to formulate in a comprehensible language what God had revealed in the experience of some people who knew Jesus and recognised the mystery of God in him, of people who experienced the power and life of the Spirit of Christ after the Resurrection. Yet its formulation was not developed until the decades immediately following the Council of Nicaea in AD 325, at which Jesus was declared to be God the Son.

The great shifts in emphasis which took place in the Catholic Church during the Second Vatican Council (1963–65) — sometimes called the Reformation of the Catholic Church — were not due to new or more facts being revealed but to new insights arising from the way in which God's action was being perceived in our contemporary history.

Private Revelation

Then there is what is called "private revelation". This term is used to mean all that is not authenticated by the Church and it can cover a wide variety of spiritual experiences undergone by individuals. In our own day we are continually receiving messages from people who claim to have received a revelation from an apparition of the Blessed Virgin Mary or some saint or an archangel, or simply through mysterious voices. The most famous of these messages in recent years are those of Bernadette of Lourdes, of the children of Fatima and of the youths at Medjugorje, all of whom claim to have seen visions of the Blessed Virgin. They all have their following. There are always people avid for "the latest message from God"! What needs to be kept in mind in hearing about these messages is the philosophical axiom beloved of St Thomas Aquinas: *Quidquid recipitur, secundum modum recipientis recipitur*: whatever is received is received according to the paradigm (or consciousness) of the recipient. In other words, one can only receive a revelation in terms of one's own knowledge and cultural background. As we said in a previous chapter, there is not a special language or a special mental gear that one employs for thinking about the Divine: it must needs be expressed with and within the limitations of our normal mental processes. It is noteworthy that in the case of the above three famous apparitions, they were all to "simple" Catholic children, so it is not surprising that the messages are unsophisticated and expressed in a traditional (or past) form of Catholic spirituality.

How should one put to the test the veracity of any private revelation? The mystery of God is a mystery of communion, or total giving and receiving in unutterable love, within the Godhead in the first place (which is what the Trinity is all about) and by extension to and with God's creation. For the Christian, therefore, the search for God is always a search for communion. So the acid test to be applied to any revelation claiming to be divine is: Does it speak to me of the mystery of God's love?

Today there is a great need for sifting and testing of what are claimed to be revelations "from the other side" in the increase of what is called "channelling". This is to be distinguished from the work of mediums who, upon request, and usually for a fee, will call up Auntie Martha or Grandpa or some other recently departed relative. Mediumship came into fashion following World War I when many people so sadly suffered the loss of young relatives. They wanted to be assured that there was a life after death. Channelling, however, is a phenomenon by which people, often unexpectedly and even unwillingly, find themselves becoming the channel for messages from "higher beings", ranging from departed human beings to the Christ or the Archangel Michael. Such channelling can be in written form (for example, *A Course in Miracles* claims to be a message from Jesus) or vocal, with the channel going into a trance as happens, for instance, to a trance healer. The messages of Lourdes, Fatima and Medjugorje can be said to be channelled messages.

The Bible

We come now to consider the best known document of Divine Revelation in the western world: the Bible. This is Divine Revelation in as much as we believe the writing to be inspired. To say it is inspired does not mean it is, in today's vocabulary, a channelled work as the Qur'an is. The Moslem belief is that the Qur'an was dictated word for word to Mohammed, who had it written down faithfully over a period of 23 years. This is why it is to be understood literally and why it is to be recited in the original language, Arabic.

The Bible is a collection of writings — a whole library, in fact — written over several hundred years. What Christians sometimes refer to as the Old Testament are the books of the Hebrew Scriptures, while the New Testament is made up of proclamations and letters written after the Jesus-event. The Bible library contains a great many styles of literature: history, myth, poetry, prayers, correspondence, prophecies, laws, regulations, epics, prose, parables, allegories, fables, dreams, visions.

The way the books are presented to us are not always as they seem. What in the Hebrew Scriptures is entitled "The Book of Isaiah", for instance, and might be supposed to be the words of the prophet of that name is, in fact, made up of three separate documents. The first (chapters 1-39) was written before the Exile, the second (chapters 40-55) was written while the Jews were in Exile about two centuries after Isaiah lived, while the last part (chapters 56-66) was written later still, once the Chosen People were back in Jerusalem.

Furthermore, we might easily imagine the books of the New Testament were written in the order in which they are presented. In fact almost all of St Paul's letters were written before any of the four Gospels in the form in which we have them today. Most probably Paul's First Letter to the Thessalonians was the first item to be written — it is believed during the winter of CE 50–51 — and his second letter to them a few months later. Our New Testament provides us with two of Paul's Letters to the Church in Corinth but there was an earlier letter, since lost, referred to in I Corinthians 5:9.

The passages of the Bible are not, as some Christians would hold, to be understood literally — at least not if one wants to be true to the original revelation. We cannot say the books of the Bible are records of Divine Revelation. They are interpretations of a revelation: interpreted with the limitations of the human author, of his personal knowledge, writing out of his "theological" paradigm, within a particular culture, at a particular moment in his people's history, with a particular purpose in mind and in a language which has since come down to us through three or four generations of translation. Even the sayings of Jesus we read in the Gospels are not verbatim but interpretations. Whilst a few of the sayings ascribed to Jesus might be translations of his very own words, or might substantially go back to Jesus, more often than not their formulation is that of the evangelist.

Professor Edward Schillebeeckx writes in his book *I Am A Happy Theologian*:

> The word of God is the word of human beings who speak of God. To say, just like that, that the Bible is the word of God is simply not true. . . . The Bible writings are human testimonies to God. . . . The new theology cannot be understood without this concept of revelation mediated by history, of the interpretive experience of human beings. When the mediation is not accepted, one inevitably slips into fundamentalism.

Whatever value we might like to give the books of the Bible as a source of light on the history and culture of a past age — a value for the scholar of history or linguistics — the spiritual value of Biblical Revelation is no other than what it offers to the contemporary reader, who is a believer, as a pointer to a way of living more fully. In other words, its spiritual value does not lie in the past but in the present.

It is important to keep this in mind when reading Scripture, otherwise we could be upset by how little we can be certain about it as a historical record, concerning the life and sayings of Jesus, for example.

While it is not possible to enter into the whole question of Biblical interpretation within these pages, the figure opposite gives an indication of just how far we are removed from what Jesus actually said. Scholars are generally agreed that Mark's Gospel was written around 70CE, Luke's between 70 and 90CE, Matthew's between 80 and 100CE, and John's around 90 to 100CE. We can see from this that what we call the New Testament is less a historical record of the person of Jesus than of the life and faith of the community of early Christians, which later became known as the Church.

Stages through which the Words of Jesus have Passed before Coming to us

Stage 1	Stage 2	Stage 3	Stage 4	Stage 5	Stage 6	Stage 7	(Stage 8)
What Jesus said.	What the Apostles understood Jesus to have said.	What the Apostles thought their listeners ought to hear of what they understood Jesus to have said.	What the first writers wrote of what they understood the Apostles to have said. Probably written in Aramaic.	What the Gospel writers wrote in Greek from oral accounts and from the Aramaic text, choosing their material with a particular purpose in mind, for their specific readership. Translating thought forms as well as words from Aramaic into Greek.	Copies of the Gospels (translated into Latin from Greek) made by medieval monks from copies of copies of copies of copies.	Our translations into English of the copies of copies of copies of the Latin or Greek.	My understanding, as I read it, interpreted by my culture, spiritual experience and "scientific" knowledge. Its spiritual value lies in how it touches me today.

It is obvious that as each linguistic translation has been made, for example from Aramaic to Greek to Latin to English, something of the original meaning has been lost at each step. What is less obvious is how the original meaning or value of words is lost with each cultural translation. A clear example is the short phrase "Son of God", perhaps the most important New Testament title for Jesus. At least it is for us as we understand the expression in our culture and with all the theological weight that expression has gathered over the Christian centuries. But we have to understand that it did not originally have the meaning in Hebrew culture which we commonly give it in the Church. Among the Chosen People the title was given to an individual or group who was close to God, under God's protection. The Jewish nation as a whole was called God's Son (Psalm 2:7), as was a devout believer. In a special way the title belonged to the King of Israel (2 Samuel 7:14). When the title is applied to Jesus in the New Testament Letter to the Hebrews — "You are my Son; today I have become your Father" — (1:5 and 5:4–5), it is in this same sense, as a specially chosen person, the author quoting Psalm 2:7. So to describe Jesus as "Son of God" was to speak of his significance rather than to account for his origins. Jesus himself uses the expression this way when, in the Beatitudes, he declares, "Blessed are the peacemakers: they shall be called sons of God" (Matthew 5:9). And Paul writes to the Romans, "Everyone moved by the Spirit is a son of God" (8:14).

Only after the Council of Nicaea in the fourth century did the phrase take on the Trinitarian meaning we give it today in the Creed as "only-begotten Son of God". In fact at Nicaea, the phrase "Son of God" was promoted to mean "God the Son". This should warn us of the danger of reading back into Scripture the theological understanding which arose at a later period, or which we have today.

Aramaic was the common language throughout the Middle East 2,000 years ago and would have been the language in which Jesus spoke to the people. (Hebrew was the religious language used in the Temple liturgy.) Many scholars believe the first written account of the Jesus-event was most probably written in Aramaic. Neil Douglas-Klotz, a scholar in Aramaic, points out in his *Prayers of the Cosmos* how very culturally different that language is from the Greek texts that have come down to us. Below is a version in English of the Lord's Prayer as Douglas-Klotz suggests it *might* have originally been prayed in Aramaic. This poetic, mystical language derives from thought processes which were holistic and so very different from our own logical, rational version.

O Birther! Mother-Father of the Cosmos,
Focus your light within us — make it useful:
Create your reign of unity now —
Your one desire then acts with ours,
as in all light, so in all forms.
Grant what we need each day in bread and insight.
Loose the cords of mistakes binding us,
as we release the strands we hold of others' guilt.
Don't let surface things delude us,
but free us from what holds us back.
From you is born all ruling will,
the power and the life to do,
the song that beautifies all,
from age to age it renews.
Truly — power to these statements —
may they be the ground from which all my actions grow.
Amen.

Non-Jewish Sources

We would be deceiving ourselves if we were to think that everything in the Bible is there by direct inspiration, given to the Jewish people exclusively and directly. Many non-Jewish writings were incorporated into the Hebrew Scriptures. Among such insertions we find historical texts, prayers, laws and wisdom sayings. God speaks through non-Hebrew prophets such as Balaam the Ammonite (Numbers 22:2–24:25) and he has special messages for non-Jews like Cyrus, Emperor of Persia (2 Chronicles 36:22-23). The Book of Proverbs contains many sayings drawn from the Egyptian dynasty and Arab wisdom. In Psalm 29 the complete non-Jewish text was taken into the Scriptures with no more than minor modifications. From an internal analysis of the text and external comparison with ancient Middle-Eastern literature we can deduce with certainty that the Hebrews were actually using the Canaanite law books in the covenant. Psalm 45 was a wedding song originally with no religious meaning. It was then incorporated into the psalter and given new meaning. In the New Testament this psalm is applied to the relationship between Christ and the Church, the Bride of Christ (Hebrews 1:8–9). On the other hand there were texts regarded at the time as equally divinely inspired which are not found in the Bible. Of 250 sacred laws of the Jews, only 80 are found in Scripture. The caves of Qumran have revealed psalms, beyond the 150 in the Bible, that were used in Temple worship. We can conclude that the Holy Spirit "uses" texts from many sources — other than from the Jewish and Christian traditions — to reveal the Divine Mystery to us.

But going beyond texts, we find that some of the beliefs of Judaism and early Christianity have their origin in other religions. For example, early Jewish belief did not regard evil as a force outside of God. Satan is a member of God's court. The story of Job shows God in partnership with Satan. When the Israelites were exiled to Babylon (after 587 BCE) they encountered the world view of the Zoroastrians of Persia who believed that there were two primordial forces constantly battling for control of the world. Thus was laid the foundation of our western dualism. It is said that the Israelites also met the concept of angels in Babylon and it was from there that they obtained the first notions of hell and heaven as places of punishment and reward. Other ideas which they first encountered in Persia concerned physical resurrection, the model of the Last Day and the vision of a messianic figure who would introduce a new age by overthrowing the Evil One.

The Development of Revelation by the Church

We have already seen how the Church, as a community, is continually gaining new insights into the "ultimate" revelation as expressed in the New Testament. Revelation is not a static set of facts but a living tradition, part of a community's ongoing story.

As the early Christian community moved west and came under the influence of Greek philosophy, it felt the need to define its Faith in declarations — the Creeds are the earliest forms — and to systematise its doctrine. The God of the Hebrew Scriptures and of primitive Christianity — a personal, relating "human" God with loves and hates — took on the God-image of Greek metaphysics referred to in impersonal language as Supreme Being, substance, first principle, unmoved mover. The study of God's being (ontology) took over from the study of God's action in history; theologians devoted themselves to trying to fathom what God is in Himself rather than reflecting upon God's living relationship with his people. As the liberal Protestant scholar, Adolf von Harnack, has said: "When the Messiah became Logos, the Gospel became Theology". Thus developed a doctrine of God. Christianity had changed from a Jewish to a Greco-Roman religion.

In our own century, with the expansion of the Church worldwide to cultures so different from our own western culture, new ways of expressing Divine Revelation are being sought. One of these ways goes by the name of Contextual Theology, based on the belief that Truth is not static but living and can therefore be expressed only in the context of time and place (see figure below). Hence our present-day search for a contemporary understanding of the word "God"!

Contextual Theology

Original Proclamation		Our Reception of the Proclamation
In the context of the		*In the context of the*
Social		Social
Cultural	⟶ 2,000 years ⟶	Cultural
Political		Political
Economic		Economic
World of Jesus' time		*World of today*

Here is an example of the way in which the (Catholic) Church has made a doctrinal shift in its understanding of Scripture as Divine Revelation. While three Church Councils affirmed that God is the *author* of both the Hebrew Scriptures and New Testament, there has been a development of thought about what the Church means by authorship. On 8 April 1546 the Council of Trent spoke of what the evangelists and apostles wrote in the New Testament as being "at the *dictation* of the Holy Spirit". On 24 April 1870 the First Vatican Council declared that what was written in the Bible was written at the *prompting* of the Holy Spirit. At the Second Vatican Council (on 18 November 1965) the Bishops declared that the Bible books were written under the *inspiration* of the Holy Spirit.

Another example: in 1950 Pope Pius XII published an Encyclical Letter entitled *Humani Generis* (all such documents take their title from the first words of the text) in which he condemned the emerging scientific theory of polygenesis (that the earliest human species evolved in different parts of the world at different times) because it denied that we were all descended from Adam and Eve, which would deny the traditional teaching on Original Sin. The Pope was starting from theology to make a point about science. Ten years later, this teaching, described not as infallible but as "theologically certain", had been quietly set aside in face of undeniable scientific evidence. A new understanding of Original Sin had to emerge, as we will see in considering the Atonement Factor.

Conclusion

We conclude with the thought with which we began this chapter: Divine Revelation has no meaning unless it is accepted by one who has faith, for the very reason that its subject is Mystery. Mystery is often presented to us as something we can never understand — at least not this side of death. This is a limited notion. In Christian tradition the word refers to that of God which we cannot comprehend in its totality (otherwise we would be God) but that we can nevertheless enter into by entering into the darkness of Divine Mystery. (We have spoken in the chapter on the Knowledge Factor of Apophatic Theology, understanding God as *not* this and *not* that.)

If we are not Deists (believing that God created once and for all and then left the Universe to its own devices) our faith will tell us that God is the great communicator. He reveals Himself by sharing Himself with us and expects our response. If we believe that Love is the creative energy — the "why" of creation — it is not difficult to accept that God-the-Lover wishes to communicate with us, his beloved.

Yes, God communicates with us, but never outside the ambit of our everyday experience. We receive his communication always through the filters of our culture, our language and our limited comprehension. The doctrine of the Trinity is a case in point. It was not a ready-made packet of Revelation but was built up from our perceiving how Jesus related to God as his Father (so we named him God the Son) and how Jesus spoke of the energy of God experienced in Love and Wisdom as the Spirit. Our Christian ancestors drew their conclusions from this and so invented our Christian God-formula which finds its place among the Trinitarian God-formulas of other religions.

God is not a human invention but our formulas for God are.

For further exploration:

Neil Douglas-Klotz (1990), *Prayers of the Cosmos: Meditations on the Aramaic Words of Jesus*, Harper & Row, San Francisco.

Chapter 10

THE CHRIST FACTOR

Who or what is Jesus the Christ? Theologians have been struggling with, arguing about, pronouncing upon this question ever since the first century — and they are still doing so. Even in the New Testament writings there are several different doctrines of the Christ, as is apparent in the writings of St Paul, St John and the Synoptic Gospels (Matthew, Mark and Luke) and of the author of the Letter to the Hebrews. Though recognisable as the same person, the Jesus of John is different from the Jesus of Matthew, because there is always a subjective content to their experience of this person.

It is not my intention to enter the Christology debate. There are plenty of books available on the subject. But any consideration of current rethinking about God cannot ignore the debate. The very fact that Christology raises so many questions shows just how fluid concepts can be about God Manifest when He is manifest in human form. How much more fluid then is our perception of God Unmanifest!

We must, however, explore this maze for no better reason than that we Christians believe the life of Jesus is the supreme way in which God is manifest to us. At the very heart of Christian belief, and at the point where Christianity differs from other closely related religions such as Judaism and Islam, is the belief that God is triune, a Trinity of "persons". We cannot even begin to understand this without our departure point being Jesus, and that for two reasons. First, because the Jesus of history is declared by Christians in the Creed to be one of these persons "made flesh and dwelt among us" and secondly, because the theology of the Trinity, which developed in the decades immediately following the Council of Nicaea in 325, grew out of a study of various sayings of Jesus. He spoke of God as Father and as distinct from himself and he spoke of God's Spirit whom he would send to be with his followers after his death. Without these references no concept of a Trinitarian God could have emerged.

The first thing I want to say, obvious though it is, but yet not clear to so many Christians, is that the name we use, "Jesus Christ", is not a pair of names like Adrian Smith, but a name and a title. This is why, in this book, I always refer to Jesus *the* Christ. Jesus or Joshua was his "given" name. Then what is the meaning of the title Christ? Christ literally means the Anointed One and, as a Greek word, was used in the (Greek) New Testament to translate the Hebrew word for Messiah.

Christ: The Icon of God

The Christ is the visible manifestation of the Divine in human form. The Benedictine mystic Bede Griffiths spoke of Christ as the icon of God, echoing St Paul's description: "(Christ) is the image of the unseen God" (Colossians 1:15). Peter de Rosa, in his book *Jesus who became Christ*, wrote: "Christ is the parable of God. He is the Image, the perfect mirror, the complete model of God." I would hesitate over the word "complete" — we can only use it relatively. If I fill a bottle with sea water, I can say it is full of the sea but I cannot say the fullness of the sea is in the bottle, neither quantitively nor qualitatively. The amount of sea present is limited by the limitation of the bottle. God cannot express Himself totally within a human person. But we can say that a human person, totally filled with Divine Life, can be as perfect a reflection of God as it is possible for us to see. Look over the shoulder of

someone looking into a mirror. You see his image; it is undoubt-
edly him, moving, living — and yet not quite a real presence, for
it is in two dimensions only and in reverse. In seeing Jesus we see
a three-dimensional image of a multi-dimensional God. A reflection of God, yes, but with a time-space limitation. Not quite the
real presence. With this limitation, the historic person of Jesus is,
in the belief of Christians, the primary or supreme Christ.

But the only Christ? Other great spiritual leaders — Buddha,
Confucius, Mohammed — are sometimes spoken of as Christs.
We do not speak of Jesus as *a* Christ but *the* Christ, for all are *the*
Christ: a manifestation of the Divine within humanity. There are
not other Christs. St Paul speaks of those possessed by the Spirit
as being Christ-filled:

> God's plan is to make known his secret to his people, this
> rich and glorious secret, which he has for all peoples. And
> the secret is that Christ is in you. (Colossians 1:27)

Clearly Paul is not speaking of the physical person of Jesus. He
says of himself: "It is no longer I who live, but it is the Christ who
lives in me" (Galatians 2:20). And elsewhere: "The Church is
Christ's Body, the completion of him who is himself completely
filled with God's fullness" — as one translation puts it (Ephesians
1:23). This embrace of all humanity in Christ is neatly described
by St Augustine: "There is only one Christ loving himself".

Today, with our new awareness of cosmology, we are speaking
more frequently of the Cosmic Christ, meaning the all-pervading
presence of God as manifested in the Universe. But again, it is a
concept without meaning except that it has its roots in the historical
person of Jesus. Teilhard de Chardin calls the Cosmic Christ the
"third nature" of Christ, meaning that the concept takes us beyond
the Divine and human natures as described at the Councils of Nicaea and Chalcedon into a third dimension, the cosmic.

In the chapter on the Science Factor we said that, according to
quantum physics theory, the composition of all being in the

Universe could be described equally well as particles or waves: matter or energy. This paradigm can help us to think of the Christ, in the historical Jesus-event, as matter but at *the same time*, in the Cosmic Christ dimension, as energy. To put it in another way: The Logos, or creating Word that we call the Son of God, Second Person of the Trinity, exists in quite another dimension from our space–time existence. During the 33 or so years Jesus was on Earth as the Christ among us, he did not vacate his "place" in heaven for that period and then resume it again after the Ascension. There was no Jesus before his conception but there was "from all eternity" the Christ.

Classical and Contemporary Christologies

The ecumenical theologian John Macquarrie in his book *Jesus Christ in Modern Thought* makes a distinction between the classical Christology of the fourth and fifth centuries when Jesus the Christ was the subject of great debates in the Church's Councils, which is often classified as "Christology from above", and contemporary Christology which seeks to understand Jesus "from below". By the former is meant that the early theologians (referred to as the Fathers of the Church), drawing their inspiration from John's mystical Gospel, took God's existence in Heaven as their starting point. It was from there that Jesus the Christ "came down" to Earth and at the completion of his mission returned to heaven "to the right hand of the Father". So long as people lived with the traditional paradigm of a Heaven "up there", a Hell beneath us and an Earth between the two, this understanding of the Incarnation presented no problem. Between his death and his resurrection, the Creed tells us, Jesus descended into Hell — at least to that "place" where the previously departed were awaiting him.

The Jesuit theologian Gerald O'Collins lists six major reasons for the swing away from Classical Christology. One of these is that the Christology "from above" no longer satisfies us. One of

the dissatisfactions is that such an understanding of the Christ begins from God. But we saw in an earlier chapter that anything we
can know about God can only be known in human thought forms.
To attempt to understand Jesus in God-terms casts doubt on how
genuinely human Jesus was. As most of us were brought up on a
catechism in the "down to Earth" mode there understandably
lurked at the back of our minds: Yes, Jesus was a human being *but*
he was God. So, yes, he had to learn his lessons like any other
child at his mother's knee *but* as God he knew it already! In other
words, we should not point to God and say Jesus is like this, but
rather point to Jesus and say God is like this.

Although the Council of Chalcedon defined what was to become the orthodox doctrine of the Incarnation, it not surprisingly
became tangled up in what is really a philosophical question
when trying to "explain" the Incarnation. It asserted that Jesus
was "truly God and truly man" without attempting to say how
such a paradox is possible. It is a neat formula but not very helpful. Did Jesus have two wills — a divine and a human — and
which made which decisions? Did he have two consciences, two
forms of knowledge, etc.? Much midnight oil has been burned by
theologians over these academic questions.

As Alistair Kee writes in his book *The Way of Transcendence*:

> The doctrine of the Incarnation has never been satisfactorily
> stated. We are familiar with the course of its development,
> but the name of Chalcedon has become synonymous with
> failure. After almost four centuries the best minds of the
> Church (some of them the ablest in the Roman Empire)
> could only agree to say that Jesus Christ was of two na-
> tures, a human nature and a divine nature. But that is no
> solution to the problem. It is simply the problem stated.
> Nor has any advance towards a solution been made in the
> remaining fifteen hundred years since then.

From what we learn from the three Synoptic Gospels, Jesus lacked
at least some of the qualities we attribute to God. He was not all-

knowing; he was not all-powerful. As regards the first, it seems that Jesus not only thought of himself as a prophet, but probably as being the last prophet. He proclaimed the imminent approach of the Day of the Lord when the Kingdom of God would be fully established on Earth. This was an expectation among the Jews of Jesus' time. So he called the people to prepare for it by repentance: "The right time has come, and the Kingdom of God is near! Turn away from your sins and believe the Good News" (Mark 1:15) and "I tell you, there are some here who will not die until they have seen the Kingdom of God come with power" (Mark 9:1). And in Matthew's Gospel, describing the signs that will herald the end of the world: "Remember that all these things will happen before the people now living have all died" (24:34). It is not surprising, therefore, that his teaching did not include any critique of the social, political (Roman occupation) and economic structures of his time, as some of the earlier Hebrew prophets had done (or as Liberation Theologians do today) because he believed the social order was soon to disappear and be replaced by God's rule on Earth. While it is generally recognised today that Jesus had no intention of launching a new religion upon the world, on a par with the Jewish or pagan religions of the Roman Empire, we are caused to question whether he even intended to found a community (today's Church) to continue his mission after his death, since he believed he was living at the end of human history.

Just as the God-problem — how to think and speak intelligibly about God — is present to every generation and to us now, so it was to Jesus. As a first-century Jewish layman he would have been brought up in the late Judaic idea of a remote God. He grew in understanding through the people with whom he came into contact and the circumstances of his life, as we all do. Coming to understand God as an intimate Father was an evolution of his thought.

Secondly, he was not all-powerful in that he was restricted by the limitations from which all human beings suffer. Would he have had the physique to climb Mount Everest or to run a mile in less than four minutes? We see his human weakness appearing on several occasions. Besides being mistaken about the timing of the end of the world — in fact he confessed ignorance about it (Matthew 24:36) — he was tempted in the desert, he felt abandoned by God on the cross, and on at least one occasion he was unable to perform any miracles (Mark 6:5).

Of course there are ingenious ways of "explaining" these texts. Were the evangelists mistaken in what they heard? Did Jesus as God really possess omniscience and omnipotence but refrain from exercising them? If this latter is so, can we claim, as the Church Councils do, that he was fully human?

Summary of the Differences between Classical and Contemporary Christology

Classical (Dominant since the Council of Chalcedon in the fifth century)	Contemporary (Twenty-first century)
Emphasises the Divinity of Jesus	Emphasises the humanity of Jesus
A philosophical statement (although based on Scripture)	Thoroughly Scriptural, picture of Jesus emerges as it did to the first generation of Christians after Pentecost
Concerned with what Jesus was, in abstract terms of substance, nature and person	Evangelists speak of Jesus in terms of action: what he did and said
Starting from our knowledge of God we discover who Jesus is as the Christ	Starting from the historical man, Jesus, to learn from him what we can of the Mystery of God
"From above down"	"From below up"
Emphasis on the Incarnation	Emphasis on Jesus' supreme act: Atonement
God "sent" his Son "down to Earth"	No longer thinking of Incarnation or Ascension as physically down or up

Jesus = God. A Divine Being who takes on a human nature	Jesus in his humanity does not = God, but is a human being who is transparent to the Divine. God was as fully present and active in Jesus as is possible for a human being
Jesus is worthy of unconditional worship	We worship God under the form of Jesus
Everything Jesus did and said is done and said by God	Jesus acts and speaks as a man
Jesus' actions and words are accurately recorded in the Gospels	Jesus is the character of whom the Gospels speak: a product of memory, reflection, revision and community experience
A full and final revelation to be guarded against corruption	Our understanding is always in the process of developing
He was omniscient and omnipotent from the womb	His perfection is relative to the limitations of his humanity. He had to grow in the understanding of himself, of his mission, of God and of other people
His miracles prove his divinity	His miracles are signs of the presence of God's kingdom
All the powers he had, he had because he was God	All his powers issued from his being a completely developed, whole human person
He brought us "salvation". Analogies of justice, ransom, a price paid, satisfaction, reparation	He brought about "At-one-ment", an evolutionary step forward in humanity's becoming more one with the Divine
In terms of repairing a past "Fall"	Future oriented

We Read the Gospels Backwards

I went through a period when my favourite author was Agatha Christie. I have to admit I very rarely got more than halfway through before I turned to read the final chapter, to learn "who done it". From that moment on I read the remainder of the plot and saw the characters in an entirely new light.

This is an analogy of the manner in which we read the Gospels. We already know the end of the story; we know just how special the main character is. Similarly, the four evangelists wrote their accounts in the knowledge of a resurrected, glorified Jesus and interpreted the Jesus-event in that light. A clear example of this is in what they tell us of Jesus' birth. No biographer writes details about a child's infancy at the time it takes place. It is only after someone has become famous that he might look back to ask if there was anything special about the birth or early childhood. Such is the case with the particulars Matthew and Luke give us about Jesus' infancy. Matthew's account contains elements to be found in folk literature: a wicked king, oriental magicians, a special star. He is not intending his readers to accept that he is relating historical events. He is putting across a theological message: Jesus is recognised by the Gentiles but not by his own people. Luke's manner of portraying Jesus was to reflect upon the Hebrew Scriptures. He is not primarily concerned with historical accuracy, as the opening words of his second chapter show:

> At that time the Emperor Augustus ordered a census to be taken throughout the Roman Empire. When this first census took place, Quirinius was the governor of Syria. Everyone, then, went to register himself, each to his own town.

In fact, the writ of the Roman Emperor did not apply in Israel since that country was not under the direct rule of Rome. Besides, when Quirinius was governor King Herod — whom Matthew named as responsible for the slaying of the Holy Innocents later on — had been dead for at least eleven years. The registration, for tax purposes, would not have taken Joseph and Mary to Bethlehem since Roman taxes were based on where people lived, not on their town of tribal ancestry. Luke's account of the birth of Jesus is based upon the infancy story of Samuel (I Samuel 1–2).

We are told nothing of Jesus' childhood years because they contain no theological message. As a boy he must have been naughty and mischievous. Boys will be boys! It is part of the process of growing in experience and responsibility. If a boy was never mischievous would he be truly human? Even among his contemporaries in the small village of Nazareth he did not show any signs of being different in behaviour from the other boys. He must have gone along with them in raiding the neighbour's orange trees! Hence the resentment against him when he returned to preach in Nazareth and assumed the role of a prophet:

> Jesus . . . went back to his home town, followed by his disciples. On the Sabbath he began to teach in the synagogue. Many people were there; and when they heard him, they were all amazed. "Where did he get all this?" they asked. "What wisdom is this that has been given him? How does he perform miracles? Isn't he the carpenter, the son of Mary, and the brother of James, Joseph, Judas and Simon? Aren't his sisters living here?" And so they rejected him. (Mark 6:1–3)

History, Faith and Myth

Not only are the Gospels a mixture of history, faith and mythical imagery but so are our Creeds. Take the words, for instance:

> (Christ) was conceived by the Holy Ghost,
> born of the Virgin Mary;
> suffered under Pontius Pilate.
> was crucified, dead and buried;
> he descended into Hell;
> the third day he rose again from the dead;
> he ascended into heaven,
> sitteth at the right hand of God the Father almighty.

Many Christians, reciting these words Sunday after Sunday, will accept them all as of the same (historical) value. Take just one expression: Mary is called a virgin. Although the virginal conception of Jesus is a traditional Christian belief of some weight we cannot know as a historical fact the intimate physical workings of Mary's womb. (Only Mary and Joseph could have known and with whom did they discuss it?) It cannot be proved from Matthew or Luke, the only two evangelists who tell the birth story, although they clearly believed in it themselves. And is it really so important? Mark, Paul and John make no mention of it in their proclaiming Jesus as Son of God. If it is so important, God would surely have given us much more certain information about it. As Hans Küng says, "No one can be obliged to believe in the biological fact of a virginal conception."

The virginal conception is not the cornerstone of Christian faith, whereas belief in the Resurrection of Jesus is. It is precisely because Jesus the Christ overcame and passed beyond death, thus empowering us to pass the same way, that gives meaning to his being our "Saviour". Yet controversy rages about what actually happened on Easter Sunday morning, and this again is because the traditional teaching, unchallenged for well over a thousand years and not in dispute at the Reformation, is faced with what science now tells us about the Universe. If we maintain that Jesus rose from the tomb with a physical body, leaving the tomb empty, we must link this belief with a literal Ascension. But the traditional belief of what happened at the Ascension requires belief in a localised heaven — not too far away — into which a resuscitated human body can be carried by clouds. The accounts we are given of the Ascension forty days after Easter, are not intended to be literal descriptions of a historical event. They are a graphic way of expressing the full integration of Jesus' humanity — and so potentially of all humanity — with the divinity of God. The earliest New Testament writer, St Paul, does not even mention the Ascension as an event, and in John's Gospel the Resurrection, Ascension

and Pentecost are all put together as an Easter event, elements of
the same Mystery. In any case, a three-tier concept of Heaven,
Earth and Hell is no longer tenable. So we think rather of Heaven
being not a place in the sky but another dimension of being; even
"here" on a different wavelength, as we spoke of it in the chapter
on the Paradigm Factor.

When Jesus rose from the dead — or as St Paul says, when he
was raised by God from death (Romans 10:9); Peter too uses the
passive voice (Acts 2:32 and 10:40) — it was not to resume his
earthly body as had been the case in the three reported incidents
when Jesus returned life to dead people, who had eventually to
face death again. He had entered another wavelength, which accounts for the fact that he "appeared" only to those people who
had had faith in him during his earthly life. (The word translated
as "appeared" is the Greek word *ophthe*, which is normally used
not for physical sightings but for inner spiritual vision.) If we take
the Resurrection narrative in a physical sense, as Luke presents it
(Luke 24:32) — but this represents a later explanation — we have
to ask such questions as: Did Jesus appear naked to his disciples,
with women among them, or are we to include the resurrection of
Jesus' garments? If his appearances were physical and not spiritual he would have appeared in the body (and clothes) that his
disciples expected to see. Yet there are three occasions recorded
when he was not immediately recognised by those who had been
closest to him.

Going back to our Gospels and Epistles is not going to help us
much to work out a Christology for our time because there is not
just one orthodox Christology presented. There are several. Again,
as I have said so often and I keep returning to the point, we cannot comprehend Truth, we can only look at different facets of it at
a time, accepting that each is only partial. For instance, for Paul
and in the early chapters of the Acts of the Apostles, Jesus was a
man "raised up by God" (Acts 2:23–32). The Gospels of Matthew,
Mark and Luke present Jesus as a miracle-worker who receives

the Spirit of God and through his obedience to God is raised to be the Christ. In the Epistle to the Ephesians (we are not sure of the author) Jesus is presented as a glorious Cosmic Christ. In John's Gospel, written much later, Jesus has become the pre-existent Word of God, a quite other-worldly figure.

The Development of Doctrine

We cannot ignore the way belief develops within the Christian community, as we saw in the last chapter, not because of more information being given us but because, under the guidance of the Holy Spirit, we are perceiving Truth at an ever deeper level. Jesus promised this would happen in his words to his Apostles gathered round the table at the Last Supper:

> I have much more to tell you, but now it would be too much for you to bear. When, however, the Spirit comes, who reveals the truth about God, he will lead you into all the truth. He will not speak on his own authority, but he will speak of what he hears, and will tell you of things to come. He will give me glory, because he will take what I say and tell it to you. All that my Father has is mine; that is why I said that the Spirit will take what I give him and tell it to you. (John 16:12–15)

Jesus was not referring simply to the coming one-off event of Pentecost, but to the continued presence of the Spirit in the world.

This is why we cannot stop at Scripture in our searching but must take cognisance of what and how doctrine about the Christ has developed, especially as expressed by the great Church Councils. However, a word of caution is needed here. These Councils never intended to give a complete summary of a particular doctrine but in each case they were summoned in order to refute current notions which they regarded (and subsequently condemned) as heresies. So, for example, in reading what the Council of Chalcedon had to say about Jesus as God the Son, we need to be aware that the aim of the Council was to combat certain current views, namely:

- That Jesus was God but not truly man. He had only the appearance of a man, his humanity being only a veil for his divinity (Docetist heresy).

- That Jesus began by being a man and became divine; he was raised in his exaltation to the dignity of adopted Son of God (Adoptionist heresy).

- That while there is a unity between the divinity and humanity, we must avoid making Jesus a distinct human person; in Jesus the living physical organism was human, but his mind or spirit was divine (Apollinarian heresy).

- That in Jesus there are two persons, the divine person of the Word and the human person born of Mary (Nestorian heresy).

- That because there is only one person, there must be only one nature in Jesus; at the Incarnation the human nature was absorbed or merged into the divine nature (Monophysite heresy).

That there should be these different views on Jesus as the Christ is not surprising when we consider (as I have done in examining the Revelation Factor) that the various writings of the New Testament were authored by different people at different times and intended for different readerships.

We are left with Questions

The fact that there are so many ways of understanding the person of Jesus the Christ raises many unanswerable questions, most of which never disturb the regular churchgoer who religiously recites the Creed each Sunday as a statement of their personal belief. Here are some of those questions:

- Of how much of Jesus' life and activities can we be certain? We are not sure in which year he was born. It is commonly believed that his "public life" lasted for three years, but this is only deduced from the fact that John's Gospel mentions Jesus going up to Jerusalem for the annual Passover on three occasions.

- We can be even less sure of actual words spoken by him. They would have been spoken in Aramaic and apart from three phrases, nothing in that language has been passed down through our Scriptures. Among the most sacred words of Jesus for the churchgoer would be those with which he instituted the Eucharist at the Last Supper. Yet Matthew, Mark, Luke and Paul all have different versions of his words. Some of his sayings are quite definitely not his originally but put in his mouth later. For instance his saying, "Whoever does not take up his cross and follow in my steps is not fit to be my disciple" (Matthew 10:38) would have had no meaning at the time he is supposed to have said it, when his future death on a cross was not foreseen.

- There is no evidence that Jesus taught or believed in his own divinity nor can it be proved that he proclaimed himself the Messiah. He is never reported in the Gospels as publicly proclaiming this role; it is not part of his message. (He does, however, seem to agree with other people's acknowledgement of his Messianic role in private on a couple of occasions.) He never said "I am God". In fact several times he seems to say just the opposite (e.g. Mark 10:18, 15:34; John 14:28, 17:3). Only twice do his disciples call him God ("The Word was God" and "My Lord and my God") both in John's Gospel and therefore of late date.

Peter, in his speech (Acts 10) to the Roman captain Cornelius, describing the high points of the Christ-event, distinguishes Jesus from God: "He went everywhere, doing good and healing all who were under the power of the devil, for *God was with him* (verse 38) . . . *God raised him from death* (verse 40) . . . and he commanded us to preach the gospel to people and to testify that he is *the one whom God has appointed judge* (verse 42) . . ."

In official Church liturgy we pray to God *through* Jesus, after St Paul's example (Romans 16:27) and so our prayers conclude, ". . . through Jesus Christ Our Lord".

- We have every reason to believe that the religion Jesus himself practised and taught was very different from the Christian religion that emerged after a few centuries, purporting to be based on his teaching, and which we recognise as Christianity today. The basis of salvation theology at the heart of the Christian message preached by St Paul is a belief in Original Sin and the consequent need to have that state of sinfulness removed by the sacrifice of Jesus on the cross. There is no suggestion in Jesus' teaching that he himself believed in Original Sin since it was not a Jewish belief, there being no mention of it in any of the Hebrew Scriptures. In fact, as we shall see in the next chapter, Jesus' own understanding of the way in which our sinfulness is forgiven is through the direct healing of the human–God relationship (as in the Lord's Prayer and the Parable of the Prodigal Son), not through the sacrifice of a mediator.

There is much to suggest the theory, heard ever more frequently these days, that the religion we have today, labelled "Christianity", owes more to the development of ideas by Paul in his letters and preaching than to Jesus' original teaching. To say this is not to diminish the veracity of Christian beliefs but to illustrate once more how, under the inspiration of the Holy Spirit, our perceptions develop, deepen, extend in time. Divine truths are not static. Consequently there is the continual need to re-express these truths in terms that are relevant to each generation and culture.

For too long now, issuing from the Classical Christology, we have over-humanised God and over-deified Jesus. The pendulum is now swinging in the opposite — one likes to think more true — direction. Set alongside other lesser manifestations of the Christ in other human beings, Jesus has made a quite extraordinary impression on human history. Moses was educated at court, Jesus in village life; Buddha was the son of a king, Jesus the son of a village craftsman; Confucius was a scholar and politician, Jesus was neither; Mohammed was a rich merchant, Jesus "had nowhere to lay his head". Precisely because his origin was so insignificant it is all the more astonishing that his influence has been so profound, so widespread and so long-lasting.

He opened the eyes and hearts of people so that they could see and experience how life might be. There was nothing more to his message than "live your humanity fully". There are no specific Jesus or Gospel values that are not also the human values that are found when humanity responds to its highest human calling. There was nothing "out of this world" either in his own life or in the life he proposed for us all.

What humanity lacked was an empowerment to live this way. Jesus, as the Christ, gave us the key to unlock the power of the Divine Mystery and make it available to us. The key lies in what Christian tradition calls "The Atonement", and it is to this I next turn.

For further exploration:

Don Cupitt (1979), *The Debate about Christ*, SCM Press.

Peter de Rosa (1977), *Jesus who became Christ*, Fountain/Collins.

Gerald O'Collins SJ (1983), *What are they saying about Jesus?* Paulist Press.

John Hick (1993), *The Metaphor of God Incarnate*, SCM Press.

John Macquarrie (1991), *Jesus Christ in Modern Thought*, SCM Press.

Keith Ward (1991), *A Vision to Pursue: Beyond the Crisis in Christianity*, SCM Press.

Bryan F. LeBeau (ed.) (2000), *The Historical Jesus through Catholic and Jewish Eyes*, Trinity Press International, Pennsylvania.

Adrian B. Smith (2002), *The Christ*, CANA Publications.

Alistair Kee (1971), *The Way of Transcendence*, Pelican, London.

Chapter 11

THE ATONEMENT FACTOR

Within the Christian tradition our perception of God must inevitably be coloured by our understanding of all that is contained in the word "redemption", since this is so central to Christian belief. According to what this word means to us we will think of God either as an ever-forgiving lover, an understanding Father or a justifier, and establish our relationship with the Divine Mystery accordingly.

In turn, our understanding of the Redemption mystery will be influenced by our understanding of what is called The Fall and of what is called Original Sin. These three related topics are each subjects of many books by contemporary theologians, because a great deal of rethinking of the traditional understanding is currently being pursued. In this chapter, I can attempt to give only the briefest outline of recent thinking and offer a contemporary explanation. Nevertheless, it is worth the attempt because this subject is such an important factor in our changing perception of God.

As a starting point, let me express, briefly, the traditional fare which most of us will have been fed in our Sunday School or Catechism class. It goes like this:

- God created Adam and Eve as the first man and woman and from this couple the whole human race came forth.

- They were given the Garden of Eden in which to live, a paradise in which there was no evil, no pain, no death but perfect harmony between our first parents, the animals and all of nature.

- There was just one thing God forbade them to do: to eat the fruit of the tree which gave knowledge of what is good and what is evil. (Where did the apple come from?)

- They did eat it — being tempted by Satan appearing as a serpent — and as a punishment were banished from Eden, and suffered other consequences of their sin: the ground would be cursed so that only by hard work would they survive, women would have trouble in pregnancy and pain in giving birth and the end of life would be marked by death, after which the body would return to dust.

- This expulsion from Paradise was known as The Fall and the evil of Adam and Eve is named Original Sin.

- Subsequently, all humanity (except Mary and Jesus) are conceived with Original Sin. It is transmitted physically through conception from one generation to the next.

- All humanity lived in the fallen state until Jesus Christ, God the Son, came down on Earth to redeem us by shedding his blood on the cross to make reparation for sin.

- Original Sin is described as a stain upon the soul but it is washed away completely should a child be lucky enough to be among the small percentage of humanity who receive the sacrament of Baptism.

This, in the main, is the traditional teaching which we as children received. And this picture was bolstered by those classical paintings by Michelangelo and others of a perfect couple — with or without fig leaves — enjoying the bliss of a perfect world. The corollary to this scenario is that God became man in Jesus because, and only because, the sinful situation of humanity had to be redeemed. So for hundreds of years — for the major part of the history of Christianity, in fact — the basis of our most fundamental beliefs (Creation, Incarnation, Redemption) was sin-oriented. But over the last decades a new, positive, creation-oriented and evolutionary scenario has arisen. In her book *Modern Mystics and Sages*, Anne Bancroft claims that modern youth is convinced that there must be more to religion than the moral life — being condemned and being forgiven by a Saviour. The same, we might add, can be said of the no-longer-so-youthful today!

The Fall

Before we can start to think about Redemption we must sort out our ideas about "The Fall" and "Original Sin" which the Redemption was said to have put right.

The last decades have seen two factors emerging which have caused theologians to rethink the meaning of these fundamental Christian doctrines. The first is the development of biblical criticism and the second is what the discoveries of science are showing us about our human origins.

By biblical criticism we mean the activity of scholars in examining biblical texts in order to discover how they are composed, by whom, in what context and culture, for what reason they were written and how different passages came to be edited together. This exercise is a moving away from a literal, fundamentalist approach to Scripture. There is no need to repeat here what I have already written about revelation and the Bible in a previous chapter. But there are certain facts we now know about the biblical basis of the traditional Fall/Redemption doctrine as presented to us in the Book of Genesis which we need to look at.

The first thing we notice is that the Creation story is told twice and in contradictory ways. The first account is found in Genesis 1:1–2:4, the second in Genesis 2:4–25. The sequence of events in the two chapters is different. Secondly, notes of the events related were not made at the time (who was present?) but written up very recently in our human history, only a few hundred years before the

Jesus-event. The second account was written before the Jews were exiled to Babylon while the first account was written during the Babylonian exile (sixth century BCE) and drew many elements from the myths of surrounding peoples, particularly from the Babylonians.

Thirdly, these were never meant to be, nor could have been, historical records nor geographical, biological or scientific explanations. (We notice, for instance, that "day" appeared before the sun was created, and so did the plants!) It is no more than a theological reflection of sixth century BCE people pondering their origins.

Fourthly, we notice that there is no mention of a Fall. In fact this is a later theological and not a biblical term. Furthermore, in the Adam and Eve story not even sin is mentioned. The first time there is any reference to sin in the Bible is in Chapter 4 of Genesis in the story of Cain's jealousy of Abel and the account of the first murder. (It is instructive to note in passing that this first mention of sin is not about damaging a human–God relationship but a person–person relationship.)

So perhaps what we have regarded traditionally as a Fall is in fact a "Rise": a step up the ladder of evolution. This is where scientific discovery can help us.

A Scientific Insight

When we accept an evolutionary account of our origins, quite a different light is shed on the biblical story. For instance, physical death could not have been a consequence of Adam and Eve's behaviour since it is in the nature of all living things, plants, animals, to die. Animals inevitably cause the death of plants and other animals in order to eat and be nourished. Physical death is not an evil but a stage of transition. Just as St Paul's references to death and dying (Romans 7:9, 8:12, Ephesians 2:1, 4, 5, etc.) were not of physical but of spiritual death (in baptism we die with Christ to sin), so the authors of the Genesis story were not accounting for biological death but the dying to a past state — an experience of separation, a loss of harmony, of primitive integrity.

What we now know about the evolution of human consciousness throws quite a different light on our origins. In the evolutionary context, the biblical idea of monogenesis (that all humanity descended from one couple) has been overtaken by the probability of polygenesis (from many couples).* This latter theory causes difficulty to Christians when they read what St Paul wrote: "Sin came into the world through one man, and his sin brought death with it" and "Just as all people were made sinners as a result of the disobedience of one man, in the same way they will all be put right with God as a result of the obedience of one man" (Romans 5:12, 19). Paul came from a tradition of monogenesis and thought of Adam as a distinct historical person, as real as Moses. He speaks of death ruling over all humanity "from the time of Adam to the time of Moses" (v. 14).

It is not monogenesis that he is trying to prove in his letter to the Romans but rather the universal application of Jesus' redemptive act. He is saying that however universal our sinfulness is, Jesus' victory over sin is greater still. "Where sin increased, God's grace increased much more" (v. 20) is the point he is making.

The Evolutionary Stages

In tracing humanity's past, the anthropologist Richard Leakey speaks of the evolution of the human species in different parts of the African continent as taking place between 7.5 million years ago, with the appearance of *Homo erectus* (when animal species could be called hominid species, walking erect on two legs), and 1.5 million years ago, by which time there had been an expansion

---

* In Genesis we read about the son of Adam and Eve: "Cain went away from the Lord's presence and lived in a land called 'Wandering', which is east of Eden. Cain and his wife had a son and named him Enoch" (4:16-17). Where did Cain's wife come from?!

of brain and our ancestors had acquired the ability to make tools. The species then evolved further, to what we call *Homo sapiens* and on to our present-day *Homo sapiens sapiens*. The emergence of *Homo erectus* was really the transition point between the earlier more ape-like species and the later distinctly human-like, living a hunter-gatherer way of life, using stone tools and harnessing fire.

Our concern here is with the Eden-state of humanity. To make sense of what I am going to say, we need to know that increasing numbers of scholars today believe that in depicting the paradise-state, the inspired writers of Scripture were not describing a past situation, but a vision and a hope of what is to come. The Bible's view of history is not a past- but a forward-looking view. The hopes and the pronouncements of the prophets of Israel were directed towards bringing about God's kind of world. Within the same paradigm, as we shall see below, the Atonement is not simply a righting of past wrong but the creation of a new humanity.

The story of our evolution in Adam and Eve symbolism is not about their being thrown out of the Garden of Eden as a punishment for "falling" but a growing up and walking out into a new state of consciousness of which they had previously "fallen" short. This is not a recent idea. The philosopher Georg Wilhelm Hegel (1770–1831) spoke of the Eden story as the "Myth of Man". For him it was the myth which described our transition from the animal state to the human state. He thought it should be referred to as "The Rise" rather than "The Fall". Ken Wilber says in his book *Up from Eden* (note the title!) for this we should thank Eve, not blame her!

Up from Eden

In the Eden setting of early *Homo erectus*, humanity was living in a state of sub-consciousness, a state which was pre-personal. Previous to acquiring language, the human being was incapable of self-reflective thought. And without self-reflective thought one lacks that self-identity which enables one to appreciate that one has a separate existence from all around. Such thought requires the tool of language. Any sense of past or future is also dependent upon self-reflective thought. Consequently, the subconscious Eden state was one of primitive harmony because of this inability to differentiate self from the rest of nature. To give a crude parallel: my pet dog is living in this pre-self-conscious state, unable to distinguish between herself and her body. Living in the present *now* with no experience of past or future, lacking reflective thought, she is therefore incapable of making a free choice. The Fall symbolises the ego emerging from a state of unconsciousness, non-self-reflectiveness, to our present state of self-consciousness: from the impersonal to the personal. In the Bible story, the Tree of Knowledge of Good and Evil (not a fruit tree but a symbolic tree) represents the acquisition of self-consciousness and consequently the acquiring of an ability to choose between good and evil.

Since the acquisition of the ability to communicate and to think by means of language are pivotal to this stage of development, it is interesting to note, in the context of human evolution, that this ability had a physical cause. In the first place, each evolutionary step was accompanied by a major increase in brain size and consequently of brain power. The brain size of a human being is three times that of the average monkey or ape. But also, each advance brought about an evolution in the vocal structure: the larynx, the pharynx, the tongue and the lips. In the pre-human mammal the larynx is high in the neck which allows an animal to breathe and drink at the same time — an ability which we have lost! In us the structure is very different and unique in the animal world. The larynx is much lower in the neck, thus creating a much larger space above the vocal chords, permitting a greater range of sounds. The human vocal apparatus can produce some fifty different sounds, compared with about a dozen for the most vocal of animals. From these fifty sounds the average individual can assemble a vocabulary of 100,000 words and an infinite number of sentences. We are communicators! (And yet how lazy we are in developing our vast mental capacities. There are half a million words in the English language but 96 per cent of our conversation uses only 737 of them!)

There has been another ingredient, according to a theory advanced by Dr Caleb Williams Saleeby in the early years of the twentieth century, which was essential to the evolution of intelligence and so of human behaviour: the evolution of caring relationships, of love. Love can only be born of freedom of choice. But before that, it presumes a sense of "the other".

The Adam and Eve in Eden myth is telling us that human creatures found their identity, their individuality, through recognising their separateness, their opposites. "Then the eyes of them both were opened and they realised that they were naked" (Genesis 3:7) describes their awakening to otherness, to difference. "That evening they heard the Lord God walking in the garden, and they hid from him among the trees" (Genesis 3:8). They experienced their separateness from God. They became conscious of moral opposites: good and evil. Becoming aware of their separation from nature, aware of moral conflict, and perceiving the often disastrous consequences of their choices, led these early humans to experience a sense of guilt. This evolutionary step was a painful birth process.

Would it not have been better, one might ask, had we never evolved, had we remained instead in the state of innocent unselfconscious harmony with nature, like the animals? But there was no choice. Scripture speaks of God posting "the cherubs and the flame of a flashing sword" in front of the Garden of Eden. There was no going back. The symbol represents God's blessing upon our journey of evolution. Humanity had to move on. The force of evolution thrust development upon us. The choice was no choice because the alternative would have been death. An illustration: the foetus is snug and protected and warm and fed in the womb. No self-consciousness, no choices to be made, no fears and worries about tomorrow, no guilt. But there is no question of staying there. Not to be born, not to be thrust out into a noisy, hostile, cold and insecure world is to die. Growth is always accompanied by pain because it involves a letting go and a journeying into the insecurity of the unknown. This was the death experience that entered human consciousness at this point: the dying entailed in the process of metamorphosis. When St Paul speaks of Jesus setting us free from sin and death (Romans 8:2) he is not, obviously, saying that there is no longer physical death (nor indeed that there is no more sin) but that Jesus gave us a reason for no longer fearing death because in his resurrection is the promise of a fuller, sinless life beyond death.

Original Sin

What we call Original Sin is no longer regarded by theologians as a particular sin committed by a particular original couple which all humanity inherits by physical generation. In fact, there is no hint anywhere in Jewish Scripture (our "Old Testament") of an inherited sin. It has never been part of Jewish belief, nor does Paul speak of sin being handed on by parent to child by generation.

Today, the label Original Sin is applied to the situation of sinfulness we are all born *into* rather than *with*, and without personal guilt. For instance, a child with a HIV-infected mother is likely to come into this world with the HIV virus. There are social and psychological influences at play as well as biological. A stressed mother, especially if she is overwrought during pregnancy and at the time of giving birth, will pass on this stress to her baby. As Peter de Rosa says in his book *Christ and Original Sin*, "Original Sin is not so much the race inheriting the sin of an individual as the individual inheriting the sin of the race".

We have to blame St Augustine for initiating the idea that it is the sin (and guilt) of the original pair that is passed down from parents to child through conception. The root of this lies in his mistranslation of Romans 5:12. Both the Good News Bible and the

Jerusalem Bible translate this verse as "death [spiritual death, as we spoke of it above] has spread to [through] the whole human race *because* everyone has sinned", and the Revised Standard Version translates it as: "death spread to all men *because* all men sinned". "Because" is the translation of the Greek word *eph'hō*. Augustine, however, was the first person to translate that word as *in whom* and this person "in whom", Augustine said, was Adam. By understanding St Paul to have written: "in whom [Adam] all men sinned", Augustine influenced the whole of subsequent theology in western Christendom, centring it on the Fall–Redemption axis. The Greek Fathers never understood it this way.

The importance of declaring Mary to have been conceived immaculate was necessitated by the Augustinian paradigm in order to safeguard the sinlessness of Mary and consequently of Jesus. In the new paradigm, we can rejoice at this doctrine, not because it makes Mary unique but because it emphasises the innocence of our own conception.

The Augustinian paradigm also required a limbo as the destination of babies who died without baptism; their inheritance of Original Sin made them unworthy of heaven. Happily, limbo has disappeared from current theology.

Redemption or Atonement?

This is a question to which I devote a whole chapter in my book *God and the Aquarian Age*. I shall try to summarise it here. It has to be said that the traditional explanations of *what* it was about Jesus' life, death and resurrection that affect our present lives and *how* the life of someone living two thousand years ago can make the difference to my life today, are not presented in ways that speak to the contemporary mind. Such explanations seem to come from a past and foreign culture. And they do.

The eminent theologian John Macquarrie reminds us in his book *Principles of Christian Theology*:

The Church has never formulated a doctrine of atonement with the same precision with which it has tried to define the person of Christ. Instead, we find several explanatory models that have developed side by side. Even in the New Testament a considerable variety of ways of understanding the atoning work of Christ is to be found.

Before proposing a contemporary understanding of the redemptive action of the Christ, let us review briefly some of the traditional explanations. Many words and expressions besides "redemption" have been used to describe this mystery: sacrifice, ransom, justification, forgiveness, acquittal, remission of sins, Jesus gave his life, shed his blood, we are saved in the Blood of the Lamb, propitiation, expiation, satisfaction, substitution — all associated with paying a penalty.

Our starting point must be an appreciation of the shattering effect the sudden death of Jesus must have had upon his closest followers. They were stunned, not only by its brutality, but by the way it came about. One moment the crowds were clamouring to hear Jesus, to be healed in so many ways, they were welcoming him into Jerusalem. He seemed to have reached the pinnacle of popularity. The next, there was a complete volte-face, they were screaming that he should be crucified. And it was all over within a couple of days. There is not one of us who is not desolated by the sudden and untimely death of someone close to us, especially when that person is our inspiration, the cause of our hope. We grope for meaning: either a spiritual meaning (it must be God's will) or a human meaning (may it be a lesson to others not to be so foolhardy). So with the Apostles: a meaning had to be found for this tragedy, and explanations soon appeared.

Traditional Explanations

It has always been the custom in different cultures to offer gifts to chiefs and kings to plead for mercy or seek forgiveness, or simply to pay homage. By analogy, traditional societies offered gifts for the same reasons to the unseen rulers of the Universe. Since these latter were the source of life, what better gift than a life, preferably a human life or, as a substitute, the life of a bull or a goat or a valued animal. This was the background to the Temple sacrifices of animals in Jerusalem at the time of Jesus. St Peter uses this argument:

> For you know what was paid to set you free from the worthless manner of life handed down by your ancestors. It was not something that can be destroyed, such as silver or gold; it was the costly sacrifice of Christ, who was like a lamb without defect or flaw. (1 Peter 1:18-19)

What could be a more fitting sacrifice to make reparation to the supreme God, the giver of all life, for the sinfulness of our forefathers, than the sacrifice of the life God would value most in all creation: the human life of his son? So from the first, Jesus' redemptive act was regarded as paying a price for past evil. This explanation is not helpful in our culture in which the giving of gifts to rulers would be misconstrued as bribery! Besides, it is difficult in this scenario not to picture a vengeful God demanding his pound of flesh like Shylock.

H. Rashdall, in his book *The Idea of Atonement*, comments:

> The various authors of the canonical [biblical] books in fact were so accustomed to the pre-Christian ideas of an expiatory sacrifice and atonement that they accepted it without going to the roots of the matter.

Soon a theory of reparation developed. From bestowing a meaning on the crucifixion to make it acceptable, the suffering was seen to possess an intrinsic value. The "sacrifice on Calvary" became the central and even unique location of Jesus' saving action. His life until then was given no other value than as a lead up to this culminating moment. But Jesus himself never gave a value to suffering as such; he never condoned it. While recognising its purifying

effect he would not accept it as part of God's plan. It was a negation of God's desire for our happiness — even on Earth. The majority of his miracles were performed to relieve people from it. He
was even impatient with suffering, healing on the Sabbath without waiting for the next day.

One of the earliest "explanations" for the death of Jesus was
given in the contemporary context of slavery — a price would be
paid to free, or ransom, a slave — based on the saying of Jesus in
Mark (10:45): "The Son of Man did not come to be served; he came
to serve and to give his life as a ransom for many." The theologian
Gerald O'Collins, SJ questions whether these words were spoken
by the historical Jesus or whether they were put into his mouth as
a consequence of this meaning being given to his death. Making
the mistake of taking metaphorical language literally, theologians
in the early Church started asking to whom was Jesus paying a
ransom. The answer could only be to Satan since, as was believed,
by the Fall humanity had submitted to the power of the devil. So
it was not humanity, in Jesus, paying a ransom to God but God
paying the life of Jesus as a ransom to Satan. Despite the unsatisfactory nature of this explanation, it was held by such prominent
men as Irenaeus, Origen, Gregory of Nyssa, Ambrose, Augustine
and Chrysostom.

It was only after 900 years that St Anselm of Canterbury
(1033–1109) proposed an alternative theory which has been taught
in seminaries and theological colleges up until quite recently,
probably because of its influence on St Thomas Aquinas. In fact,
Anselm was the first writer to devote a treatise to this topic.
Within the culture of medieval Europe, if a subject dishonoured or
abused the authority of his lord, he would be punished or made
to pay some form of satisfaction pronounced equivalent to the
harm done. So Anselm developed his explanation based on the
idea of satisfaction, which briefly runs like this. Because it was the
infinite God who had been offended by Adam and Eve's disobedience, the required satisfaction had to be infinite in value. A

human being, a mere creature, could never offer this, but a human being who had infinite worth because he was also divine, could. So Jesus, as both man and God, was able to make satisfaction to God on humanity's behalf. Besides appearing to be a commercial deal, the objection to this explanation was that it seemed to imply that God demanded the cruel death of his son. What kind of loving Father was that? Even St Paul, wishing to emphasise the love of God manifested in Jesus, frames his example in terms of Jesus dying for our salvation:

> Even when we were still helpless, Christ died for the wicked at the time that God chose. It is a difficult thing for someone to die for a righteous person. It might even be that someone might dare to die for a good person. But God has shown us how much he loves us — it was while we were still sinners that Christ died for us! By his death we are now put right with God; how much more, then, will we be saved by him from God's anger! (Romans 5:6-9)

This explanation no longer carries weight for us who live in an entirely different, a democratic, social order.

Another explanation, named "vicarious atonement", emerged among the reformers in the sixteenth century. By this time the idea of injustice had shifted from being an act against a ruler, and therefore subjective, to being understood as an objective act in such a way that punishment was no longer at the whim of the ruler. Justice applied to the ruler and to the subjects equally. Punishment had to be paid but it could be paid by someone else on behalf of the guilty person. One is reminded of the Polish priest, Maximilian Kolbe, in the German concentration camp during the Second World War, stepping forward to offer his own life in place of a father of a family who had been condemned to die. Again, this theory of substitution, of God punishing himself in the form of his Son, is not satisfactory today: punishing the innocent in place of the guilty. Besides, if A is to represent B, B must agree to his doing so and A must undertake the task freely. If substitution is to have a redemptive value it is in this sense of representation, not substitution in the manner in which a footballer might be sent onto the field to substitute for an injured and unconscious player who is quite unaware of the substitution. Such substitution is purely passive. Gerald O'Collins rightly points out that a guiltless person can suffer from the sins of others, and can suffer for others, but cannot literally carry the moral guilt *of* others.

Finally, there is the Moral Influence theory first propounded by Peter Abelard (1079–1147) and held by some contemporary liberal Protestant theologians, John Hick for instance. The theory is that what Jesus endured in his excruciatingly painful death reveals God's self-sacrificing love which moves people to respond with repentance and gratitude, with faith and love. It evokes people's felt need for divine forgiveness. However, this theory falls down on two counts. First, God's moral sacrifice is not necessary as a means of inspiring our sense of wrongdoing; and secondly, this relegates Jesus' role to that of a mere exemplar compatible with Socrates, the Buddha, Confucius and so many others.

Jesus' Own Understanding

How did Jesus himself regard his death? How free was he to accept or reject it? If we are to believe the Gospel writers, he foresaw the form it would take. Did he regard it as having salvific value? According to his words at the Last Supper it would seem so. "This is my blood of the covenant, which is poured out for many" (Mark 14:24). But as we have seen in a previous chapter, these eucharistic words are quoted differently in different Gospels. We just do not know to what extent the eucharistic liturgy of the early Church modified what Jesus actually said the night before he died. If Jesus did not consider himself to be the incarnation of God nor God the Son nor the Second Person of the Blessed Trinity — and as we have seen, there is no reason for presuming that he did

— then he would not have thought of his death as being the required redemptive sacrifice for all humanity.

What does seem evident is that he went to his death freely. He allowed events to take their course in the Garden of Olives, rebuking Peter for his pathetic demonstration of opposition. At the moment of dying he was still in command of his life, "he yielded up his spirit" (Matthew 27:50) and according to Luke he died with the words "Father, into your hands I commit my spirit" (23:46). This was in accord with what he is reported to have said earlier in his life: "No one takes my life away from me. I give it up of my own free will" (John 10:18). So he was not a passive victim of his Father's wrath and nor was his death premeditated as a death wish, a form of suicide. We can only understand his acceptance of his death as the culmination of the drive that directed his whole life: obedience to the mission given him by his Father to manifest God's design for creation (which Jesus referred to as God's Kingdom) to the extent that his proclamation, and even more, his manner of living by the values he proclaimed, led inevitably to a confrontation with the religious authorities who were challenged to the point of seeking his extermination. The crucifixion was demanded by human beings, not by God. It highlights our injustice, not God's justice. His acceptance of his death and the manner of it was the final demonstration of his life being a witness of his message: "The greatest love a person can have for his friends is to give his life for them" (John 15:13). Had Jesus, quite understandably, yelled from the cross, "What you do to me is an unforgivable sin. You will burn in Hell for this", it would have been the antithesis of his teaching about forgiveness and love. There could have been no Resurrection. It would have been a contradiction of resurrected life.

The Healing of Damaged Relationships

If we today are to make any sense of our "redemption" by Jesus it must be in terms of love, not by using analogies of justice, ransom, satisfaction, reparation, buying-back or substitution. And it was not just in his death but in his whole life — his manner of living coupled with his preaching — that he put across the message of love. Among the theologians of the Eastern Church the total mystery of the Christ, from birth, through life, death, and resurrection to ascension had a redemptive value, of which the Incarnation was the decisive saving action. The Eastern Orthodox Churches think of salvation as transformation: transferring, uplifting our purely human state into the divine. This is why, of all the words used to describe this mystery, I prefer the word atonement if that is understood as our *at-one-ment* with God: the healing of our broken, deficient relationship with the Divine and the attaining of that union with God for which Jesus prayed at the end of his life: "that they may be one, just as you [Father] and I are one" (John 17:22). The word "salvation" comes from the same root as "salve" that we rub on our wounds for their healing. The remedy for sin in the Bible seems to be more one of healing a wound than of punishing a wrong.

For us and our contemporaries, the mystery of Atonement needs to be understood within the evolutionary paradigm. Once we accept that the Fall was not a fall into a lower state from a higher but a falling short of what we are destined to become — a breakthrough into a higher state — then we can understand the Atonement brought about by Jesus the Christ as another great evolutionary step forward. We have already described the Eden myth as being about an evolution from a state of subconsciousness to a state of self-consciousness — from the physical to the mental. Atonement is the process of humanity's becoming increasingly conscious. The Christ event marks the transition from the state of self-consciousness to that of super-consciousness, to the predominance of the spiritual — at least potentially. We are shifting the meaning of Redemption from a negative one of deliverance from sins to a positive one of a release of inner creative power to enable us to grow to the fullness of our personality: to become the complete persons God always intended us to be. Personal evil is the

deliberate refusal to become whole, or as Carl Jung would express
it, the refusal to face up to our shadow side.

Jesus' overriding concern was to bring about the unity of humanity and God, which inevitably included the forming of the
human–divine relationship, yet we never find him even suggesting that for this a mediator was necessary. He tells us that forgiveness is always on offer if we will only accept it. We are already forgiven in God's eyes. What is required of us is conversion,
metanoia, the putting on of a new mind. In the parable of the
Prodigal Son (Luke 15:19–32) the father did not demand a blood
sacrifice to appease his sense of justice before welcoming his son
back into the family. The father took the initiative and expressed
forgiveness just as soon as the son was seen to be returning. In the
Lord's Prayer, the only condition required for receiving God's
forgiveness is that we be prepared to forgive others equally gratuitously. The redeeming act in both cases is the healing of a severed relationship. Again, in the parable of the Pharisee and the tax
collector (Luke 18:13–14) the latter "standing far off, would not lift
up his eyes to heaven, but beat his breast, saying 'God be merciful
to me a sinner'". Jesus says: "I tell you, this man went down to his
house justified." Yet again, in the parable recounted by Matthew
(18:23–35), the "wicked servant" who had a great debt was let off
the debt quite gratuitously by his master with no question of re-
payment or punishment. He was named wicked because in his
turn he would not forgive one of his fellow servants who owed
him a trifling sum. The master came to hear of this. "You should
have had mercy on him just as I had mercy on you," he says. Jesus
concludes the parable with the words: "This is how my Father in
Heaven will treat every one of you . . ."

The fact is scarcely understood by Christians today that the
great breakthrough in our spiritual evolution which Jesus brought
about — that which is behind his introducing us to an "Abba" relationship with God — is the truth that we do not need a mediator
between God and ourselves.

Jesus never spoke of himself as a mediator.* Almost the only place in the New Testament where Jesus is referred to in this role — as a priest — is in the Letter to the Hebrews, a letter written by an unknown author, addressed to a Jewish Christian community and therefore explaining Jesus' death in terms of the Jewish priesthood and Temple sacrifice with which his readers will have been familiar. Other New Testament writings (1 Peter 2:9, Revelation 1:6 and 5:10) speak of the whole People of God becoming, through Christ, "a kingdom of priests".

Although Jesus tried to put us into this direct and intimate relationship with God, so many of us within the Church are still influenced by a primitive human need which originated at the time — between 7500 and 5500 BCE — when our ancestors shifted from being a nomadic fruit-gathering, hunter people to settled communities developing agriculture and animal husbandry. It was at this point of our evolution that priests and shamans appear on the scene as required mediators between the powerful celestial gods and frail humanity. They were responsible for religious rites and (often human) sacrifices to placate angry gods or to win favours and fertility. As long as some streak of this "fear of God"

---

* "I am the way, the truth and the life; no one comes to the Father except by me" (John 14:6) are oft-quoted words of Jesus by those who champion Jesus, and in turn the Christian Church, as the unique mediator of salvation. There are other words of Jesus which seem to support his role as unique mediator between humanity and his Father, for instance: "I am the gate for the sheep . . . whoever comes in by me will be saved"; "I am the good shepherd who is willing to die for the sheep" (John 10:7–11). Many contemporary theologians (e.g. Maurice Wiles, John B. Cobb, K. Rahner, R. Panikkar) affirm that the Logos of Christ, eternal and universal, has been incarnated in Jesus of Nazareth. All these quotations are from the Gospel of John who applies them to the Christ, the Logos, Divine Word, "and are wrongly taken to refer exclusively to a particular human being", Jesus of Nazareth. "Like other statements in the same Gospel (such as 'before Abraham was, I am') they are to be understood as referring to the Logos rather than Jesus the first-century historical figure" (Maurice Wiles). The Christ existed before the world originated: Jesus was born in human time. Jesus was a Jew: the Christ was not.

remains in us, we will continue to regard the ministers in the Church as go-betweens, expecting them to have more power in interceding with God on our behalf, as dispensers of God's forgiveness and as exclusive channels of divine energy through a sacramental system which they control.

Today we are more aware of offending other people than we are of offending God because we more easily define ourselves in relation to other people than in relation to God. We no longer think of salvation in personal terms, of saving *my soul* (after I die) but of a cosmic redemption by which the whole of creation is raised towards its Omega Point, its final consummation, from which we, the whole of us, can benefit here and now. This surely is in keeping with the notion of God's Kingdom described by the author of the Letter to the Ephesians (1:10): "This plan, which God will complete when the time is right, is to bring all creation together, everything in the heavens and on Earth, with Christ as head."

A Contemporary Explanation

In conclusion, I offer an "explanation" of Jesus' atoning action which is more in keeping with contemporary thinking.

One of our deepest human aspirations is to grow, to develop, to become more. In my book *God and the Aquarian Age* I describe sin as whatever prevents growth — our own, other people's or the evolving of creation, God's plan. In the measure in which we deprive ourselves or are deprived of love in relationships we are hampered in our growth. Nothing gives us greater delight than the satisfaction of experiencing that we have overcome some blockage, some obstacle to our becoming more fully human.

In the world of science and technology our creativity and inventiveness can never be halted. We will go on and on making new discoveries, inventing new methods, however dangerous and whatever the potential for possible destruction, it seems. Physically too we are always striving beyond our present attainment.

Hence the Guinness Book of Records! It seems also to be characteristic of human nature to require one of our species to break
through the barrier of human limitation in order to empower others to follow. (Rupert Sheldrake has built his theory of biological
evolution — Morphic Resonance — on this principle working in
the animal world.) Such empowerment is not a gift from without
of a power not already possessed. It is the liberating or release of a
God-given gift already present but hitherto untapped. There are
plenty of examples of this process at work. Let us look at just two.

Over the thousands of years that people have been plying between Dover and Calais it was only in the nineteenth century that
anyone succeeded in swimming the Channel. Since Captain Webb
did it, hundreds of others have done it — 423 people had accomplished the feat by 1992 — some even there and back. A few years
ago a twelve-year-old boy did it, and within twenty-four hours a
second boy of twelve had followed. In 1875 Captain Webb took 21
hours 45 minutes. The present record is held by Californian Penny
Lee Dean, who crossed in 7 hours 40 minutes. No one had ever
succeeded in reaching the summit of Mount Everest until it was
reached by the New Zealander Edmund Hillary and his Sherpa
guide Tenzing Norgay on 29 May 1953. Now that the barrier to
this particular human achievement has been broken it has become
an annual event. In 1990, an Italian made the ascent alone and
without the benefit of oxygen equipment. One day in April 1993,
38 people stood at the summit after queuing! Between January
and June 1992 more people reached the peak than in the 25 years
following the first achievement. The first British woman to succeed, Rebecca Stevens, on 17 May 1993, was only one of 15 climb-
ers in two days! At the end of May 1998 Tom Whitaker reached
the summit on his third attempt. He had lost a foot in a car accident 19 years previously.

To lift humanity out of its state of disintegration and raise it to
a higher state of spiritual evolution there needed to be one person
who would break through that barrier and in doing so empower

the whole of humanity to follow the same path. Teilhard de Chardin explains that as the whole of creation moved dramatically forward and upward, Jesus marked a unique leap from the lower level of matter towards a higher spiritual unity. He not only marked the leap; he was the cause of the leap. He was able to do this because as the icon of God he was the perfection of humanity, free of the inner enslavement to which we are all held captive: that false ego. One characteristic of Jesus that shines through the Gospel account is his complete integrity. He was completely himself, completely authentic, not coerced by any slaveries. In other words, he was completely and unswervingly the person God intended him to be. He was so sure of his own worth in his Father's eyes that he did not need to seek his identity in a role or along any unauthentic paths. Unlike us, he never capitulated to any outside pressures. As one of us who has broken free of the captivity to personal slavery, he has empowered us to break through our own anti-growth barriers to integral liberation, so that evil need no longer hold us in bond. This is the path of our "salvation", our becoming at-one with God. We are enabled to have such an identity with the Christ that we are able to say with St Paul: "It is no longer I who live, but it is Christ who lives in me" (Galatians 2:20).

In this perspective we are not — as so many Christians still are — looking backwards towards the Jesus of two thousand years ago as if he were God's afterthought when His creation plan went wrong, but forwards, to Jesus as the personification of the fulfilment of that plan. Jesus himself, like the prophets before him, was forward-looking. To say, as our liturgical prayers do, that Jesus came to save us from our sins is to view him in a negative perspective: to appreciate him only in the context of sin. Whereas he came to establish our harmony with God, within ourselves, among us and between us and all creation. Not to restore but to raise up. As the great theologian St Thomas Aquinas expressed it: "The Son of God became human in order that humans might become gods and become the children of God" (*Compendium Theologiae*. 214).

What is anti-relational, anti-harmony is sinful, whereas his Kingdom message is of a world in harmony, a world that he has empowered us to make a present reality. We contribute to this forward thrust to the extent that we are attuned to this divine energy.

Perhaps a more suitable word for Atonement is Attunement!

For further exploration:

D. Wiederkehr (1979), *Belief in Redemption: Concepts of Salvation from the New Testament to the Present Time*, SPCK, London.

Denis Edwards (1986), *What are they saying about Salvation?* Paulist Press, USA.

John S. Spong (1994), *Resurrection: Myth or Reality?* Harper Collins.

John Dominic Crossan (1995), *Who Killed Jesus?* Harper, San Francisco.

Ken Wilber (1983), *Up from Eden*, Routledge and Kegan Paul, London.

Peter de Rosa (1967), *Christ and Original Sin*, Geoffrey Chapman, London.

Chapter 12

THE MORALITY FACTOR

The way in which we understand evil, morality, ethics, sin and how we relate these to God is a good indication of the belief paradigm out of which we operate: whether it be a top/outside downwards paradigm or a from-the-centre outwards paradigm. Do we believe that our ethical codes were given us by Divine decree — as in the manner in which Moses received the Ten Commandments on tablets of stone on Mount Sinai — or do we regard them as rules for behaviour originating from the human experience to enable groups of people to live together as pleasantly as possible? Are the Commandments a set of arbitrary rules imposed upon us like a school test to see which of us can qualify for eternal happiness and which of us fail? Are deeds evil because there are commandments forbidding them or are some acts intrinsically harmful to our human nature and for that reason they are listed as forbidden and given a divine seal?

Evil

Before considering the origins of our ethical codes, we must clarify what we mean by evil. In ordinary parlance the word is used loosely to describe anything which causes us to suffer. Disasters which are natural, such as plagues, earthquakes, famine, as well as those of human origin like car crashes, Chernobyl-size explosions, sinking ships — broadly named accidents — are often classed

among the evils which befall us. These are all causes of our suffering which are exterior to us and are part of our condition as human beings with limited capacities. (We have not yet acquired the
intelligence to invent the crash-proof car!) To these we can add the
physical or mental pain inflicted upon us by our fellow human beings: war, torture, slavery, rape, abuse in any form.

Then there is the suffering we bring upon ourselves and others, the cause of which arises from within us on account of our
pride, possessiveness, hatred, desire for revenge, envy, insecurity,
lust for power.

Evil is a Human Creation

Disasters are often referred to as physical evils. But we name them
"evils" only in the sense that they cause us to suffer. And they are
only relatively evil: what seems evil to us might be regarded as
beneficial by another.

What we are speaking of as evil here are the effects of deliberate *human* behaviour. What we call *moral* evil. The suffering
caused by moral evil is a human creation. There is no evil in the
animal world because evil arises from free choice. What animals
experience is pain inflicted from outside — from natural disasters
or from human intervention in the animal kingdom or from their
natural condition as animals. We cannot speak of evil done when
one animal inflicts pain upon another. Evil is a human creation.

But having said that we need to qualify the statement by saying
that evil is a negativity, a negative energy, arising from our misuse
or excessive use of positive energy. It is energy gone wrong. As a
negative entity it has no existence in its own right. No matter how
real is our experience of evil, or rather, of its effects, it has no existence other than being the "flip-side" of creative energy. Some
analogies will clarify this. We are only too familiar with holes of
every shape and size, from a hole in our sock to a bomb crater. We
would not deny their existence. But in fact a hole has no existence

of its own. It is a negativity. It is an absence of something. I cannot go along to the local DIY store and tell them I want to build a lily pond in my garden and so would they please deliver a hole 3×2×1 metre! There is no such thing, scientists tell us, as cold: there is zero heat, an absence of heat. And yet we are very aware of suffering from cold. Similarly, there is no such thing as darkness: there is an absence of light. Yet in each of these cases, despite a hole, the cold and the dark having no existence of their own, we can be affected, caused to suffer, perhaps even meet our death on account of them.

Evil is Whatever is Anti-Life

It is a coincidence that *evil* is *live* spelt backwards! Evil is all that is anti-life, anti-growth, whether it be damaging to our personal growth towards fulfilment or preventing the growth of other people, or hampering the evolution of our planet Earth: cosmic evil. If I say evil is death-inducing I am not speaking only of natural death, so I am not confining the word "growth" to physical growth. Today there has sprung up a culture which regards physical death as the ultimate evil. All possible and even the impossible attempts are taken to prevent it, keeping a deteriorating human body "alive" with sophisticated technology instead of allowing the person a dignified death. I believe this attitude arises from our spirit-denying culture, our loss of belief in the continuation of life after passing through death. Someone has perceptively observed that in Victorian times, when people died younger and at home with the whole family, including the children, gathered at the bedside, death was a familiar sight and spoken about openly. But no one spoke about sex. Today everyone speaks about sex but no one speaks about death. The dying are removed from the family circle and taken to hospital where they often die alone, then the body is almost secretively removed from the ward.

Evil entered human life at the point where our consciousness evolved to that stage where choice became possible. This was when the evolving human being acquired consciousness of self: became self-reflective. Self-consciousness enables us to differentiate other beings as separate from ourselves and from each other. Recognising differences causes fear. Other beings become a threat to us, which leads to conflict and suffering and anti-growth behaviour. The Eden Tree of Knowledge of Good and Evil is symbolic of freedom of choice. In the Gnostic gospels the serpent is a symbol of wisdom, inviting Eve to enter into greater consciousness, while in the Genesis account of "The Fall" God is depicted as a dictatorial father demanding total obedience which includes forbidding Adam and Eve a basic human liberty: freedom of choice. They cannot exercise their right to make a free choice until after they have acquired a knowledge of good and evil. Incidentally, a curious feature of this story is that God warns of the consequence of acquiring the knowledge of good and evil. It is death: "you shall die"; whereas the serpent foretells that the result will be their becoming more god-like by their knowing good and evil, by their acquiring free will. In the myth, God's prediction was wrong: the serpent's prediction was right!

Evil is Inevitable

A child grows by expanding her experience outwards from a small world, rebelling against constraints, venturing beyond further and further boundaries. Rebellion is part of the process of growing up. While acknowledging that the presence of evil is not a necessary part of creation, we have to admit that in the process of human growth, it is, however, inevitable. Self-consciousness gained in the Eden period of our evolution gave us the possibility of making mistaken and often disastrous decisions. It was the price we had to pay for evolving. The process of attempting to bring about unity, harmony — the Omega point of creation — inevitably, in our under-developed human state, causes wastage, breakage, damage and destruction.

As evil is a negativity, not having existence in its own right, it is only brought into existence when we give it a reality by believing it is real. I have often contended that Christians of the Pentecostal, Charismatic strain in the Church are so intent on identifying evil, on searching for its causes, on exorcising evil spirits whose presence they detect behind every misdemeanour, that they are actually giving reality to evil and thereby creating the very thing they are wishing to eliminate; they are extending its influence.

Thought generates energy. We bring about what we think about, or so we do when our thoughts are powerful enough. When God thinks, his thoughts take on existence. Thus creation is God's thought in continual actualisation. Negativity is created by negative thoughts just as positivity is the product of positive thinking. As we frequently hear it said these days: "We create our own reality." By believing in evil — by seeing devils everywhere — we are giving effectiveness, a reality, to evil. We are spreading the effects of evil, just as someone going around extinguishing the lights is giving a reality to darkness.

St Paul had the right approach:

> Fill your minds with those things that are good and that deserve praise: things that are true, noble, right, pure, everything that we love and honour and everything that can be thought virtuous. (Philippians 4:8)

In today's phraseology: "Think positively."

Good or Evil

But how do we decide what actions and thoughts are true, noble, right, pure, honourable, virtuous and worthy of praise? The three great Faiths originating from the Near East which claim Abraham as their spiritual father — Judaism, Christianity and Islam — regard the Ten Commandments as their moral template. And yet how different is each religion's application of them. Each claims that its own code of ethics is divinely inspired. Since God is unlikely to give different sets of laws to different groups of people who exercise the same power of decision-taking issuing from the same development of consciousness, it is clear that even if we subscribe to the belief that there is such a thing as Divine Law, we have to acknowledge that there is also an element of human interpretation of such a law.

As a foundation for structuring a framework of human law, a particular ethic, appeal is often made to Natural Law. (Natural Law, which is a moral law, is distinguished by western philosophers from the Law of Nature which is the predetermined, non-chosen way all creation follows, e.g. the Law of Gravity, the Law of Reproduction, etc.) An obvious example of Natural Law often quoted is the prohibition on killing another human being. The ordinary person has a natural, deep revulsion to taking another person's life. That is easily said. But if we probe a little, we are forced to question this. There have been times and cultures which have regarded cannibalism and human sacrifices as entirely proper. And we do not have to go far back in history. Still today there are those that champion war and the new technologies of war have moved from the killing of opposing combatants to the wiping out of whole cities and peoples. There are the acts of genocide, or "ethnic cleansing", as we politely call it today, practised upon the Jews in Nazi Europe, upon the Armenians in Turkey, upon the Kurds in Iraq and Turkey, upon the Tibetans by the Chinese, by opposing tribes in Rwanda. It is only recently that some countries, and some countries only, have abolished capital punishment. Until now the death penalty has been regarded worldwide as a legitimate punishment.

Who is to say what is "natural" in law? I return to the basic thesis of this book: there is not a special divine decree to enlighten us that enters our world from outside creation, but that all we know of the Ultimate Mystery, of the divine action upon and with creation, is none other than that which we learn from within, and can only be in terms of our human condition. What we call Divine Revelation is the interpretation of our human experience of the Divine.

Ethical Codes are a Human Creation

Ethical codes are created by groups of people in order to ensure that their living together will be as harmonious and fruitful as possible. Consequently we find different standards of moral behaviour practised in different cultures at different times in history. What often happens is that a certain way of behaving is discovered to be required sociologically but then a religion canonises it. For instance, humanity has discovered the genetically and emotionally destabilising effects upon children born out of an incestuous union. Consequently, one finds in most African tribal law that marriage is forbidden between immediate blood relatives. The Church has canonised this by writing it into its Canon Law.

So who or what are the human agents which shape our moral laws? For much of this information I am indebted to the research done by Oliver Thomson published in his book *A History of Sin*. He finds that apart from a few exceptions where "dramatic changes in moral direction are achieved by individual leaders" — and he cites Jesus and Mohammed as examples — "the majority of moral concepts are created and imposed by anonymous groups or successions of people working slowly to achieve their ends". He lists seven main categories. I add two more.

1. Dictators, hereditary monarchs and military oligarchs have cultivated a death-or-glory military ethic based on blind obedience and bravery, to the point of self-sacrifice. (Do we not find this ethic reflected in the writing of that soldier-saint, Ignatius of Loyola?)

2. Priests and prophets. Where they have not been in collusion with the ruling power, this group more than any other has contributed to the development of an altruistic ethic and condemned violence and self-indulgence.

3. Political revolutionaries who have generally been reactionaries to exploitation and have promoted an ethic of personal freedom and equality.

4. Lawyers and professional lawmakers add to the ethical code by arriving "at practical solutions to numerous moral dilemmas which are neglected by philosophers". Today moralists cannot keep pace with the progress of science, particularly in the fields of medical technology and genetic engineering.

5. The promoters of economic welfare. They set a moral tone by rewarding production (the work ethic), encouraging pride in skill and by proposing profit as the ultimate goal. But also within the economic community we find the trade union leader applauded for opposing technological progress. The cotton trader was allowed to pursue a moral code which included slavery.

6. Teachers, social workers and academics have in our day taken over the role of moral educators, which was previously that of the clergy. Their influence on the younger generation is immense.

7. Minority pressure groups such as the Campaign for Nuclear Disarmament, Save the Whale, the anti-slavery movement, the suffragettes, the Movement for Women's Ordination, whether they be political, moral or religious pressure groups. Each creates its own sub-ethic which often has a disproportionate influence on the nation as a whole.

8. The arts and the media. The influence of rave parties and their permissiveness, the videos and DVDs available to households, the weight given to editorial comment in newspapers. All these create acceptable standards of behaviour. Since the media is now quite international they have a cross-cultural influence. The moral values of western soap operas are conveyed to audiences in rural survival situations in Third World countries. Those who own and control the media have immense power to create new ethical standards.

9. Finally, the drive for market domination pursued by the transnational companies, whose only aim is profit, has led to a largely consumerist ethic.

On a smaller scale, we find a lot of ethical sub-systems operating within larger societies. We have all had experience of medical codes and school rules, the Citizen's Charter, business codes, and the Highway Code. There are sports rules and Trade Union codes. We even speak of a criminal code: "honour among thieves". Then of course there are conventional codes such as table manners by which a child is taught what is wrong or right, but which in fact are purely modes of cultural behaviour. No one way of holding a fork is any better, easier or morally superior to any other.

An Ethical Progress

Is there any way of measuring whether there is progress in ethical behaviour from one era to another? Indeed has there been any progress at all? A yardstick for the Christian who believes that God's creative plan "is to bring all creation together, everything in the heavens and on earth, with Christ as head" (Ephesians 1:10) is to ask whether we can say humanity is displaying an increasing love of neighbour, becoming more united at an altruistic level.

Oliver Thomson claims from his research that although moral attitudes keep changing "it is not easy to see any clear line of progress in human moral history", on the basis of people being more kind and less cruel to their fellows. He goes on: "Moralities which are strong provide reactions in the opposite direction; moralities which create one kind of normality create another kind of deviation."

While writing this chapter I watched with horror a television documentary about child slavery in the carpet factories of Pakistan. How could human beings be so insensitive to the suffering of their children? Then I recalled that it is not so many years ago when young children were treated in a not dissimilar way in the factories and mines of western Europe. Slavery, which began as an institution when Egyptians enslaved their conquered enemies (around 2500 BCE) was condoned in the time of Jesus and legislated against only in very recent history. The earliest record of racism also comes from Egypt in the reign of Pharaoh Usertsu III (1440–1412 BCE), when he set up a pillar at the southern end of his kingdom and decreed that no black people should pass it. Only in recent decades has there been such an effective outcry against the racial laws at the southern end of the same continent that apartheid has had to be dismantled. But racism still persists under other names: "ethnic cleansing" in former Yugoslavia or "tribal warfare" in Rwanda and Burundi.

While there are many examples that could be quoted as "progress", we have to ask whether violence is really diminishing or whether it is simply taking other forms. A final quotation from Oliver Thomson reminds us that we cannot assume automatic moral progress throughout human history:

> The Punans of Borneo, the Arctic Eskimos and the Djahai of Australia never made war. A remarkable achievement in thousands of years and not equalled by many more advanced societies. Other primitive tribes were free from slavery, prostitution, polygamy, cannibalism, infanticide, human sacrifice and many other habits found in civilised societies.

And yet, taking the moral measure of the world today on the Christian yardstick of "bringing all creation together", can we not recognise that there never has been previously, *on a world scale*, such concern about and campaigning against so many injustices inflicted upon our fellow human beings, not to mention those inflicted upon the animal world? Besides abolishing slavery on the grand scale, most of the western world abhors capital punishment; we have the Geneva Convention to dictate how prisoners of war should be treated; we campaign against the use of nuclear and chemical weapons; we donate gifts with enormous concern and generosity to alleviate victims of famine; we feel guilt about the crippling debt the First World has imposed upon the Third World; we deplore the suffering caused to children by manifold forms of abuse; we are indignant about the spread of pornography; we are increasingly alert to the many forms of inequality between women and men. The list is endless.

Yes, I sincerely believe that, despite localised signs to the contrary, humanity as a whole is displaying an increasing love of neighbour, and not for selfish reasons but because of a sense of the oneness of all humanity, and of a more widespread sense of oneness with Mother Earth.

Teilhard de Chardin foresaw that the next great evolutionary step from mineral to plant to animal to humanity, now that human beings have developed their individuality, is the step towards community: the development of the unity of the human race, of a communal consciousness.

Sin

Are some forms of behaviour labelled sinful because God has decreed that they are? Or has society found that certain behaviour is injurious to human well-being and therefore invoked the authority of God to enforce a taboo?

At an early age we were taught that "sin is an offence against God". This coloured the development of our personal scale of values. There was the implication, which in our innocence we automatically took on board, that everything which we were told was "wrong" or "bad" was sinful and therefore displeasing to God, even such misdemeanours as not saying "please" or crossing the road without looking both ways or forgetting to brush our teeth. We were smacked for these, so they must be morally wrong and therefore sinful and therefore hurting God. Or so we reasoned. In any case, they were classed under "disobedience" and teacher said that was a sin. This notion of sin gave birth to a concept of a God who is to be feared because eventually it will be not our parents but God who will punish us. I am sure that for many Christians, perhaps for the majority, their idea of God is influenced, if not actually formed by what they have been taught about sin. In fact, our idea of sin should follow from our perception of God.

Despite what we might have been taught in Sunday School or Catechism class, we cannot hurt or displease or anger God. If we were able to influence God's attitude towards us — and this is as true of pleasing God as of displeasing God — we would have a power over God, which is nonsense.

So how are we to understand sin? We can only speak of something being an offence against God analogously if it is an offence against humanity and against our own potential, our future growth. Jesus spoke of God's plan for creation (in terms of the Kingdom of God which was the main thrust of his teaching) as the building up of relationships.

Sin therefore can best be understood as a breakdown in relationships. The word "sin" is shorthand for the destruction or rejection of love. We have already seen how Jesus speaks of forgiveness in terms of healing relationships, of being open to unconditional love. The noun which best describes the quality of God's Kingdom, God's reign, is "harmony". Purposeful disruption of harmony produces evil, the negation of the positive energies of love.

This breakdown of relationships, this cause of disharmony, happens at different levels: between person and person, within our own person, between humanity and the environment. It can be caused singly or collectively. We call such an act sin because it is disruptive of God's ordering of creation, of creation's evolutionary progress towards the Omega point, the completion of God's design.

We cannot sin against God directly. We can only sin and bring about the consequences of sin in the context within which we live. True, Jesus spoke of the sin against the Holy Spirit as being unforgivable (Matthew 12:32). The Spirit is the Spirit of unity, the source of love, the supreme relater. To refuse the Spirit of Love by deliberately being closed to the Spirit's promptings is to refuse the loving advances God makes to us. Such an act is not unforgivable on account of a divine decree but because it is the very antithesis of openness. It is a choice to be non-loving, to be closed-in upon oneself, non-relating. Such persons deliberately exclude them-selves from God's plan for the harmony of creation. And therein lies their punishment.

God's Punishment

We picture God punishing human beings in the way we punish each other — so often vindictively: an eye for an eye and a tooth for a tooth. Too readily are prisons regarded by the general public as primarily places of punishment. "He caused suffering so he must be made to suffer", we hear the victim of an assault say in a television interview. God does not need to be vindictive!

It is truer to say we are not punished *for* our sins but *by* our sins. We are "punished" by being allowed to suffer the unhappy consequences of our actions. Such suffering is of value to us only if it is recognised and accepted as a lesson for our future.

We have created a God in our image. We ourselves are angry and judgemental and punishing so we project this behaviour onto God. We are fearful of anger and judgement and punishment so we are fearful of God.

Fear: Our Greatest Obstacle to Love

If love of neighbour — a precept expressed by every religion — is the nucleus of all morality and ethical systems, its greatest obsta-cle is fear. It is often thought that the antithesis of all fear is cour-age. True, courage is the opposite of *physical* fear. But the opposite of *moral* fear is love. St John reminds us: "Perfect love drives out all fear" (1 John 4:18).

On the many occasions I have been facilitating the gatherings of different communities, communities of priests and of nuns in particular, who meet to plan their future, the moment arrives when they try to identify their "Key Problem" — the fundamental cause of what is going wrong in their life together. As often as not, that Key Problem is identified as *fear*. Fear to be themselves, fear to be open with one another, fear of change in their lifestyle, fear of their future, fear of rejection if they should reveal a personality weakness. Fear is an exceedingly strong behavioural motivation. Fear is crippling; it stifles creativity.

So many of us Christians have received our religious initiation on the basis of "The fear of the Lord is the beginning of wisdom" (Psalm 111:10). The phrase "fear of the Lord" which occurs so frequently in the Hebrew Testament is hardly ever mentioned in the New Testament and only once on the lips of Jesus (Luke 12:5). The word "fear" is better translated by "awe" or "respect" or "admiration". In fact, the Good News Bible translates that verse of the psalm: "The way to become wise is to honour the Lord."

It is worth quoting that passage from St John's First Letter in full:

> We ourselves know and believe the love which God has for us. God is love, and whoever lives in love lives in union with God and God lives in union with him. Love is made perfect in us in order that we may have courage on Judgement Day; and we will have it because our life in this world is the same as Christ's. There is no fear in love; perfect love drives out all fear. So then, love has not been made perfect in anyone who is afraid, because fear has to do with punishment. (4:16-18)

The Judgement of God

That passage raises the idea of a final judgement. This is a subject which the classical religious artists have really exploited. Their paintings feed our imagination with images of divine weighing scales upon which are loaded all the good deeds of our life and all the evil deeds. Then there is a fearful hush in the heavenly court while we and the angelic choir hold our breath as we wait to see which way the scales tip, and then . . . a judgement is pronounced which will determine our eternity. No wonder we are so afraid of death, and of God.

The evil we have created — but also the good and love we have created — are not cumulative in the sense of our putting them into a deposit account. They affect us here and now. They make us what we are today. Their only influence on us as we face death lies in how they have caused us to become the loving or hating people we are at the moment of dying. This, according to John's Gospel, is how Jesus explained it:

> Whoever believes in the Son is not judged; but whoever does not believe has already been judged because he has not believed in God's Son. This is how the judgement works: the light has come into the world, but people love the darkness rather than the light, because their deeds are evil. Anyone who does evil things hates the light and will not come to the light, because he does not want his evil deeds to be shown up. But whoever does what is true comes to the light in order that the light may show that what he did was in obedience to God (John 3:18–21).

We are "obedient to God" when our wills are in harmony with the way in which the Divine Will is manifested to us through the continuing day-by-day process of creation.

For further exploration:

Oliver Thomson (1993), *A History of Sin*, Canongate Press, Edinburgh.

Richard Holloway (1999), *Godless Morality*, Canongate Press, Edinburgh.

Hans Küng (1990), *Global Responsibility: In Search of a New World Ethic*, SCM Press, London.

Chapter 13

THE NEW SPIRITUALITY FACTOR

There are three intertwined factors which are witnesses to the appearance of a "new" spirituality — a spirituality more appropriate for the times in which we live — and so to a new way of regarding and relating to the Divine Mystery.

1. There is the vast compendium of items which the media classify under an umbrella title: "The New Age Movement".

2. There is the opening of dialogue between the world's great religions, and, as a consequence, a growing appreciation of the spiritual wealth of other Faiths.

3. There is what is being called "The New Mysticism" manifested by the increasing popularity of different meditation techniques being employed by people seeking to make a journey inwards.

What Do We Mean by Spirituality?

We need to be clear about our use of the word "spirituality". It is often confused with spiritualism. By spirituality we mean that aspect of our nature — complementing the physical and psychological aspects — which awakens us to wonder, gives our lives meaning and calls us towards our higher self, usually expressed as a relationship with the Transcendent. The spiritual is part of our make-up as human beings, indeed the eternal part. However, our spiritual aspect does not belong to some nether world. Our spiritual journey is one with our emotional, psychological journey.

We also need to distinguish spirituality from religion. Religion is a human creation and has arrived comparatively recently in human history, the earliest of the great religions being less than four thousand years old. By religion we mean a particular framework, which includes a belief system, a moral code, an authority structure and a form of worship, within which people find nourishment for the spiritual aspect of their lives and explore their spiritual journey with others.

In its concern for the ultimate questions about life, spirituality needs to express itself in a number of ways:

- In a search for answers: through reading, reflecting, attending lectures and courses, etc. (Spiritual searchers are unanimous in testifying to the way in which the right guidance — through a randomly selected book, a chance word or encounter, an inspiration — enters their lives at the exact moment it is needed to enable them to take the next step in their journey.)

- In rituals, particularly for absolving, cleansing, expressing forgiveness and harnessing or appeasing unseen powers.

- In actions to express being in control of oneself and one's situation.

- In prayer (in the broadest sense) in an endeavour to communicate beyond our time-space limitation, whether it is addressed to a higher being or in the form of séances or channelling.

- In meditation in order to raise the mind to a higher plane.

Religion is not a structure parachuted down to Earth by God as a constituent element of creation. It is a structure invented by human beings to enable us to give form to these expressions and so to feed the spiritual aspect of our lives. As can happen, and so often does, with all structures that are not regularly evaluated, from being originally life-giving sources they become life-draining. Our energies are not vitalised by them any more; our energies are tapped and eventually drained simply to maintain them.

The latter half of the last century saw hundreds of thousands of people leaving the form of Christian religion they were born into and exploring further afield to find their own means of spiritual growth because the beliefs proposed so authoritatively no longer seem to ring true — they are at variance with people's experience — and their spirituality is not being nourished by what the Churches are offering.

Let us consider some of the signs we can observe around us that cause us to believe that a new spirituality is emerging, a new attitude to and a new way of relating to the presence of the Divine in our lives.

A New Era of Consciousness

I had thought of entitling this chapter "The New Age Factor". What is meant by "The New Age"? It is a name applied to a wide variety of theories, attitudes and practices that point towards our entering a new era of consciousness. This phenomenon has numerous manifestations. I have in my library a New Age Dictionary giving an explanation of some 450 words, phrases and names that are associated with the New Age.

A variety of these manifestations can best be seen by a visit to one of the New Age shops that are appearing in our cities. There we find books on witchcraft, on complementary medicine, on a variety of healing techniques, on the Tibetan Secret of Eternal Youth and Zen meditation, on hypnotism, colour therapy, the occult and on spiritual channelling. We notice Tarot cards for sale and advertisements for a Hatha Yoga holiday on a Greek island, for a lecture on Tai Chi alongside an announcement of the next meeting of the local Green Party. On the opposite side of the street is a health food shop. Yet these are just a few, very few, of the elements of this multifaceted phenomenon. The media have used the label "New Age Movement" to cover an enormous range of human interests, speculations, activities and, in some cases, alternative lifestyles.

Whatever our reaction to these manifestations, one thing we cannot properly do is simply to ignore the whole New Age scene. A couple of decades ago it was just a fringe concern of a few people we labelled "weird" and their activities came to our attention only as conventions at Glastonbury or at Summer Solstice gatherings at Stonehenge. It did not really intrude upon our everyday lives. But in recent years what was decidedly marginal has emerged as a contemporary subculture arousing the interest, and often involvement, of "respectable" people — perhaps our friends among them. Do we not know people who have benefited from acupuncture or reflexology, who have become vegetarians, who practise some form of eastern meditation or attend Yoga classes? The rise in concern for ecology and "green" matters is another aspect of the same movement. It is referred to as a "movement" in the sense that it is a growing feature of western culture, attracting increasingly more people, not because there is any particular organisation promoting it or development policy being pursued.

What's New?

But is it so new? Many aspects of it are a return to the earliest nature religions and pre-scientific health treatments. Since history was first recorded humanity seems to have been looking forward to a Golden Age. The human being has an innate longing for an age of peace and love, of justice and plenty — a return to the harmony of what was believed to be a superior way of life in Eden. Our New Testament holds out the promise of a new Jerusalem: the vision of "a new heaven and a new earth" (Revelation 21). Millenarianism has constantly reappeared in one form or another. It seems that we are incapable of living fully in the present because we regard the present as the low point between the high of a Paradise in the past and the high of the Kingdom of Heaven in the future.

It is sometimes argued that while every period of history has felt itself to be on the verge of something new, it is only in retrospect that a past era can be judged to have been a turning point in the path of humanity. However, our present New Age supporters are convinced that what is happening in our own time is more than an improvement in our human condition: it is, as they call it, a "quantum leap", a new evolutionary step.

Since the turn of the century there have been lone voices announcing that humanity is on the point of a great leap forward — the Jesuit scientist Teilhard de Chardin among them. Previous evolutionary leaps have been in the physical order: from matter to plant life to animal life to intelligent (human) life. This new step, this quantum leap, is claimed to be of another order, an evolution into a new level of consciousness. That last word is important because it is the key to what it is all about.

The development of our consciousness is precisely what is new. The leap we took out of the mythical Eden from sub-consciousness to self-consciousness is now being followed by a further leap to super-consciousness. We are evolving from a physical to a metaphysical vision of reality. From viewing our world as purely physical, as scientists and western religions have done, we are beginning to appreciate the presence of consciousness in all matter. The "Gaia Hypothesis" of James Lovelock — that planet Earth is a single, living, self-regulating organism — is witness to this. We are moving beyond the limitations of our rational minds, beyond what we learn through our five senses, beyond the boundaries of space and time, to the exploration of inner, deeper realms. We are stretching the boundaries of our consciousness. It is at this point in our history that we are moving beyond our physical potential to explore our spiritual potential.

A Seeking for Wholeness

We have already mentioned the dualism from which we in the West suffer: the either/or of natural/supernatural, sacred/profane, spiritual/material, body/soul, good/evil, heaven/hell. We owe this to the legacy of Platonic philosophy, not to our religious heritage. Hebrew thought, expressed in both the Hebrew Bible and in the

Christians' New Testament, was holistic. So, for example, when St Paul in his letters writes about the body and the soul, we of western culture employing the dualistic thought form interpret him to be contrasting body and soul or even to be setting one against the other. However, when St Paul speaks of the body he is most times referring not simply to the flesh and bones of a person but to the whole complex living organism in its physical context. Similarly, when he speaks of soul he is not referring to the vital principle of the person's biological activity, but to the whole person with his vitality, his consciousness, his intelligence and volition, in the same way that a vicar might speak of there being 823 souls in his parish without implying that his parishioners are disincarnate!

Vedic and Hindu concepts and those of the other great eastern religions are also holistic rather than dualistic or analytical.

It is not by accident, therefore, that many westerners in recent years have adopted eastern spiritual values. This has nothing to do with becoming a Hindu or Buddhist: it is an attempt to transcend the dualistic and analytical nature of western culture in order to integrate the holistic experiences they are encountering.

This is sometimes expressed as a return to "right-brain" thinking. The brain has a left and a right hemisphere. The left hemisphere is said to analyse, discriminate, measure, it names and organises. Its thinking is linear going from A to B to C, from cause to effect. The right hemisphere sees in wholes, it synthesises, unites, detects patterns, comprehends the totality of A to Z. It is the creative, intuitive, non-rational part of the mind. The former is said to predominate in the masculine mind and the latter in the feminine. Our western culture has, since the sixteenth and seventeenth centuries, favoured rational knowledge over intuitive wisdom, science over mysticism, competition over co-operation, always enforced by our masculine-dominated society. Today there is a move to redress this imbalance, not by letting the pendulum swing the other way but by the cultivation of the whole mind. This is coming about by increasing numbers of people taking up the practice of deep meditation and other exercises to deepen consciousness, and also by a deliberate education policy to cultivate the creative, unifying, non-competitive potential of children. I am meeting so many parents and infant teachers who remark to me that today's small children seem to be much more "aware", "connected", intuitive than the previous generation.

One of the consequences of restoring the left–right brain balance is witnessed in the feminist movement. In its external form this is manifested in the promotion of women, but in its essence it is a renewed appreciation of the feminine qualities of the mind (intuition, co-operation, compassion, emotionality, creativity, empathy) in both men and women in a society in which the male rational, power-seeking, aggressive, competitive, exploitative, logical mind has predominated for so long and produced our patriarchal, hierarchical society.

A by-product of this is a renewed appreciation of the feminine aspect of God, often expressed as the Divine Mother. In both Hebrew and Christian Scriptures we can find feminine images of God: a dairymaid, a laundress, a midwife, a baker woman, a nurse, a homemaker, a mother hen.

In the field of health we notice a movement away from curing (being concerned with the diseased part of the body only) to healing: concern for making the whole person more healthy, taking into account their emotional life, the stresses they suffer, their environment, their family history. Our seeking for wholeness looks for ways to bring our body, mind and spirit into greater harmony.

A New Relationship to Creation

Another aspect of the new sense of wholeness is a more widespread understanding of the place humanity has in the total picture of creation.

Until recently our western culture has caused us to see ourselves as standing outside nature, from which vantage point we observed it, dominated it and exploited it. Now we are feeling ourselves to be an integral part of nature, of which the life-force is essentially one, though appearing in billions of different forms, in consequence of which what affects one part of creation in some ways affects all others. This accounts for our current increasing concern for the environment and the health of our planet. The rising interest in "green" issues, the increasing popularity of the Green Party, debates on ecological matters: all these are manifestations of a new attitude towards creation. I believe the spark which kindled this particular blaze were those first pictures of planet Earth sent back to us by the Apollo mission in the mid-1960s. The sight of our only home as a tiny, isolated, fragile but beautiful planet with no territorial frontiers or separate countries in evidence, touched us deeply. Previously our planet was seen as a hostile environment, a place of struggle against the brutal forces of nature in order to survive. Now we are beginning to appreciate our partnership with the Earth as the producer which can meet all our needs. We call her Mother Earth.

Another level of experiencing our interrelatedness is in the growing sense that all persons form one human family and that our interdependence is such that a tragedy befalling one nation or people affects us all. The immediate response of people at one side of the globe to the sufferings of people at the other side — despite differences of colour, religion, language and politics — is evidence of this, never better illustrated, perhaps, than in the overwhelming response to the victims of famine in Africa through "Live Aid" and "Band Aid" in the mid-1980s, and to the ethnic crisis in Rwanda in the 1990s. Perhaps for the first time on Planet Earth we witness the potential of the power of goodwill as a mass force.

The Interconnectedness of the Whole Cosmos

Linked closely to ecology is astrology. Leaving aside the fun aspect of reading one's horoscope in the daily paper, astrology is emerging as a respected science by those who appreciate that, like ecology, it is based on the belief in the interconnectedness of all creation. Behind the natural human curiosity to know what the future holds in store for us is the serious conviction that stars and planets have an influence on each other through energy fields, including those which influence our lives on Planet Earth. Unconsciously we allow the sun to affect us. It gives us our seasons, our temperatures, our day and night hours. We plan our holidays, our journeys, what we are going to wear according to our expectations of these. What is less widely known is the influence the sun has on the Earth's magnetic field. The sun goes through an eleven year cycle of solar activity, one feature of which is the appearance of sun spots. When sun spots are active, the weather is warmer, when they disappear it is colder. The irregular cycle of sun spot activity affects our magnetic field, causing such phenomena as variations in the length of the crop-growing season, the growth pattern of trees, the blood-clotting rate in human beings and the number of admissions to mental hospitals! In March 1989 there occurred the most severe magnetic storm ever recorded. It cut off electricity supplies to six million people in Quebec and put a nuclear power station out of action for 42 hours.

Every schoolchild learns that the gravitational pull of the moon influences our tides. And we are only too aware that some minds — animal as well as human — are affected by a full moon.

With today's knowledge of gravitational and other forces in the Universe, about the rhythms and cycles of the constellations, it is not surprising that people accept more easily than a few decades ago that these "outer" influences do affect all aspects of life on this planet as on any other. Even around the skin of our Earth the weather patterns are so sensitive that, according to Ed Lorenz, a meteorology professor who made a study of air movements in the atmosphere, the flapping of a butterfly's wing in Rio could lead to a hurricane in New York! He named this phenomenon, whereby weather systems exhibit a great sensitivity to initial conditions, with very different outcomes arising from infinitesimally different starting points, "The Butterfly Effect"! We just cannot even begin to comprehend the extent to which all aspects of our lives are influenced by factors outside ourselves, near and far. Nor, conversely, the extent of our influence on all else.

Interfaith Dialogue

Thanks to the ease of communication between east and west, to the multicultural and multi-faith nature of western society today, there is increasing dialogue between the adherents of the world's major religions. In our schools children learn about Faiths other than their own, so the understanding of the treasures of different religions will enable them to have a greater respect for and appreciation of people who think differently on religious matters from themselves. At the highest level, we are witnessing unprecedented gatherings of religious leaders to discuss matters of common concern: justice, peace, population and development, ecological and world issues.

We have already distinguished between spirituality and religion. As a (recent) human creation, religion is a means, not an end in itself. Long before human beings arrived at an understanding that their ultimate destiny is to be in union with the Divine, the God-head, they groped towards an experience of and contact with pure spirit, reaching out beyond themselves, towards an undefined Something which transcends the boundaries of ordinary experience. Over the last 4,000 years, humanity has felt the need to express the inner energy of the spiritual (the esoteric) in an external (exoteric) form we name religion. While the esoteric is unique and found in every religion as its source, but beyond all formulation, it seeks expression in diverse ways in different Faiths. We all originate from the same source, the mind of the Creator, and we are all destined for the same ultimate experience of unity with the Divine, but each religion provides a different route for making that journey. Even within Christianity we see that the evolution of our understanding of the esoteric which Jesus introduced to humanity expresses itself today in so many different forms of Christian Church. (There are said to exist 423 different Christian denominations in the world!)

All religions are explorations into and applications of the Fundamental Truth or Perennial Philosophy, as Leibniz called it. This cannot be known by sense or reason but by the experience of the soul in its depths. The Dalai Lama has written:

> Every major religion of the world has similar ideas of love, the same goal of benefiting humanity through spiritual practice, and the same effect of making their followers into better human beings.

Expressions of Love in the World's Great Religions

Bahai: Love Me that I may love thee. If thou lovest Me not, My love can no wise reach thee.

Buddhism: Let each one of us cultivate towards the whole world a heart of love.

Christianity: Beloved, let us love one another; for love is of God.

Confucianism: To love all is the greatest benevolence.

Hinduism: One can best worship the Lord through love.

Islam: Love is this, that thou shouldst account thyself very little and God very great.

Jainism: The days are of most profit to those who act in love.

Judaism: Thou shalt love the Lord thy God with all thy heart and thy neighbour as thyself.

Shintu: Love is the representative of the Lord.

Sikhism: God will regenerate those in whose hearts there is love.

Taoism: Heaven arms with love those it would not see destroyed.

Zoroastrianism: Wo/man is the beloved of the Lord and should love in return.

The Second Vatican Council reminded us that the religions of the world are not mere philosophies but attempts over centuries to respond to the mysteries of the human condition (*Lumen Gentium*, 17).

No Religion is Complete in Itself

All religions are partial. There is ever present the danger of getting stuck in one groove, believing it is the only true religion, and not being open to encounter other expressions of Truth. No religion is complete in itself. Each is a sign pointing in its own way to the Divine Mystery.

A story from India tells of a simpleton approaching a wise man to ask where the moon is. The sage points to it but the simpleton looks only at the finger! All Creeds, ethics, rituals belonging to any religion are no more than fingers. We have to look beyond them to encounter reality. There are so many pointing fingers, but if they seek Truth they will all point in the same direction. Each religion is a particular but incomplete manifestation of unmanifest Truth.

The parable of the six blind men encountering an elephant for the first time is often told today. One man approached the tail and declared he had found a rope. Another felt the ears and stated this object was an immense fan. Yet another took hold of the trunk and warned his companions it was a snake. The fourth ran into a tusk and shrieked that it was a spear. The fifth encountered a leg and pronounced that this "thing" was a tree, while the last walked into the side and announced it was a wall. All were convinced they were right, and they were, within their limited understanding and interpretation — yet none was right.

Each religion has some aspect of truth to contribute to all the others. No single one is absolute or totally comprehensive in itself. It may be unique in its manner of expressing truth but it cannot claim to be unique in pointing the way. It can do no more than point beyond itself to some greater reality. The revelation of each is a treasure to be shared, not a private possession to be defended. Religious wars arise precisely from the mistaken idea of one religion that it possesses the latest revelation and is superior to all others. Such thinking creates a desire for religious supremacy.

If the superiority of one religion over another is sometimes claimed on the grounds of revelation, its followers might also be tempted to claim superiority on the historic grounds that it has been more successful than any other in fulfilling humanity's deepest aspirations. But none in fact can claim this. There are certainly no grounds for Christianity, for instance, to claim to have produced more saints in proportion to membership, nor to having given witness to a higher quality of saintliness than any other religion. Nor has it brought about more peace, more justice, more community. Its record of suppression, of belligerence, of intolerance and triumphalism is indeed much worse than some of the religions of the East! Christians are estimated to be 32 per cent of the world's population yet they receive 62 per cent of the entire world's income and they spend 97 per cent of it on themselves. What kind of witness is that?

Aldous Huxley in *The Perennial Philosophy* writes:

> Because Christians believe that there had been only one Avatar, Christian history has been disgraced by more and bloodier crusades, interdenominational wars, persecutions and proselytising imperialism than has the history of Hinduism and Buddhism.

And he goes on:

> The level of public morality has been lower in the West than in the East, the levels of exceptional sanctity and of ordinary individual morality have not, so far as one can judge from the available evidence, been any higher.

With the exception perhaps of Islam, there is today an openness on the part of the major religions to learn from each other. In the past few decades Christian theologians have been engaged in an interfaith dialogue. Their level of dialogue depends upon their theological stance regarding the traditionally claimed uniqueness of Christianity.

Those who believe Christianity contains the fullness of truth have no doubt about its unique position as superior to all other religions. This view is to be found among evangelical theologians whose dialogue with other Faiths is restricted to sociological, environmental and similar world concerns. They are opposed to any form of worship together, and their motive for dialogue is really to gain a point of entry for evangelising. But this is an extreme position.

A second group — the majority of theologians today including, for instance, Hans Küng — would hold that while all religions can be channels of salvation for their followers, nevertheless Christianity is a superior religion and the gift of salvation for all humanity is mediated by Jesus the Christ whether the recipients are aware of this or not. However, they acknowledge that the insights of other religions can throw a refreshing light on Christian revelation. In other words, we can come to a deeper appreciation of our own Faith through dialogue with other religions. This much was said in an official Vatican document in 1991:

> Through dialogue they [Christians] may be moved to give
> up ingrained prejudices, to revise preconceived ideas, and
> even sometimes to allow the understanding of their faith to
> be purified. (Dialogue and Proclamation, N. 49)

Those who hold this view have no hesitation in taking from other traditions what will be of value to their Christian practice, as for instance, adopting eastern methods of meditation as a form of Christian prayer.

Dom Bede Griffiths, the Benedictine monk who spent 38 years living in an ashram in India, would be one of this group. His *Rivers of Compassion*, subtitled *A Christian Commentary on the Bhagavad*

Gita is not a Christian interpretation of the Bhagavad Gita but a drawing from it of insights to enrich the understanding of our Christian tradition. "I want to show how it can be a practical spiritual guide to a Christian", he wrote in the Introduction.

A third category of theologians — as yet few in number — would regard each religion as a valid path to the Divine Mystery because each is a search for Ultimate Truth within its own cultural history. Each has been likened to a particular well which draws its water by different means from the same underground source. This theological position is not saying that all religions are equally good for anyone, but that all are imperfect and limited and some are more appropriate to a particular time and culture than others. Not all wells provide equal accessibility to water at all times. One prominent theologian who would be in this category, making a leap into the future, is Raimundo Panikkar, son of an Indian Hindu father and a Spanish Catholic mother, who holds Doctorates in Science, Philosophy and Theology, and made interfaith dialogue his particular concern.

Finally, there is the level of mysticism. Every major religion has its mystics who dialogue out of a higher state of consciousness: a state beyond any particularities.

The New Mystics

The two deepest and most pervading dynamics in the human person are inward towards transcending and outward towards relating. The first draws us irresistibly towards the source of all consciousness, all being, all energy, beyond ourselves, towards the Greater. The second attracts us towards building up relationships: towards unity of person with person, of person with nature and with the cosmos.

While the Eastern religions (Hinduism, Buddhism, Taoism, Confucianism) are principally mystical, experiencing God as Being, the three religions of the West (Judaism, Christianity, Islam) experience God in action, in dialogue with humanity, partnering us in our history. As a consequence, the former are pronouncedly mystical religions, while the latter are principally active. The former are a uniting force in the world; the latter, with their doctrines, divide us.

We have spoken in a previous chapter about "myth". The words "myth", "mystery" and "mysticism" derive from the same root, the Greek word *musteion*, to close the eyes or the mouth. They conjure up the notions of darkness or silence. Evelyn Underhill (in *Practical Mysticism*) defines mysticism as:

> The art of union with Reality. The mystic is a person who has attained that union in a greater or lesser degree; or who aims at or believes in such attainment.

This, of course, applies as much to those who adhere to no religion as to those who choose a religion as their path.

The sexual experience is the nearest that many people ever come to a mystical experience. Our sexuality arises from a sense of incompleteness and causes a longing for wholeness, just as spirituality is an urge towards wholeness, an attraction towards the Divine. The spiritual instinct, like the sexual instinct, can follow a path which is joyful and rewarding or perverted and destructive.

It is curious that while some people are attracted to a religion as a path towards the Ultimate Mystery, there are others, we in the West particularly, who seek religion as an escape from mystery, who are looking for an "explanation" of Ultimate Reality. Reality, like God, is an absolute value, one we can never grasp in its totality. We cannot possess Reality. Reality, like God, possesses us. I am reminded of a simile offered by Albert Einstein:

> In our endeavour to understand reality we are somewhat like a man trying to understand the mechanism of a closed watch. He sees the face and the moving hands, even hears its ticking, but he has no way of opening the case. If he is ingenious he may form some picture of a mechanism which could

be responsible for all the things he observes, but he may never be quite sure his picture is the only one which could explain his observations. He will never be able to compare his picture with the real mechanism and he cannot even imagine the possibility of the meaning of such a comparison.

To follow on from this quote, there is of course the man who, in his attempt to understand, opens the case, and removes all the pieces, one by one. At last he can see exactly how it works — except that it doesn't work anymore! His attempt to "solve" the mystery has merely destroyed it.

People take either a predominantly mystical or a predominantly active path towards Ultimate Reality. Not that one is exclusive of the other. St Paul surely followed the active way yet he had his mystical experiences, among which was his vision on the road to Damascus. In an autobiographical note he speaks of his experience in the third person:

> I know a certain Christian man who fourteen years ago was snatched up to the highest heaven (I do not know whether this actually happened or whether he had a vision — only God knows). I know that this man was snatched to paradise . . . and there he heard things which cannot be put into words, things that human lips may not speak. (2 Corinthians 12:2–4)

Western Christianity had its high point of mysticism in the thirteenth and fourteenth centuries. Both Germany and England produced famous mystics. In Germany: Mechtild of Magdeburg (1210–1280), Meister Eckhart (1260–1327), John Tauler (1300–1361), Gertrude the Great (1256–1302) and Henry Suso (1295–1306). In England: Richard Rolle of Hampole (1290–1349), the unknown author of *The Cloud of Unknowing*, Walter Hilton (d. 1346) and Dame Julian of Norwich (c.1342–1416). But since the Enlightenment of the seventeenth century, interest in mysticism has waned — until our own time, that is.

It is not without significance that today as we stretch ourselves beyond the confines of Planet Earth, to relate with other bodies in our solar system, as we journey into outer space, there is a journey being taken in an opposite direction by increasingly more people, to explore the depth of their inner space. To do this many are following the different paths of eastern meditation that we described in the chapter on the Consciousness Factor.

Inner Awakening

Meditation is a means to inner enlightenment that enables the nervous system to shed unhealthy stresses and thus evolve towards more refined levels of acting, feeling, being. It should be natural and spontaneous for us to act in this way. Most of the time, though, this does not happen because we act out of a level of consciousness that hinders rather than fosters our growth as holistic people. Nevertheless, we all have glimpses of this inner depth, however fleetingly, and it is good to remind ourselves of this potential for inner growth.

We may feel small and separate selves, alone and struggling to exist, but we are really part of the great cosmic whole. At a moment when life's pressures are not noticed, we may suddenly become aware of this oneness. It could happen anywhere, on an escalator, in the garden, listening to music, in any number of different ways. For a brief moment we "let go" completely and transcend. These are rare occasions which happen spontaneously and are not normally repeatable.

Such experiences will tend to awaken deep spiritual feelings which we may not have connected with previously, ones that may have been repressed in childhood through fear or guilt, through religious indifference in the home or peer group pressure. These feelings may have remained underdeveloped through a spiritual vacuum in our faith development, or for some other reason, but they are there, deep within us, nonetheless, as part of God's design. Transcending cannot take place without the awakening and integration of these feelings.

In the past, meditation was considered to be exclusively religious in nature. Therefore only people who had a highly developed religious sense were considered capable of doing it. Moreover, the ability to meditate was deemed to be a divine gift which God, and only God, bestowed on those he chose. Any hint of human beings developing this capacity for themselves was considered blasphemous and even idolatrous (worshipping a god of the mind created by oneself).

This misguided understanding of meditation is largely the fruit of our western dualistic thinking, where matters of the spirit are always considered to be in opposition to, and in conflict with, our lower nature.

All religions, however, have as one of their goals the release of those blockages (sins) which inhibit the realisation of the fuller life which God intends for all people — even on Earth.

The concept of transcendence is known and treasured in all religions. It is an experience open to everyone, artist, atheist and lover alike. It is nature's supreme blessing yet it is also the supreme paradox. We instinctively desire to transcend known boundaries, but the Unbounded, Unknown may inspire the restricting element of fear, which is why we need guidance. It is an experience of bliss when found, and is sought again, yet the harder we try for it the more it eludes us.

The "Letting Go" of Transcendence

Skills and techniques are helpful: they awaken the inner potential. But this inner power is not something we can manipulate to our own liking. While it can only lead to the rediscovery of our true selves, it can take us along paths that challenge us in ways we may not like, inviting us to leave behind habits and behaviour that hinder rather than enhance our lives. Meister Eckhart wrote:

"God expects but one thing of you, and that is that you should come out of yourself in so far as you are a created being and let God be God in you."

Spiritual progress is made through the growing awareness of the unreality of so much of ourselves and of the Godhead as all-embracing Reality. The Christian symbol of the Cross (not favoured by some today) is a constant reminder of the need to die to one's false self in order to transcend to Reality. This is at the heart of the teaching of all religions — the need for inner silence, inner struggle, inner emptiness, inner transformation — found in Christian Centering Prayer, the Sufi "Zhikr" (remembrance of God), Buddhist mindfulness and Hindu knowledge of "advaita" (non-duality).

None of us is fully enlightened, but all of us could be. This is the challenge left us by some of the great spiritual leaders of civilisation. Our world today, in the throes of new evolutionary expansion, is calling for a greater need for transcendence. In effect, this means greater numbers of people desiring and opting for a more intuitive and enlightened way of loving, acting and living.

The focus of today's new spirituality is the recognition of God's presence — God Immanent — within ourselves, within humanity and as a dimension of our world. We are rediscovering what our ancestors were so aware of: the presence of the sacred in all creation. This is in contrast with the spirituality in which people of my generation were brought up, which has less appeal today: an other-worldly spirituality reaching out to a God beyond this sinful world. This shift accounts for today's global environmental movement of respect for Planet Earth and — recognising as St Paul did, that our bodies are the temples of the Holy Spirit — the health and fitness movements to relieve stress and the current concerns about the poisons we consume through polluted air, artificially cultivated food and drugs of every kind.

Jesus Launched this New Age

As Christians we believe that the mission of Jesus the Christ was to raise humanity to a new level of spiritual evolution. (In the Fall-Redemption paradigm this is expressed in terms of Salvation.) He foresaw that, elevated to this new level of consciousness, which would give rise to new attitudes and in turn to new ways of acting and relating, we would be attaining God's design for creation, which Jesus named the Kingdom of God. St Paul expressed it this way: "When anyone is joined to Christ, there is a new world, a new creation" (2 Corinthians 5:17). And in another letter he promises: "We shall become mature people, reaching to the very height of the Christ's full stature" (Ephesians 4:13). This is a promise that our destiny is to live in what today we would call a state of "Christ Consciousness". (This does not mean being conscious *of* Christ but possessing the same consciousness that Jesus enjoyed, that of the Christ.) Jesus expressed his own level of consciousness to his closest friends at the Last Supper — a state of Unity Consciousness. Although he speaks of the Father (God) as greater than himself (John 14:28) he tells of his experience of a state of continual union with God: "I am in the Father and the Father is in me" (John 14:11).

Our twenty-first century spirituality could not be better summed up than in the words of the Belgian priest-author, Louis Evely: "Jesus' greatest liberation is to have freed us from religion! He wanted us all to have free, direct and joyful access to God."

Jesus foresaw that his message was too much for even his closest followers to comprehend at the time, so he promised that the Spirit of God would reveal his message to us when we were capable of being receptive to it (John 16:12–15). There are many signs today that humanity is on the verge of a breakthrough into a higher consciousness. Perhaps only now are we sufficiently mature to begin to take the full, challenging, exciting message of Jesus to heart. As we see the development of extraordinary natural powers among more and more people — there are already a few people like Sai Baba in India who can perform the same miracles that Jesus performed — we recall the words of Jesus: "Whoever believes in me will do what I do — yes, he will do even greater things . . ." (John 14:12). The wonders, miracles that he performed (healing, raising from death, power over the elements, multiplications) did not issue from any power outside his human nature but from the fact that he was such a highly evolved human being. Otherwise his promise, that such powers are available to us too, would have been false. As a Christian, it is my belief that he was the most highly evolved person that it is possible for anyone on this Earth to become. In this he was the most perfect human image of the Divine.

Yet his very goodness aroused such jealousy among the religious leaders who saw their authority threatened by his popularity, and foresaw the political and social danger of his denial of the hierarchical paradigm by his "being all things to all people", that it inevitably led to his execution. And ever since, mystics have had a rough passage. They become inner-directed, self-authenticating, acting out of a highly developed intuition and with a deep inner conviction which gives them their own authority. In their mysticism they rise above the divisions that separate religions. Islamic mystics especially have suffered from their openness to other paths. The new mystics of today cannot expect any better treatment as they show up the futility of trying to lead our world forward at the present gross level of consciousness.

Spirituality is not a special department of life, as the rationalists and scientists have led us to believe over the last few decades in the West. It is a higher intensity of aliveness. Spirituality is not about keeping rules, fasting, martyrdom, obligations, self-denial. It is about delighting in the wonder of life, playing, rejoicing, taking risks, being able to laugh at obstacles and at oneself, having fun.

St Bernard writes of his experience in one of his letters:

> What I know of the divine sciences and Holy Scripture, I
> learnt in woods and fields. I have had no other masters
> than the beeches and the oaks.

And in another letter:

> Listen to a man of experience: thou wilt learn more in the
> woods than in books. Trees and stones will teach thee more
> than thou canst acquire from the mouth of a magister.

To be spiritual means to be fully alive and alert to God's Spirit in-
forming everything, since the very word spirit means life-breath.

What we have seen as two separate departments of life in the
past — secular life and religious life — is going to be bridged in
future by a hunger for spirituality: by increasingly more people
having a spiritual attitude to the whole of life, and living life to
the full. In his *Letters and Papers from Prison*, Bonhoeffer spoke of
his natural sympathy with non-religious people and insisted that
"to be a Christian does not mean to be religious in a particular
way . . . but to be a man". "I have come," said Jesus, "that you
might have life — life in all its fullness" (John 10:10). We are not
human beings trying to be spiritual but spiritual beings trying to
become more fully human.

For further exploration:

On the New Age:

William Bloom (ed.) (1991), *The New Age: An Anthology of Essential Writings*, Rider.

Michael Cole et al. (1990), *What is the New Age?* Hodder & Stoughton,
London.

Vatican (2003), *Jesus Christ, the Bearer of the Water of Life: A Christian Reflection on the New Age*, Catholic Truth Society, London.

On Interfaith Dialogue:

Maurice Wiles (1992), *Christian Theology and Inter-Religious Dialogue*, SCM Press.

Bede Griffiths (1987), *River of Compassion: A Christian Commentary on the Bhagavad Gita*, Amity House, New York.

On the New Mystics:

Bede Griffiths (2003), *Return to the Centre*, MedioMedia, London.

Peter Spink (1991), *A Christian in the New Age*, Darton, Longman & Todd, London.

Chapter 14

THE FAITH FACTOR

It is fitting that the final factor to be considered, among the many factors which collectively are causing us to rethink what we mean by that short but power-loaded word "God", should be that of faith.

Ultimately, the meaning we give to our world, to the totality of creation, the interpretation we make of our experiences, the sense we give to life, derive from the mental construct to which we subscribe, our belief paradigm, our faith.

God values us for our love, not for our belief. The purpose of our belief is to fuel our love. Belief is no more than a means to an end. Our beliefs, our knowledge, can give God nothing. Our love is what God rejoices in.

Within the Church the word "faith" is used with two different meanings. The expression "The Faith" is used to mean the set of truths which are proposed for our belief, as in the exhortation "Keep the Faith". *Fidem servate* is a phrase I remember well: it was the motto of my Prep School! It is in this sense that it is used in the phrase "handing on the Faith".

The alternative meaning of faith is that of an act of the will. It is my personal paradigm constructed by my beliefs, by what I choose to believe. In this meaning my faith is different from your faith or anyone else's because each of us constructs our own belief parameters.

I am writing this chapter while staying in an Anglican vicarage and in front of me on the desk is a book entitled *How to Give Away Your Faith*. It is about methods and techniques for winning over others to one's own belief paradigm, with the implication that the giver has "the True Faith".

Faith: Life's Orientation

Faith, in the second meaning, the way in which we are using the word here, is not an assent to a package of truths. It is much deeper than that. It is not simply a head concern. It is a total life concern. It is the foundation of my whole life. It is that which gives an orientation to my life, sets my course: that which gives me meaning and purpose and a reason for living. So to ask, "What do you believe?" is a question about a collection of notional assents, the items of a Creed. A deeper question to enquire into a person's faith paradigm would be "What do you believe in?", even though this too can only be answered by a list of expressions. (To believe *in* is to trust, to have confidence in someone or something. The very word *con-fidence* means *with faith*.) We can only communicate ideas, not experiences, still less a totality of experience. To this latter question we would expect to be answered by a list of absolute values such as "I believe in justice, love, beauty, etc.", those values which can be grasped only partially because they contain an element of the transcendental, as different from relative values which change according to time and culture, such as the laws of a particular country or the ordinances of a particular Church.

Truth is one of those absolute values. As we have seen in an earlier chapter, we can never grasp Truth in its entirety but have to deal with it mentally in parts, as truths. All of us as human beings, by our very nature, are set on a course towards discerning and embracing Truth more fully. Not the pursuit of true ideas but of that which is true. It is not a straight path but has many twists and turns, ups and downs, and its share of blind alleys. And all the while our search is causing us to readjust our faith paradigm. We are always pointed towards the same horizon but it can often seem that with each adventurous step we draw no nearer. There are sadly those who have ceased to journey. They have either accepted to believe they have arrived because they have taken on board someone else's faith baggage, lock, stock and barrel, because they cannot bear the insecurity of being a seeker, or they have come to the conclusion that there is no horizon towards which to journey.

My personal faith is my personal paradigm for living. It is my mental construct which enables me to answer the why, what and whither of life to my satisfaction. Each of us has our own. I have no right to impose mine upon another, nor to make a value judgement about other people because their faith differs from my own. This principle is the basis of interfaith dialogue — which is wider than inter-religious dialogue! Dialogue can only be between persons, not between institutions or religions. People can only hold a faith dialogue out of their own experience of their religion. It follows that we cannot comprehend the best or the ideal of any religion simply on the understanding of it (still less on the communication of it) by those in dialogue. While Truth is an objective reality, the understanding of it that we grapple with — expressed as truths — is subjective. This latter is the level at which we dialogue.

Our Faith Interprets Our World

There can be no objective view of God. Every perception is subjective, with all its human limitations. I cannot say my perception is right, yours is wrong. Every generation has to create the image of God that makes sense of their world. This is our spirituality, our search for meaning. In the last chapter we differentiated between spirituality and religion.

Formal religions will continue to be of value to us for as long as they are able to evolve with the evolution of human consciousness. Any religion that holds that its expression of beliefs and values has eternal existence is doomed to fossilisation because it has ceased to answer the deepest questions about life in the light of contemporary experience.

We can see a parallel in science. There are no "brute facts" as the rationalists of the Enlightenment supposed. There are only interpreted facts, conditioned by the social and cultural paradigm out of which the scientist operates. The major ideologies of the last hundred years — Marxism, Fascism, Capitalism, National Socialism — which for many devotees are quasi-religions in that they provide the motivation for their lives, mistakenly employ the techniques of science in an attempt to convince people that they are objectively and uniquely true. As the late Dom Bede Griffiths reminded us:

> All scientific theories and all religious doctrines are in fact symbolic structures. In each religion the symbolic structures work by opening the human mind to the transcendent Reality, to the truth. The symbolic structures within the religions each have their unique value but all have limitations because they are socially and culturally conditioned. (*The Tablet*, 16 January 1993)

Within Christianity we can notice shifts that have taken place in its symbolic structures. The God of the Hebrews and of early Christianity was regarded as a God who acts. God was considered principally as a God who relates to the Chosen People. As the infant Church stretched westwards, there grew the tendency to define the faith and to systematise doctrine. Ontology (the study of God's Being) became more important than religious history (God's deeds). Under the influence of Greek metaphysics, God was referred to as Supreme Being, unmoved-mover, substance, first principle. Reflection upon what God is in himself became more important than reflecting upon the relationship of God to people. Knowledge of God through experience was replaced by rational knowledge. An illustration of this is found in comparing

Jesus' Sermon on the Mount, which is an appeal to a way of conducting our lives without any specific mention of precepts, with the arid formulation of truths in the Nicene Creed, a list of doctrinal statements which make no reference to the way we live.

The late David Bosch, the South African theologian, reminded us in his book *Transforming Mission: Paradigm Shifts in Theology of Mission*, that with the non-arrival of the Last Day (the *parousia*) so urgently announced by Jesus and after him by St Paul, the sense of excitement among Christians at the thought of living in the Last Times evaporated. The urgency of announcing God's imminent reign turned into a proclamation that Jesus was the Christ and that following him was the universal way — the only true religion for all people. The desire to strive to bring about "a new heaven and a new earth" was transformed into working for a reward in "the next life".

By the end of the first century the young Church had taken into its vocabulary and liturgy concepts typical of the Roman Emperor, the military, the Greek mystery religions, the theatre and Platonic philosophy.

The development of Christian belief throughout the Church's history has largely been due to challenges to that belief by so-called heretics. The word "heretic", in Greek *hairein*, means to choose. God's special endowment to human nature is the ability to choose. Only a being free to choose can respond to love and God wants lovers, not robots. It was an absolute necessity that we be free creatures in our search for God. This freedom must be preserved at all costs and be allowed expression in order that humanity may continue exploring into Truth. Theologians ought to have pinned to their desks for their consolation the reminder of Thomas Huxley: "It is the customary fate of new truths to begin as heresies"; or, as Alistair Kee puts it:

> The distinction between orthodoxy and heresy is not that
> one is true and the other false, but rather that the latter is a

minority view. And this is what heterodoxy means. (*The Way of Transcendence*)

The reason why I personally choose to be a Christian and not a Hindu or Muslim is not because I have accepted the Church's package as my only way to salvation, nor because I believe Christianity is the true way and that all other ways are false; but because at this point in my life it is the paradigm which provides me with what I consider to be the most acceptable explanation of what life is all about. It inspires me. There are times when I feel distinctly uncomfortable with the manner in which truths are expressed in liturgical prayers and more especially in some of the traditional hymns. But on these occasions I transcend the words and experience the Truth as present in the context in which the words are said or sung: in the life of the community of which I am a part. I am uplifted by the underlying faith of the community and by the way they live their truth in practice. I am nourished by the "atmosphere" of a worshipping community, experiencing the awareness of the spiritual through a combination of music, silence and the sense of wonder in the presence of the Divine. I feel at home in this community because I accept the identity which the Christian understanding of God generates among us. Not that I deny God's presence or activity in other religions which are given *their* identity by *their* understanding of the Divine Mystery.

Faith is a Freedom

No one can force faith upon us. Like love, it has to be freely accepted or it is simply not faith, it is mental programming or brainwashing. We can surrender our belief-freedom by taking on board an institution's complete belief system and making it our own. But this comes about only because we have freely chosen to hand over this element of our personal power to another.

The Church can appear to offer a belief packet with a take-it-or-leave-it label. In its extreme form, there is a minimum packet labelled "Truths necessary for salvation"! It is one thing for the Church to propose doctrines to us as clarifications of Revelation, as an aid to help us enter more deeply into the Divine Mystery. It is another thing to demand our total acceptance of the doctrines proposed as a condition for our eternal salvation.

If I value my faith paradigm I can offer my insights to another. I can never impose them. I can share with others why it is adequate for and of value to me. To do more is to proselytise.

Faith is described by the Church as a supernatural gift. It is supernatural, as distinct from natural, only for those who preserve the natural/supernatural dualism. We can understand it as a gift in as much as we accept all aspects of humanity and creation as gift of the creator. The expression is open to misunderstanding if it implies that God gives faith to some people and denies it to others. This would hardly be compatible with the Christian understanding of God's design for the whole of humanity as expressed by the author of the Letter to the Ephesians:

> This plan, which God will complete when the time is right,
> is to bring all creation together, everything in the heavens
> and on earth, with Christ as head. (1:10)

Faith is also described by spiritual writers as our response to God. God offers us a gift of a relationship with Him: we accept it. It is our response in the sense that by an act of our will (which faith is) we show our willingness to be open to the spiritual, to the transcendental dimension of life.

Ultimately, we believe something because we want to accept it as true. However, a Christian might argue, the Church says we must accept this and that because they are true. Yes, we reply, we accept what the Church says is true because we have already decided to accept the Church as our mentor. But this does not mean that we take on board every doctrinal statement unquestioningly. It only has a value to us in so far as it relates to where we are on our spiritual journey. I believe in Jesus, not because the Church has pronounced him to be God the Son, but because the experience of Jesus in my life justifies my faith in him.

We Create Our Own Beliefs

It would be quite wrong to attempt to measure the spiritual depth of Christians by their acceptance of the Church's teaching, their orthodoxy. Doctrines are offered us as a means to access the Truth. To give them greater weight than that is to give the products of religious experience a greater value than the source of religious experience. Yet how often do Christians, confronted with a new insight, assess it according to the theological baggage they carry rather than referring it to their inner experience, their intuition.

We create our own belief paradigm. The objects of our belief (truths) flow from three sources.

1. There are those which are genetic. They are deep in our genes as human beings and express themselves most often through instinct. For instance, the instinctive reaction (of some) on seeing a spider. It is caused by the unreasoned belief that the sight of a spider spells danger. We do not go through a mental process to acquire this belief but we do go through a mental process to discount it, to be rational about it. We can decide not to believe there is any danger in the appearance of a spider.

2. There are beliefs into which we have been indoctrinated. They have been passed on to us by parents, teachers, clergy and others in a parental role. When we were children we needed this help to build up our belief paradigm. It was the foundation of our value system. But if we are adult in this respect — which is not the same as being grown-up! — we will be continually sifting through this baggage, discarding, readjusting and adding to it.

3. Then there are beliefs arising from our own experience. We see the sun setting and we see it rising next morning. We

believe it is going to do the same tomorrow. Our experience of its regularity is the basis of this belief, rather than the scientific explanation that the appearance of rising and setting is caused by the Earth rotating round the sun every twenty-four hours.

Let us apply these three sources to our faith in the Divine Mystery.

1. There seems to be an instinctive sense of the Divine, of the transcendental among all tribal peoples. It is something very deep in the human psyche. In whatever way we may rationalise about this belief, it does seem to be universal and gives us cause to speak of the spiritual as equal to the physical and mental as ingredients of human life.

    Investigation shows that deep spiritual experiences and awareness of God's presence are more common among young children than we adults suppose. They do not speak of them because they presume that everyone else has the same experience. As the ability for analytical thought develops in adolescence these experiences diminish and are often forgotten.

    It is astonishing how many self-declared atheists call for help from some higher intelligence/energy/being when faced with a sudden or unmanageable crisis! This is because very few self-declared atheists are really *a-theistic*, that is, they have proved to their own satisfaction that there is no God or Higher Being. Most self-styled atheists have not arrived at their position because they have encountered any obstacles that prevent them believing in God but simply because they have not had any spiritual experience that might lead them to suppose that there might be a God.

2. Most of us in the western world were brought up with some Christian teaching. We were given beliefs about God. As children we took them all on board and it did not worry us that

we did not understand them. These are the beliefs we need to question — their expression especially — before we own them as adults and build up our current faith paradigm.

3. This is the way in which we experience the Divine directly, perhaps in some peak experience, some moment of transcendence. Such glimpses are the foundation of our faith. We cannot verbalise them but they are tremendously real to us. This intuitive knowledge of the Divine provides the bridge between indoctrinated revelation (the truths we are taught) and rationalisation by which we try to make sense of them. This intuitive faith experience is so powerful that it dispenses with the need to base our belief on rational arguments, on "proofs for the existence of God".

We create our own belief paradigm. All our experiences, spiritual and other, are given meaning and value by our faith paradigm. We edit our experiences to fit our preconceived ideas. For instance, two men tell you they have had an apparition of a beautiful woman. One is in a psychiatric hospital, the other a fervent churchgoing Christian. You will assume that the former had a hallucination, a sexual fantasy perhaps, while the latter was privileged with a vision of the Blessed Virgin Mary.

Our faith paradigm, on the other hand, is continually being adjusted by the experiences which come to us from both outside and within ourselves. Our human experience is always our starting point — it cannot be otherwise — and so it is the complete scenario of our faith. There is no beyond-the-human, extraterrestrial access to knowledge of the Divine or of anything else. My faith as a Christian is not based upon any certainty derived from my reading the New Testament, but what I read in its Gospels and Letters of the way the early Christian community experienced the Jesus-event provides me with a context from which I can draw an interpretation of my own spiritual experience that makes sense to me.

The faith experience of each of us is continually changing. As St Paul wrote: "When I was a child, my speech, feelings and thinking were all those of a child; now that I am a man I have no use for childish ways" (1 Corinthians 13:11). As a child I was certain about the faith-facts I was taught. Everything was in black and white. As an adolescent I was concerned about detail, which led to questioning what did not seem to fit my mental picture neatly. In my mature years I am woolly about most faith-facts — there are more grey areas than stark black and white — but this no longer worries me. My faith is still the compass for my life's journey. Our belief paradigm is built up and adjusted over a lifetime. It is not a static "given".

I like Tennyson's words from "In Memoriam": "There lives more faith in honest doubt, believe me, than in half the creeds."

Three Categories of Christians

Many Christians today would recognise themselves as falling into one of three categories, which are commonly labelled *conservative*, *liberal* and *radical*. The defining point of each is their understanding of the nature of God and of the God–humanity relationship.

The conservative group probably represents the largest number of churchgoers. They are distinguished by their loyalty to the doctrines they were taught as children. Their belief that these are unchanging provides them with an anchor-point in a life that offers less and less security on account of the rapidity of change all around us. For this reason they do not want to see change in the religious domain of their lives — in moral values, in biblical interpretation, in formulations of the Faith, in the ways and words of worship — because they rely upon this one unchanging rock of stability.

The Path to a New Faith Paradigm

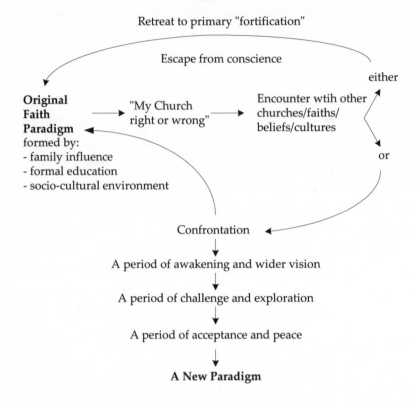

In the mid-1990s, the long-awaited English-language edition of *The Catechism of the Catholic Church* was published. It is the first authoritative compendium of Catholic belief to be published since the catechism of the Council of Trent in 1566, and it is surprising — some would say saddening — how much of the Trent catechism it echoes. Perhaps its most alarming aspect is that it allows of no grey areas. Everything is in black and white. Is this the reason why the French edition became a bestseller in France, available in airport bookstalls, while the English translation sold 100,000 copies in Britain within a month of its publication? Is it providing Christians with a longed-for sense of security in a turbulent world? The late Dom Bede Griffiths wrote about the project before it was published:

The new Catechism of the Catholic Church attempts to put the content of the Catholic Faith into rational, discursive terms. The aim is illusory because the *content* of the Catholic Faith, in common with that of the other great religious traditions, transcends all rational, discursive thought.

Liberal Christianity appeared in the nineteenth century with the growth of biblical criticism. Liberals, for instance, rationalise about the miracles of Jesus. Everything was opened to questioning and what was accepted previously as symbolic had to be explained in rational terms, or explained away. While belief in the supernatural and in a God outside creation was maintained, such beliefs had to be understood in the light of the emerging scientific world view.

In more recent years, a third category of Christians has come into prominence: Radical Christians or Christian Humanists. In Britain the followers of Don Cupitt who launched the annual *Sea of Faith* conferences are prominent members of this group. They describe themselves as non-realists. They believe that the world of the supernatural is a human invention to explain the inexplicable. They have given up belief in an objective personal God and in a life beyond the grave. They explain how this is really a more authentic form of Christianity. They still claim to believe in God but for them the word means the sum of the highest human values by which they direct their lives: love, goodness, justice, knowledge, wisdom, beauty, etc.

Anthony Freeman, an Anglican priest who calls himself a radical Christian, rightly points out in his book *God in Us: A Case for Christian Humanism* that in hanging on to former expressions of belief in today's changing world is not in fact to preserve continuity with the past because there is no such thing as a timeless truth: "To say the same thing in new circumstances is to say something different." As we have seen in previous chapters, the words in which ancient doctrines were enshrined change their meaning.

As must have become apparent during the course of this book I maintain that we are at that point in the development of human consciousness where we feel it is essential, if we are to be true to our own experience, to rethink and restate our beliefs in terms of the new cosmology. But that is not to say that we are required to abandon that which is beyond the humanly explainable.

It seems to me that there is a dimension of human consciousness that is so universally witnessed, among people who are pre-technological as much as among the technological, that yearns for a spiritual dimension to life that cannot be satisfied except by that which is beyond the created realm. Indeed, the meeting of science and mysticism today, which we have referred to already, is one indication of the insufficiency of pure science and rational knowledge to satisfy these deep human aspirations.

God Is

Because we no longer feel able to say "God is out there" we are not thereby saying there is no objective God, as some "Sea of Faith" members do, including not a few clergy. We are saying God *is*. God is within creation (God manifest) and God is beyond creation (God unmanifest). This is not a contradictory statement if we understand God to exist in a different dimension, on a different wavelength, from ourselves. During one of the non-religious retreats which I lead, we shared what the word "God" meant to each of us at this moment of our spiritual journey. My own contribution was to say that I experience the Divine as a presence. One of the participants, a retired Anglican priest in his ninetieth year, who had no belief in a divine "being", asked how I could experience a presence unless I believed in a he, she or it as present. I replied that just as "sensitives" have a sense of a "presence", an atmosphere, in a room without any knowledge of what that presence is, so I appreciate a presence which I call "Divine" without feeling any need to objectify it.

We recall the Book of Exodus account of how God described Himself when He appeared to Moses in the burning bush: "I am

who I am"; and Moses is instructed to go to his people saying:
"The one who is called *I am* has sent me to you" (3:14).

> Who is God? I can think of no better answer than, He who
> is. Nothing is more appropriate to the eternity which God
> is. If you call God good or great or blessed or wise or any-
> thing else of this sort, it is included in these words, namely,
> He is. (St Bernard)

Jesus' Revelation of God as Father

The heart of the "Good News" that was the message of Jesus to
humanity he encapsulated in the expression "The Kingdom of
God". We might describe this in contemporary language as the
total harmony of all creation as God wills it to be. The great breakthrough Jesus made in bringing this Kingdom dream a step nearer
reality was in introducing the God–humanity relationship as one
of parent to child. He himself called God his father and even addressed God with the familiarity of the Aramaic term "Abba", the
equivalent of "Daddy". It is hard for us to appreciate how blasphemous such a way of addressing God appeared to the Jewish
leaders until we recall that at the time of Jesus, God was held in
such awe that he was never addressed by name. At that period in
Jewish history God was more remote and majestic than in previous eras. No wonder such familiarity with the Divine fuelled the
charge of blasphemy with which he was accused and which finally led to his execution.

In humanity's spiritual evolution, the teaching of such
human–Divine intimacy was a great leap forward, as was the
Kingdom-vision and the value system of that vision to which Jesus introduced us. Because the Church has retained the concept of
God as "Our Father" in its liturgy, we might be led to believe that
this revelation was the ultimate stage of our spiritual evolution. It
was not. It was simply the next stage which was appropriate two
thousand years ago.

"The Faith" has frozen Jesus' words for all time and all cultures, forgetting that he was a man of his own times and culture. It was not meant to be the ultimate nor the total expression of Godhead. We have to employ models to enable us to come to terms with mysteries. It is as if Jesus was saying, "I will give you a model of how to relate to God: as a child does to their father."

With the development of the behavioural sciences we understand that maturity calls for us to grow beyond the child–parent dependency to an adult-to-adult relationship between people. This is well brought out by Transactional Analysis which helps us to analyse our relationships in terms of child, parent and adult and presents the adult-to-adult as that of the mature relationship.

To get stuck at the level of the Father–child relationship to God can become a form of idolatry. We would be transforming what is no more than a model into a reality. It is not even a model that appeals to everyone. For someone who in their childhood suffered abuse from their father or stepfather, this model can be a real obstacle. We might find it more helpful on our journey to human maturity, to envisage God as a friend — our closest friend — rather than as a father or mother.

The Lord's prayer, the "Our Father", is not the epitome of the ultimate revelation of the God–humanity relationship. In fact the prayer was only introduced into Christian liturgy in the third century after Tertullian had made that claim for it.

We can detect from the Gospels that for a chosen few Jesus did teach a much deeper, a mystical, relationship with the Divine. "The knowledge of the secrets of the Kingdom of God has been given to you, but to the rest it comes by means of parables", he said to his close disciples (Luke 8:10). Mark writes:

> He spoke the word to them [the crowd] as far as they were capable of understanding it . . . but he explained everything to his disciples when they were alone (4:33–34).

From among the Apostles, Peter, James and John were given more advanced teaching and allowed a mystical experience on Mount Tabor: the event we call the Transfiguration (Matthew 17:1–9). Jesus even said he would not "give to dogs what is holy or throw [his] pearls before swine" (Matthew 7:6).

Since the Evangelists and St Paul wrote for the general public, their writings do not include the private instructions the disciples received. As the young Church grew, she created a single code of doctrine that was meant for the masses. Thus we might be forgiven for thinking that Jesus' introducing us to a parent–child relationship to God was the height and totality of his teaching about our relationship with the Divine Mystery.

Our Bottom-Up Knowledge of God

Let us return to our original thesis: anything we know about God comes not from outside human life and experience — from an extraterrestrial source — but is part of human life and experience. We cannot exist outside our own reality, yet nevertheless we feel drawn to something beyond.

The traditional "proofs" for the existence of God are not as conclusive to contemporary scientific minds as they were to the medieval philosophers. However, taking a "bottom-upwards" approach to the transcendental, as I have done throughout this book — starting from human experience instead of the theologian's top-downwards approach, which starts from Revelation — we can notice that there are experiences common to all humanity which point us towards a belief in "The Other", "The Beyond".

In his book *A Rumour of Angels* Peter Berger lists five of what he calls "signals of transcendence: phenomena that are to be found within the domain of our 'natural' reality but that appear to point beyond that reality". I will list these briefly, with my own comments and then add a further two myself.

1. **An argument from order.** We experience an underlying order in the Universe, despite often seeming chaos. We have a trust that "everything will be all right in the end". The mother comforts her child who has experienced some tragedy with the promise "It's all going to be all right" without any assurance that it is. The mother is not lying to the child but is transcending the present grief and expressing her belief that there is an underlying order in the Universe that it makes sense to trust. Many times each day we rely on the certainty of mathematics which is based on a presumption of the existence of order. The Universe is ultimately trustworthy. This gives people hope that there is something to rely upon beyond the threat of death.

2. **An argument from play.** Play is an escape from the seriousness of reality. It invents its own rules: it takes us into another time dimension. Watch children completely engrossed in play. It is usually a joyful activity. It takes us to a realm beyond reality into the dimension of eternity.

3. **An argument from hope.** Unlike the creatures of the animal kingdom, we are creatures oriented towards a future. We live with the belief that the future can be better. We strive — and promote revolutions! — to bring about a better world. It is hope that gives meaning to our suffering and makes it bearable. "The profoundest manifestations of hope are to be found in the gestures of courage undertaken in defiance of death." A refusal to accept death as ultimate extermination is rooted in our very humanity.

4. **An argument from damnation.** We experience a universal attraction to goodness and a revulsion of evil. Our outrage at the atrocities of Hitler, Stalin, and other dictators is an intuition of the moral rectitude that we have a right to expect. It highlights our human sense of justice. We feel that such atrocities are so grievous that they "cry to heaven for vengeance" — that the death of the perpetrator is an insufficient retribution, that a

greater, equivalent expiation is required, beyond this present life. It is significant that Christianity provides damnation for the perpetrators of evil.

5. **An argument from humour.** Humour is a characteristic of human life. It is a perceived incongruity in our experience which reflects the imprisonment of the human spirit in the world. Animals seem comic to us only because we imbue them with human characteristics. Our cheerfulness, our jokes, break into our most tragic moments: in the midst of grief at funerals or in the desperate situation of warfare. Our humour implies that our imprisonment is not final but will be overcome.

6. **An argument from growth.** The number of self-improvement courses of every description now on offer bear witness to a basic human desire to grow, to become more. Nothing gives us greater pleasure than to discover a new talent, a latent gift, to be more self-confident, self-assured, to feel we have overcome an inhibition . . . that we have grown a little. We are never content to stop at the present, but feel we are called to something greater in the future.

7. **An argument from adventure.** There is something deep in all of us calling us to reach beyond the boundaries of our present capabilities, our present skills, both as individuals and as the human race. To be adventurous. This is never more obvious than in children who will take physical risks to do something beyond what they have previously achieved. It is illustrated in humanity's drive to explore further and further into space, to transcend our present limitations.

Revelation does not tell us anything about God beyond the human experience. It tells us about ourselves. We see ourselves mirrored in the concept of God that we entertain because that concept derives from our human experience. We say God is perfect justice because, drawing on our experience of imperfect justice, we can conceive of the possibility of perfect justice as an ideal towards which we are journeying.

Faith is a Risk-Taking Journey

The classic definition of Faith we find in the Letter to the Hebrews (11:1): "To have faith is to be sure of the things we hope for, to be certain of the things we cannot see." This invites us to commit ourselves to something which is never totally disclosed. Therein lies a risk!

Faith is never a static "given" but a risk-taking journey. The emotional experience we may have received from religion in childhood has dried up. We cannot go back to that. To attempt to do so would maintain us in spiritual infancy. Perhaps the popularity of much that is labelled by the media as "New Age" is pursued because people are looking for this emotional quasi-religious experience outside formal religion. If we do not continue to be seekers throughout life, if we believe we have arrived because we "know" the Faith, we have put a full stop to spiritual growth, indeed to life. There is no life without growth.

There is a danger for practising Christians that they are more intent upon looking backwards than looking forwards. The annual celebrations of Christmas, Easter and Pentecost tend to focus the mind on the past historical event rather than on the consequences of that event for us today. The Patriarchs and the Prophets of Hebrew Scripture were forward-looking figures as indeed were the Chosen People as a whole. They looked forward to a Promised Land and to a coming Messiah. (Only one person looked back — Lot's wife — and we know what became of her!) Jesus was forward-looking to the coming about of the new world order of justice and peace and harmony which he called the Kingdom of God.

In refashioning our perception of God, in moving forward from what until now has been the traditional Christian concept of God as Father, we are not being disloyal to the tradition. Nor are

we being disloyal to Jesus the Christ who introduced our religious
ancestors to what was for them an entirely new — and one might
say, presumptuous — God–humanity relationship. The Jesus concept of God was but the latest step in a long process of discovery.
Over the previous two thousand years, the Hebrew people had
moved from understanding their god to be in relationship to their
tribe as other gods were to other tribes, to acknowledging that
their god who had delivered them from Egypt was more powerful
than and of a different category from the gods of the Egyptians —
a superior god. Then came the post-Exile understanding of there
being just one God, creator of the Universe and of all humanity
but with whom they had been chosen to be a People with a special
relationship. (The Genesis account of creation was written during
this period.) Then came Jesus who invited his listeners to enter
into an even closer, intimate, relationship with God.

It is often said that the God of pre-Jesus times was a despotic
racial God. This is untrue. It should rather be said that the Hebrews were insensitive to the God of love. God never changes
through the ages: humanity changes in its perception of God. And
we will continue to do so.

To maintain today and for all time the concept of God that Jesus proposed to us would be to diminish the God–humanity relationship because one of the partners to this relationship has
changed over the years. And we are continuing to change. We are
currently moving into a new consciousness. We are moving into
the era of the Spirit. So the relationship has to be reforged. If not, as
in so many marriages where partners never renegotiate their original relationship despite their growth, maybe along diverging paths,
there will be a divorce. In our case a divorce between a new-
consciousness humanity and a God who has become meaningless.

In fact, for a large percentage of people in the western world
the divorce has already taken place. Not because they have had a
row with God and decided to break off the relationship but

because their understanding of God is such that he bears no more relevance to their lives. They have simply drifted apart.

As one theologian writes:

> There can be times when we do not think that we are still believers. Perhaps at such times we are learning to let go of underdeveloped or inadequate or even untrue images of the God our hearts are seeking. (Brian O. McDermott in *Faith in the God of Jesus Christ*)

We have to confront the fact that when the time comes that it is no longer helpful to address God as Father, the present form Christianity takes, with which we are so familiar — in its Creeds and in its Liturgy — will have to change radically. It will become a Spirit-centred religion. This is not a denial of our God-centred Jewish roots, nor of our Father-centred Jesus relationship, but the growth of a new shoot from that stock to a new blossoming.

And further on still in human history, I suspect, the Spirit-centred religion period will prepare the soil for the next great step: religionless spirituality. And humanity will not have to wait another two thousand years!

Is that a presumption? We have already noticed that formal religion is a comparative newcomer to humanity's spiritual journey. Do we not already see signs that structured religion — its rituals, its theological systems, its temples and cathedrals, its moral codes, its scriptures, its legal and social institutions — is beginning to fray? Structured religion — whichever religion — is a human construct that is no more than a means to an end, a help offered on our spiritual journey for as long as that help is required. God does not reveal religion; God reveals Himself. When we die, it is irrelevant what religion we were guided by: God is interested in us as persons, not as religionists. (It is curious that we are so concerned that after death we be buried alongside our co-religionists that we divide our cemeteries accordingly! Does our religious affiliation really matter at that point in our pilgrimage?)

The Three Shifts in the Perception of Our God-relationship

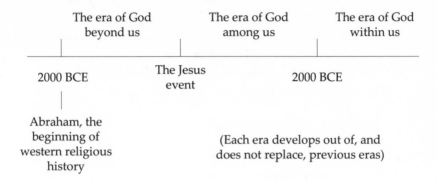

The era of God beyond us	The era of God among us	The era of God within us

2000 BCE   The Jesus event   2000 BCE

Abraham, the beginning of western religious history

(Each era develops out of, and does not replace, previous eras)

Religious structures can so often impede rather than enable spiritual growth. This was recognised by most spiritual reformers and prophets. They attacked or severely criticised the religious environment in which they found themselves. This is as true of Jesus as of Luther or Wesley, as true of Gautama the Buddha as of Mohammed, as true of Amos and Isaiah as of Karl Bath. As Wilfrid Cantwell Smith wrote in 1962 in *The Meaning and End of Religion*:

> It is as Christians' faith in God has weakened that they have busied themselves with Christianity; and as their personal relation to Christ has virtually lapsed that they have turned to religion for solace.

And he goes on:

> One has even reached a point today where some Christians can speak of believing in Christianity (instead of believing in God or in Christ); of preaching Christianity (instead of preaching Good News, salvation, redemption); of practising Christianity (instead of practising love). Some even talk of being saved by Christianity, instead of by the only thing that could possibly save us, the anguish and the love of God.

Jesus was not interested in Christianity but in God and people. He proclaimed a new "Way" of living, not a new religion. He told the woman of Samaria at the side of the well:

> Believe me, woman, the time will come when people will not worship the Father either on this mountain or in Jerusalem. But the time is coming and is already here, when by the power of God's Spirit people will worship the Father as he really is, offering him the true worship that he wants. God is Spirit, and only by the power of his Spirit can people worship him as he really is. (John 4:21, 23–24)

∞

All are parts of one stupendous whole
whose body nature is and God the soul
— Alexander Pope

For further exploration:

Cyprian Smith (1987), *The Way of Paradox: Spiritual life as Taught by Meister Eckhart*, Darton, Longman and Todd, London.

Teilhard de Chardin (1971), *Christianity and Evolution*, Collins, London.

Lloyd Geering (1994), *Tomorrow's God*, Bridget Williams Books Ltd., Wellington, New Zealand.

Lloyd Geering (1999), *The World to Come: From Christian Past to Global Future*, Bridget Williams Books Ltd., Wellington, New Zealand.

Adrian B. Smith (2002), *A Reason for Living and Hoping: A Christian Appreciation of the Emerging New Era of Consciousness*, St Paul's Publishing, London.

Adrian B. Smith (2002), *A New Framework for Christian Belief*, John Hunt Publishing, Hampshire.

Ken Wilber (1998), *The Marriage of Sense and Soul*, Gill and Macmillan, Dublin.

Epilogue

Do not look for God outside yourself,
for the God which you seek does not exist.
God manifests in us as light in our spirit,
Sweet warmth in our heart,
And strength in our will.
Look within for the living God and be thankful.

Ask that God may live in you,
that he may manifest through you.
Only God can transform human beings.
Everyone is seeking the meaning of life.
The meaning of life lies in communion with God.

The Great Beings, Geniuses and Masters of Humanity
are those in whom God lives.

God is the goal of life;
it is he we are seeking.
God is the beloved of the human soul.

Peter Deunov,
the great seer of Bulgaria.